# RESILIENCE AND TRANSFORMATION

# RESILIENCE
## AND
# TRANSFORMATION

## Preparing Australia for Uncertain Futures

Edited by Steven Cork on behalf of Australia21

**CSIRO**
PUBLISHING

Australia²¹
SHAPING THE FUTURE

National Library of Australia Cataloguing-in-Publication entry

    Resilience and transformation : preparing Australia for
    uncertain futures / edited by Steven Cork.

    9780643098121 (pbk.)

    Includes bibliographical
    references and index.

    Social prediction – Australia.
    Resilience (Personality trait) – Australia.
    Resilience (Ecology) – Australia.
    Political planning – Australia.
    Australia – Economic conditions – 21st century.
    Australia – Social conditions – 21st century.

    Cork, Steven John.

    303.49

Published by
**CSIRO** PUBLISHING
150 Oxford Street (PO Box 1139)
Collingwood VIC 3066
Australia

Telephone:   +61 3 9662 7666
Local call:    1300 788 000 (Australia only)
Fax:          +61 3 9662 7555
Email:       publishing.sales@csiro.au
Web site:    www.publish.csiro.au

Front cover: image by iStockphoto

Set in Adobe Minion 10/12 and Stone Sans
Edited by Janet Walker
Cover and text design by James Kelly
Typeset by Modern Art Production Group
Printed in China by 1010 Printing International Ltd
Reprinted in Australia by Doculink Australia Pty Ltd, 2010

**CSIRO** PUBLISHING publishes and distributes scientific, technical and health science books, magazines and journals from Australia to a worldwide audience and conducts these activities autonomously from the research activities of the Commonwealth Scientific and Industrial Research Organisation (CSIRO).

# Contents

## HEALTH AND EDUCATION

## ENVIRONMENT AND SOCIETY

## DISASTER PREPAREDNESS AND RECOVERY

# *Foreword*

Brian Walker

Since the beginning of the 21st century, interest in the notion of resilience has expanded rapidly. As a science, largely in the domain of ecology and natural resource management, it took off in the 1970s. There was a parallel, older interest in resilience in the field of psychology, centred on the characteristics of individuals and the environments they lived in, which together determine how people cope or fail to cope with stress and trauma. These two discipline areas have recently come together, with insights from both informing new thinking.

Aside from these scientific developments, in the last few years resilience has become of great interest to people who are concerned with the future of regions, of nations and of the world. New centres and institutes of resilience are appearing. To those not involved in this development resilience appears to be a new buzzword, with phrases such as 'resilience is the new sustainability'.

This is unfortunate for it gives the impression that resilience is a fad. But the emergence of resilience in science and practice is not a fad. It is occurring because of a rising concern amongst scholars and policy makers about trends in the consequences of economic growth and globalisation and our declining capacity to cope with unexpected shocks accompanying them. It is not faddish for practitioners and politicians to worry about how resilient we are in the face of the very rapid and disturbing global and regional changes we see all around us. Resilience is not a panacea, but it is a very important consideration in national, regional and global policy and practice. It is a very important development that needs to be understood, and this book has been written to put the concept of resilience into a wider policy context.

It is not difficult to see why interest in resilience has emerged. Insights from scientific developments have led to awareness that ecosystems, social systems and linked social–ecological systems (such as agricultural regions, urban complexes or commercial fisheries) behave like complex adaptive systems. That is, they are self-organising within limits. There are two important outcomes of this systems behaviour: (i) it is not possible to control the dynamics of such systems rigidly (they shift and change and reorganise if one part is held constant, or 'optimised') and, furthermore, attempting to do so reduces their ability to absorb shocks (i.e. they need to change and vary in order to remain resilient); and (ii) there are limits to how much such systems can change and still recover – the measure of a system's resilience is the size of a shock, the amount of change which that system can absorb and still continue to function in much the same kind of way.

This increasing scientific understanding and awareness is occurring at the same time that society's leaders are becoming increasingly concerned about our ability to cope with a number of looming global and regional-scale threats – climate change, pandemics, market collapses, peak oil, ocean acidification, collapsing fisheries, water 'wars', terrorist activity, to name some.

We cannot prevent or even predict most of them. Defence and security organisations recognise that bigger walls and more armaments are not the solution; the priority is to enhance our capacity to cope with whatever shocks occur. In other words, the need is to build resilience. We need a resilient food production system, resilient energy, water and transport systems, resilient cities and health and education systems. And the signs are that many of these systems are less resilient now than they have been.

Though reference to 'resilience' now appears in various vision and mission statements of government departments, it is not yet being applied or researched widely in policy development in Australia. Europe is somewhat ahead – the UK Resilience initiative undertaken from the Cabinet Office, the Dutch Research Institute for Transitioning, the Stockholm Resilience Centre and Cranfield Univeristy Resilience Centre being examples. In the USA, indications are that interest in resilience is about to expand rapidly. It is therefore very timely that Australia21 has initiated this inquiry into Australia's resilience and what it means for our strategic development. The inquiry began with a round table in Sydney in 2007, which resulted in an Australia21 working paper ('How resilient is Australia?').

This book follows that initial effort. The chapters are an eclectic mix, chosen to cover a range of issues in which resilience plays a central role. They are not intended to be a complete or definitive set, but collectively they raise the issues that Australia needs to address, at all levels of society, if we are to develop along a trajectory of non-declining human well-being.

One aspect of resilience not included in this book concerns the resilience of indigenous societies and what they have to offer our understanding of resilience. In March 2009, Australia21 participated in a workshop, organised by the Resilience Alliance at Hinchinbrook in Queensland, on this topic. It involved indigenous people from several parts of the world and resilience scientists with whom they were associated. The proceedings are not yet available for inclusion here but there were many interesting insights. Small societies anywhere are prone to being locked into various kinds of 'traps' out of which it is very difficult to escape and the participants in this workshop identified a number of them that occur in different indigenous societies around the world. I await with great interest a statement being prepared by the indigenous participants on their perspective of resilience.

I conclude by reiterating my opening comments. Resilience is not some new fad and it should not be seen as the solution or the way to approach development. It is one important way to help resolve the difficulties we face. What is needed in Australia and in the world today is an attitude of complementarity in regard to proposed solutions to our problems – how can resilience, together with other, economic, social and technological, approaches help? It is not that other solutions are wrong; the problem is that all the individual solutions are partial and bringing consideration of resilience and complex systems dynamics will increase our chances of finding durable solutions.

I commend this volume to all those with an interest in Australia's future.

*Dr Brian Walker is a Research Fellow at CSIRO Sustainable Ecosystems, Chair of The Resilience Alliance (www.resalliance.org) and an Australia21 Board Member.*

## About the editor

Dr Steve Cork is an Australia21 Fellow and Leader of this resilience project. He is also an ecologist and futurist who, over the past 26 years, has been a senior researcher with CSIRO and played a lead role in developing ecological scenarios for the world's future in the United Nations' Millennium Assessment. He now works as a private consultant and as Adjunct Professor in the Crawford School of Economics & Government at the Australian National University.

## About the Australia21 Advisory Group

The idea for and overall development of this publication was undertaken by an internal Australia21 group. This group comprised Dr Steve Cork, Dr Brian Walker, Paul Barratt AO, Richard Eckersley, Em Prof Bob Douglas AO, Dr Lynne Reeder.

## About Australia21

Australia21 is a non-profit organisation whose core focus is multidisciplinary inquiry on issues of strategic importance to Australia in the 21st century. It is committed to:

- promoting interdisciplinary and inter-institutional discussion to germinate new frameworks of understanding on issues of significance to Australia's future

- building networks between leading researchers, community, business leaders and policy makers

- improving community understanding of the factors that will contribute to a better future for Australia.

For more information, visit www.australia21.org.au.

# OVERVIEW

# CHAPTER 1

# Introduction and synthesis of key themes

Steven Cork

'Resilience' is a word on many lips at the moment. It is used in disciplines as diverse as engineering, medicine, ecology, economics, education, defence, business and law. The risk management profession, for example, is currently emphasising organisational resilience as a key component of preparing for future challenges and opportunities. Where 'sustainability' was a prime focus for policy relating to interactions between the environment, society and economies for many years, the concept of resilience is being introduced as a way to ensure that ecological and social systems are able to find their way towards sustainability (whatever societies decide that is, in the future) in the face of potential shocks, some of which can be partly anticipated and some of which will come as surprises. Various chapters in this book comment on the appearance and interpretation of 'resilience' in policies and strategies for the environment, health, welfare, national security, law, education and business, among other areas.

The popularity of this term comes in part from the recognition that attempts to predict and control the future have been largely unsuccessful, in whatever field of human endeavour they have been attempted. There is comfort to many in the idea that they can do something tangible about preparing for the future by building the capacity of people, societies and ecosystems to deal with whatever emerges. This comfortable feeling, however, has led to uncritical application of the term in many fields. In the business literature, for example, it is easy to find lists of actions to take to improve organisational resilience but it is difficult to find empirical or theoretical underpinnings for this advice. Rita Parker (Chapter 4, this volume) explains how it is possible for an organisation to 'tick the resilience boxes' but still not be resilient because it does not understand the intangible aspects of the concept. Similarly, Cork (Chapter 15) points out that although all major environmental strategies developed by Australian governments make resilience a key component of the problem definition and the proposed solutions, few are either explicit about what it means in terms of governance and management or fully apply resilience thinking in implementation plans.

The broad application of the concept of resilience has, however, been questioned by some critics. Some point to a perceived lack of theory associated with the concept or the impression that the concept is being offered as the solution to all of society's problems. Others question how it is different from other concepts (e.g. 'capacity building' or 'adaptability') that have come before it. Advocates of the concept point out that resilience should not be considered a panacea, and that a body of theory is emerging that explicitly addresses how resilience thinking relates to other ways of dealing with current and future challenges and itself questions many of the ill-informed applications of the concept.

Research brought together under the umbrella of the Resilience Alliance (Resilience Alliance 2009; Walker and Salt 2006) has revealed a number of principles about resilience that provide a strong basis for dialogue about what resilience might mean in different situations. These principles reveal that some 'common sense' interpretations of resilience are ultimately unhelpful because they lead to logical inconsistencies. A perfect example is the idea that resilience is about resisting change. Research on how social and ecological systems have responded to change in the past shows that resisting change is a recipe for a system to be overwhelmed by it and to lose its essential functions and identity. Thus, most recent definitions of resilience have been couched in terms of systems responding to perturbations by changing, within limits, while retaining their essential functions, structures and 'identity'. These and other principles are discussed in some detail in Chapters 15 and 17.

But Australia21 recognises that being prescriptive about any theory or practice will not bring about desirable change. Resilience thinking advocates diversity of ideas. People with different backgrounds, skills, experiences and world views will want to come to grips with the concept of resilience in their own ways. Thus, in preparing this volume we invited authors to define and interpret resilience from their own perspective. We asked them to consider what factors confer resilience within the systems they study and what trends they think are emerging or underway with respect to the resilience of these systems. Many common messages have emerged, which are discussed in the following chapter on key themes and policy implications.

With the rapid expansion of interest in resilience across all sectors of Australian society and internationally, it is understandable that people involved in different initiatives are often unaware of one another's activities. Diversity of approach is to be encouraged but lack of communication is a problem to be addressed. This volume and the previous initiatives by Australia21 to bring people interested in analysing resilience together (Cork *et al.* 2007, 2008; Cork 2009) are attempts to improve the sharing of knowledge about the issues surrounding this concept through open dialogue. We hope this volume will encourage further dialogue about how well Australia and Australians are preparing for the next few decades and beyond.

# References

Cork S (2009) 'Brighter prospects: Enhancing the resilience of Australia'. Australia21, Canberra, <www.australia21.org.au/pdf/A21%20Brighter%20Prospects%20Report.pdf>.

Cork S, Eckersley R and Walker B (2007) 'Rapid and surprising change in Australia's future – Anticipating and preparing for future challenges and opportunities on the way to a sustainable Australia'. Australia21, Canberra, <http://www.australia21.org.au/pdf/Tipping2007.pdf>.

Cork S, Walker B and Buckley R (2008) 'How resilient is Australia?'. Australia21, Canberra, <http://www.australia21.org.au/pdf/Resilient08.pdf >.

Resilience Alliance (2009) *Research on Resilience in Social–Ecological Systems – A Basis for Sustainability*. Resilience Alliance, Stockholm, <http://www.resalliance.org>.

Walker B and Salt D (2006) *Resilience Thinking: Sustaining Ecosystems and People in a Changing World*. Island Press, Washington, DC.

# CHAPTER 2

# Policy implications

Steven Cork

## Abstract

This chapter summarises and synthesises the thinking from the rest of this volume. A detailed summary of advice and recommendations is presented, followed by a shortlist of overarching recommendations and some discussion of these. This shortlist includes:

- learn from the substantial information on resilience that now exists
- apply governance processes that promote rather than inhibit resilience
- identify *what* is resilient *to what* pressures
- recognise that resilience is about more than good risk assessment
- recognise that resilience can be not only desirable but also undesirable
- address declining reserves.
- consider 'systems' at scales above and below the one currently under scrutiny
- develop a new approach to national security, prosperity and well-being
- develop nation-building response plans to address interrelated challenges
- take steps to achieve energy and water use efficiency, carbon-neutrality, eco-efficiency, green productivity, especially with respect to Australia's cities, and satisfaction of human cultural and other social needs

## Policy makers are increasingly focusing on resilience

Thinking about resilience has proceeded apace in business circles and academia over the past 5–10 years. This has included advice to policy makers about issues as diverse as environmental, organisational, governance, health and economic resilience, to which Australia21 has made several contributions (Cork *et al.* 2007, 2008; Cork 2009). It is impossible in the space available here to review the many ways in which the concept of resilience is finding its way into policy forums. The following examples give a flavour.

Australian policy makers have begun to focus on the challenging question of how resilience thinking can be applied not only *in* policies but also *to* the policy development process itself. For example, most major policies for environmental management in Australia include social and ecological resilience as key objectives (see Chapter 15, this volume). Similarly, the

Council of Australian Governments has endorsed resilience measures in early childhood development and the health sector and recently agreed to a *'new whole-of-nation, "resilience" based approach to natural disaster policy and programs, which recognises that a disaster resilient community is one that works together to understand and manage the risks that it confronts'*. This agreement has led to a 'National Disaster Resilience Statement' (Council of Australian Governments 2009).

The Attorney General of Australia recently announced the renaming and refocussing of its 'Critical Infrastructure *Protection*' program to 'Critical Infrastructure *Resilience*' (my emphasis) with a focus on organisational and disaster resilience. A 'Resilience Community of Interest' has been established between businesses and Commonwealth, State and Territory Government agencies with the objective of *'promoting the concept of organisational resilience within the business community generally, and critical infrastructure in particular, for the purposes of building a more resilient nation'* (TISN 2009). This community of interest worked with members of the business and risk management communities to run a 'National Organisational Resilience Framework Workshop' (TISN 2007). The Risk Management Institute of Australia's (RMIA) recent national conference focused on 'The Road to Resilience' (RMIA 2009). The 'Torrens Resilience Institute' was recently established in Adelaide (Torrens Resilience Institute 2009). Numerous organisations focus on resilience in New Zealand, including 'Resilient Organisations', which brings together *'engineering disciplines and business leadership aimed at transforming NZ organisations into those that both survive major events and thrive in the aftermath'* (Resilient Organisations 2009).

Internationally, resilience is prominent in research and policy forums at a range of scales from global to local (e.g. Millennium Ecosystem Assessment 2009; Resilience Alliance 2009) and in government and business debates (e.g. Cabinet Office UK 2009; Cascio 2009; International Resilience Project 2009; Skandinaviska Enskilda Banken 2009).

## Summary of advice and recommendations from individual chapters

As with all debates about policy, there is an inevitable gap between what people outside government think policy makers should do about resilience and what government policy makers think is feasible and attractive. Table 2.1 summarises the advice offered by the authors of the chapters in this book. Some of that advice is directed at government and some at industry and broader society. Most of the authors have considerable experience working in, or with, government policy agencies. Nevertheless, we do not pretend that the advice is definitive; it is a starting point for ongoing dialogue with professional policy makers about how to address the substantial challenges and opportunities that resilience thinking presents.

**Table 2.1**    Summary of advice and recommendations for the chapters of this volume

| Chapter | Advice/ recommendations |
|---|---|
| **Organisations and economies** | |
| **3**<br>**Organisational resilience**<br>**(Barratt)** | Apply the principles of effective and resilient organisations by learning from analyses of recent failures to deal with crisis situations and ensuring that all organisations with a regulatory or functional contribution to make perform their intended purpose to the required standard by ensuring that:<br>• they have a clear mission, are adequately resourced and adequately governed<br>• they have staff that is adequately trained and has appropriate authorities and resources<br>• there are clear relationships with other relevant organisations<br>• there are systems in place to ensure that the governing body and leadership are in control of the business at all times and have timely notice of any shortfalls in performance |
| **4**<br>**Managing for resilience**<br>**(Parker)** | Recognise that today's complex global environment of enhanced communication, new security threats and unforseen events demands a level of organisational resilience that goes beyond traditional defensive management tools such as business continuity planning and risk minimisation. This requires:<br>• recognition of the interdependencies of vertical and horizontal operations<br>• taking a hard look at organisational attributes including leadership and adaptive capability<br>• considering the distinction between defensive resilience (which includes traditional business practices that focus on known or anticipated challenges and opportunities) and offensive–strategic resilience (which is achieved by adopting a capability-based, anticipatory and adaptive approach that prepares an organisation for any disruptive event – whether it was planned for or not) |
| **5**<br>**Australia's economy**<br>**(Gruen and Quiggin)** | Increase national savings and the resilience of the Australian economy through, for example:<br>• investing some of the dividends of recent windfalls (including offshore)<br>• continuing and even expanding the policy of compulsory superannuation<br>• encouraging more conservative prudential policies for Australian financial institutions that keep aggregate borrowings from overseas sufficiently low to reduce the risk of a systemic failure arising from a credit crisis<br>• calibrating capital adequacy requirements and/or prudential rules on borrowing with greater sensitivity to the economic cycle<br>• providing a simple deposit-taking service that would give citizens a low cost and relatively liquid means of placing their savings with government in return for some reasonable interest payments as well as a means of making payments to others in the same system<br>• expanding government operations to protect against illiquidity in financial markets beyond the core banking markets within which current central banks now operate<br>• implementing a full-scale independent commission on the financial system |
| **Governance and security** | |
| **6**<br>**Governance and**<br>**robustness**<br>**(Marshall)** | Make governance systems more robust by transforming them towards polycentric systems (i.e. comprising multiple decision-making centres retaining substantive autonomy from one another) by, for example:<br>• applying the principle of subsidiarity – allocate each governance responsibility to the lowest level of governance with capacity to exercise it<br>• establishing multifaceted policies that encourage leadership at all levels of society, ongoing clear communication of 'resilience thinking' to lay people, sponsorship of deliberative forums that encourage the 'surfacing' and respectful challenging of outmoded beliefs, rewriting the textbooks and curricula for school and university education and making the most of those opportunities that do arise to craft polycentric governance arrangements, learn from them and celebrate their accomplishments<br>• actively experimenting (politicians and officials) with polycentric arrangements of such scale and scope that the risks are affordable to them<br>• considering alternative resourcing to allow participation of civil groups in polycentric arrangements, limiting reliance on government funding |

| **Governance and security** *continued* | |
|---|---|
| **7**<br>**Security, prosperity and resilience**<br>**(Behm)** | Develop a new security logic that addresses the emergent strategic discontinuities, the huge shifts in power balance and the new threats to national well-being that reside in the complex cocktail of nationalism, ideological competition, terrorism, pandemics, global warming and the growing prospects of a global competition for energy and water, by, for example: |
| | • expanding the traditional approach to national security from a concentration on the power of the state to include the rights of its citizens to live rewarding, fulfilling and prosperous lives<br>• developing a robust framework for national governance that supports the national security and prosperity programs but remains independent of the cyclical changes of government<br>• establishing processes that recognise a single point of accountability with responsibility to consult all who should be consulted, to canvass all the issues fairly, dispassionately and professionally and to produce clear and implementable recommendations that are the personal responsibility of the official preparing the advice<br>• helping the community to understand the nature of the attack on values and to accept that an appropriate response is not to apologise for what Australia stands for but to promote those values<br>• taking a 'whole-of-government' approach to security policy that integrates 'soft' power initiatives with 'hard' power capabilities and recognises that the drivers of national prosperity – education, infrastructure investment, health and the growth of social capital – are central to any evolved concept of national security<br>• investing in government's capacity for long-term strategic thinking<br>• considering how best to liberate the considerable intellectual resources that reside in universities, industry, business and the corporate world, as well as the public services, by increasing the number of parties to the national security conversation – providing not only 'contestability' but also creativity and imagination<br>• removing barriers between and within the departments of state that hinder development and implementation of holistic security policies |
| **8**<br>**Global financial system**<br>**(Buckley)** | Make the global financial system fairer, reducing the extent to which it favours the powerful and therefore disempowering the feedback loops that make the current system so resistant to change by, for example: |
| | • promoting lending to developing countries in their own currencies<br>• granting more debt relief to more poor countries<br>• stopping the socialisation of private-sector debt in debt restructurings<br>• introducing a fair and independent arbitration process for sovereign bankruptcy<br>• moving towards a different global reserve currency, perhaps an instrument crafted from a basket of currencies |
| **Energy and settlements** | |
| **9**<br>**Peak oil**<br>**(Dunlop)** | A resilience approach to peak oil will require: |
| | • an honest public acknowledgment by Australian governments and business leaders of the real challenges we now face<br>• urgent education campaigns to inform the community and gain support for the hard decisions ahead<br>• establishment of an emergency, nation-building response plan to place the economy on a low-carbon footing, minimising the consumption of oil, including: a major focus on energy conservation and energy efficiency; large scale conversion to renewable energy; major investment in efficient public transport, rail, bus, cycling, etc., and an immediate halt to investment in freeway and airport expansion; a rapid phasing out of high carbon emission facilities such as coal-fired power stations unless safe carbon capture and storage can be introduced within 10 years; urgent introduction of high-speed broadband to minimise travel and improve communication efficiency; continued investment in low-emission technology; a focus on biological, as well as geological, carbon sequestration; a rapid reform of the tax system to remove perverse incentives that encourage oil use and carbon emissions |

| 10<br>**Resilient cities**<br>**(Newman)** | In order to create resilience in cities, globally and in Australia, there will need to be:<br><br>• renewable energy strategies showing how to tap local resources progressively<br>• carbon-neutral strategies that can enforce energy efficiency, integrate with the renewables strategy and direct the carbon offsets into the bioregion<br>• distributed infrastructure strategies that enable small-scale energy and water systems to flourish<br>• biophilic or green infrastructure strategies that include the photosynthetic resources of the city and which can enhance the green agenda across the city through food, fibre, biodiversity and recreation pursuits locally<br>• eco-efficiency strategies linking industries to achieve fundamental changes in the metabolism of cities<br>• 'sense-of-place' strategies to ensure the human dimension is driving all the other strategies<br>• sustainable transport strategies |
|---|---|
| **Health and education** | |
| 11<br>**Personal health**<br>**(Douglas)** | Introduce issues of resilience, learned helplessness and control into our thinking about health and health care and their significance for the way health services are managed and, especially:<br><br>• encourage research to understand if control of one's own care is an important modulating factor in relation to health outcomes<br>• take the results into account in reform of the health system |
| 12<br>**Early childhood**<br>**(Burgess)** | There is currently underway in Australia considerable reform activity, in terms of resources, time and policy development in early childhood development systems and services. Resilience thinking provides a way to identify barriers and harness positive drivers of change in this reform process. Key recommendations note that:<br><br>• there is now a large body of evidence demonstrating that integrated, family-centred policies and programs produce the most effective and efficient outcomes in early childhood development. Australia must ensure that its various systems can work together to achieve this<br>• Australia must begin a process of mapping and understanding its early childhood development systems, and their interactions, to identify the specific elements that relate to early childhood and to try to identify facilitators and barriers to these elements interrelating effectively<br>• the push for reform, with the provision of supporting resources, is a key enabler of change, as is the now very large bank of evidence around the importance of the early years<br>• the importance of the willingness of stakeholders to come together to drive reform should not be underestimated<br>• resilience theory alerts us to the high levels of potentially undesirable resilience that appear to exist in the old systems and the need to overcome this resilience if desirable changes are to be achieved<br>• while significant reform processes have begun at State and Commonwealth level to bring the early childhood care and learning systems together with the education system, the policies and processes for linking these with the health and child protection systems are much less clear<br>• a number of major policy initiatives have been developed by the Federal and State Governments and it is now time to consider how they can be effectively implemented |
| 13<br>**Population health**<br>**(Eckersley)** | We need to think of health not just as an individual illness that requires treatment, but also as an issue having national, even global, causes and consequences that need to be addressed urgently to avoid potentially catastrophic outcomes. Recommended actions include:<br><br>• pay serious and urgent attention to indications of declining social, physical and emotional well-being among young Australians<br>• think of health as more than a matter of healthcare services (including increasing the proportion of the health budget allocated to prevention and public health and removing the bias against mental health)<br>• reorient education to give it a clearer focus on increasing young people's understanding of themselves and the world to promote human growth and development, not just materially, but socially, culturally and spiritually<br>• set stricter standards for the corporate sector, especially the media and marketing industries, to guard against moral hazard and psychological harm<br>• work to change the stories or narratives by which Australians define themselves, their lives and their goals, including making better health (in the broadest sense), not greater wealth, the nation's defining goal |

| Health and education *continued* | |
| --- | --- |
| **14**<br>**Education**<br>**(Lewis** *et al.***)** | A shared, bipartisan national vision for education in Australia, which is independent of the three-year electoral cycle and takes a long-term strategic perspective, is essential. Such an approach should prepare Australia to deal with likely future drivers of change in education this century. It should include:<br><br>• preparing young people to be flexible as part of global production and knowledge systems<br>• fostering creativity<br>• rethinking funding structures to encourage flexibility<br>• encouraging innovation in training and education<br>• encouraging long-term planning<br>• moving on from the old paradigm of 'public' versus 'private' education<br>• accepting that there are many ways we can educate people in Australia and they should be valued, and that we must concentrate on developing every Australian to their full potential to enhance individual worth, social capital and the 'public good' |

| Environment and society | |
| --- | --- |
| **15**<br>**Social–ecological systems**<br>**(Cork)** | Policies for building and/or maintaining social and ecological resilience, which are high priorities in most major government and non-government strategies for managing Australia's natural resources, must aim to encourage diversity, modularity and tightness of feedbacks (manifested as a variety of skills and ideas, connectedness, openness, reserves of resources, and governance systems that match appropriate people and organisations with the scales and locations of different challenges and opportunities). Recommended actions include:<br><br>• investment in research to improve our understanding of the dependency relationships between humans and ecosystems and the factors likely to influence each in the future<br>• being transparent about the policy problem (implementation of most environmental–social strategies by government and non-government organisations appears to be directed by political, economic and other constraints that are not explicitly acknowledged and mostly work against resilience)<br>• avoiding partial policy and management solutions by thinking about how immediate problems are related to processes operating across difference scales of time, space and jurisdictional responsibilities and by encouraging interdisciplinary, inter-organisational and inter-jurisdictional cooperation where appropriate<br>• building on steps towards 'regional models' to transition to governance systems that give decision-making authority and resources not only to central agencies but also to organisations and people that operate close to environmental change so that changes are detected and responded to effectively<br>• avoiding the downsides of and narrow interpretations of 'efficiency', which powerfully erode ecological and social resilience |
| **16**<br>**Climate change**<br>**(Barratt** *et al.***)** | Policies that are resilient in the face of climate change should:<br><br>• receive sufficient support across the political spectrum that a change of government is not likely to produce radical change in the policy<br>• be practical, implementable and equitable so that no significant sectors of society feel that they are carrying a disproportionate share of the burden or receiving an inadequate share of the benefits<br>• be applicable if matters do not turn out quite as we expect (i.e. covering as wide a range of credible outcomes as possible relating not only to changes in temperature, precipitation and weather patterns, but also to changes in our terms of trade, changes in the economic, social and environmental circumstances of countries in our region, and increasing demand upon the humanitarian capabilities of the Australian Defence Force and Australian NGOs)<br>• include measures that are directed to extracting carbon from the atmosphere, rather than just abating emissions, and that enable Australia to adapt to the changed circumstances including any irreversible tipping points that the world climate system might pass<br>• be consistent with all of the knowledge and evidence that we have, even if there are gaps in our knowledge that we have to fill as best we can with informed judgements and even if this evidence flies in the face of conservative or ideologically held views of the way things are and the way they therefore should remain (waiting for 'perfect' knowledge will probably ensure phenomena that threaten a resilient future)<br>• command wide public understanding and support from the public, who understand there is a problem and agree that action must be taken and understand the arguments for the particular measures that are adopted to address the problem (policy that is not understood by the public cannot be considered resilient) |

| 17<br>Global change<br>(Grigg) | Give serious consideration to guidance by earth-systems scientists on those aspects of global change that are of most concern.<br><br>Pay attention to the explanations from resilience thinkers about why our current institutions are failing us and consider their ideas about the kinds of institutions that would be more effective, particularly:<br><br>• understanding the significance of system interconnections and especially barriers that prevent integrated approaches<br>• developing global ethical principles that have the potential to allow humanity to build bridges where currently there are barriers |
|---|---|
| **Disaster preparedness and recovery** | |
| 18<br>Biosecurity<br>(Prowse) | Two central elements that will determine Australia's national capacity to respond adaptively to biosecurity threats in the future are developing and maintaining an adequate pool of trained personnel and the way information is generated and shared. Policies and actions to address these elements should include (noting that AusBIOSEC is a policy initiative by the Commonwealth and State Governments providing a framework of common principles and guidelines to enable biosecurity arrangements to be applied consistently across Australia):<br><br>• ongoing consolidation of biosecurity activities across plants, insects, animals and aquaculture sectors, including co-location of complementary animal, food and human science<br>• enhanced planning and simulation exercises to identify biosecurity response needs and to set priorities<br>• continued improvement of information management<br>• broader responsibility in the community increasing industry involvement in disease surveillance and in the management of outbreak responses<br>• encouraging the biosecurity community to take advantage of new technology to collect and analyse diverse sources of information and to accept that alternative sources of information are of value and complement traditional information about threats<br>• building on existing initiatives to achieve an appropriately sized workforce with adequate skills and capabilities<br>• careful evaluation of new technologies to ensure scarce resources are wisely spent<br>• adopting a cross-sectoral and cross-jurisdictional 'one-health' approach, requiring genuine interdepartmental and inter-agency collaborative research and operational programs that develop the human disease, livestock disease and wildlife disease networks at research and operational levels |
| 19<br>Pandemic preparedness<br>(Douglas) | Build on the preparation for a serious influenza pandemic, and the whole-of-government approaches that have been evident in Australia's response to swine influenza, to enhance the resilience of Australia's pandemic preparedness by, in the longer term:<br><br>• reviewing Australia's constitutional arrangements, bringing the community into the planning process and expanding our thinking and planning beyond government<br>• preparing the community for a broad range of possible pandemic agents and the likelihood that pandemic assault could occur at the same time as other future systemic shocks<br><br>More immediate actions include:<br><br>• calling a national pandemic planning summit that brings civil society from across Australia into a planning exercise that expands ownership of pandemic planning from government to the community at large and from influenza to a broad suite of pandemic scenarios<br>• developing a series of 'hypotheticals' in communities across the nation, in which community leaders are encouraged to experiment with the ideas for managing catastrophe in their community (e.g. 'how would we cope with an 80% attack rate and a 50% death rate from the release of small pox virus in our town or city?')<br>• involving the community (perhaps starting with high school students) in an open discussion about who should be the first recipients of limited supplies of life-saving drugs and prophylactic vaccines in their school and community<br>• developing some realistic media productions about what makes some societies able to adapt and transform in response to catastrophic events while others spiral into chaos<br>• promoting discussion in schools, hospitals, churches and small businesses about 'first-aid community plans' for what to do if 40% of the population suddenly becomes seriously ill with a highly contagious infectious disease<br>• developing plans for substantial 'surge capacity' in the availability of emergency beds to care for victims of a fast moving pandemic |

| Disaster preparedness and recovery *continued* | |
|---|---|
| **20**<br>**Communication**<br>**(Nicholls)** | Recognise that good communication (two-way dialogue, hearing as well as speaking and being willing to act on the mutual exchange of information, opinion and expressed wants and needs) among communities and government or other agencies is essential for building and maintaining resilience in a risk environment, or when dealing with disaster and its aftermath.<br><br>Apply the principles of good communication to build community resilience in disaster and disaster recovery by:<br><br>• assisting in preparation and mitigation through carefully designed communication campaigns<br>• engaging in two-way dialogue about response during a crisis<br>• contributing to and, where possible, expediting recovery through a combination of information and dialogue<br>• learning from communication successes and failures in disasters such as the Canberra bushfires of 2003, the Victorian fires of 2008, the 11 September 2001 attacks in the USA and New Orleans' response to Hurricane Katrina in 2005 |
| **21**<br>**Transforming adversity**<br>**(Citraningtyas)** | Enhance Australia's capacity to deal with disasters, by not just enhancing the capacity of systems to deal with the unexpected but also enhancing the capacity of the people and creating integration between people and formal systems. This can be achieved by:<br><br>• catering to the needs of families in places where people work and study, just as families have adapted to the requirements of work and study<br>• paving the way to better negotiation of expectations and greater collaboration by enhancing communication between components of the system<br>• facilitating flexible partnerships that take into account persons as a whole and a part of community units as a way to reduce personal versus professional conflicts<br>• reforming formal systems to go beyond professional roles, clear job descriptions, mandates and hierarchies, so that that focus on people, relationships, families and communities as a whole in all aspects of life<br>• not waiting for disasters to bring an end of civilisation as we know it, but transforming our civilisation, and ourselves |

## Key themes and overarching recommendations

In Box 2.1, I present a shortlist of recommendations that I think captures the cross-cutting advice emerging from the chapters. These are elaborated on below. There are many other recommendations that could be included from the literature on resilience, but I have restricted myself to what has been said in this volume. The shortlist is intended to stimulate dialogue rather than be a definitive recipe for achieving a resilient Australia.

### *Recognise, and learn from, the substantial body of information that now exists on personal, organisational and societal resilience in the face of recent and past environmental, social and economic challenges*

Barratt (Chapter 3) draws on several case studies to illustrate lessons that can be learned from past failures of organisational processes and to draw inferences about how to build and maintain resilience, especially in the public sector. Parker (Chapter 4) summarises a wealth of experience from public and private sector organisations. She makes the point that resilience needs to be more than good risk assessment (i.e. asking 'what if?') – it needs also to prepare an organisation culturally and emotionally for unexpected events and trends. There is a warning to all groups of people who seek to assess and manage their resilience: be cautious of 'tick-the-box' exercises that focus only on obvious and readily measurable (usually structural) attributes but can overlook less tangible, but vital, aspects of resilience.

Gruen and Quiggin (Chapter 5) seek lessons from recent upheavals in the global financial system and conclude that Australia's resilience was, at least partly, conferred by lucky decisions and policies. Nevertheless, this luck yields insights into what decisions could be made in the

## Box 2.1    A shortlist of overarching recommendations from this volume

- Recognise, and learn from, the substantial body of information that now exists on personal, organisational and societal resilience in the face of recent and past environmental, social and economic challenges.
- Develop and apply societal and organisational governance processes that promote rather than inhibit resilience.
- Invest appropriate time and resources identifying what is resilient to what pressures whether in the government or other sectors, recognise that resilience is about more than good risk assessment and expand the scope of preparing for the future to include the ability to deal with the unexpected and unimaginable.
- Recognise that resilience can be not only desirable but also undesirable.
- Address declining reserves: consider what levels of reserves of human and other resources and diversity of ideas and approaches are needed for a resilient Australia and take steps to increase these where levels are too low.
- Consider 'systems' at scales above and below the one currently under scrutiny.
- Develop a new approach to national security, prosperity and well-being.
- Develop nation-building response plans to address a number of interrelated challenges across all sectors of Australian society.
- Especially with respect to Australia's cities, take steps to achieve efficient energy and water use, carbon-neutrality, eco-efficiency, green productivity and satisfaction of human cultural and other social needs.

future to achieve resilience of Australia's economy. Buckley (Chapter 8) concludes that there are many economically and ethically undesirable aspects of global financial governance, demonstrated by recent lending decisions, that are perpetuated by strong 'undesirable' resilience in the system. Buckley concludes that, in this case, our aim should be to break down the system's resilience rather than enhance it.

Eckersley (Chapter 13) draws lessons from trends in population health and concludes that the ability of Australians to cope with the future would be enhanced if the artificial distinction between mental and physical health was removed and if the ways in which we describe our lives and aspirations were based on a broader understanding of well-being than the current one, which is based strongly on economic prosperity.

Nicholls (Chapter 20) distils lessons – from terrorist attacks and natural disasters in the USA and from bushfire disasters in the Australian Capital Territory and Victoria – about how well-designed communication can help communities prepare for and recover from disasters.

A lesson that is emerging from the convergence of physical and social sciences is the importance of recognising the different psychological responses to highly threatening situations, including active denial, passive denial, blame, vested interests and narrow perspectives (Barratt *et al.*, Chapter 16).

Other chapters draw on examples but they also develop assertions and theory about the nature of resilience and what steps are required to address Australia's needs that must be tested by looking at past examples and setting up experiments to test future initiatives.

*Develop and apply societal and organisational governance processes that promote rather than inhibit resilience and actively experiment with new governance approaches*

Almost every author in this volume identifies aspects of current governance arrangements, across all sectors of Australian society, that appear to be working against resilience. Although different authors base their discussion on different definitions or conceptualisations of resilience, there is strong agreement about the attributes of governance and institutional arrangements that are needed to prepare Australia for future challenges and opportunities (Box 2.2). All authors express concern that some or all of these attributes are declining or at worryingly low levels. The list in Box 2.2 is very similar to the attributes of resilience identified by recent research and summarised in Chapter 15.

Gruen and Quiggin (Chapter 5) conclude that Australia's economy is much more resilient to minor economic shocks than it was a generation ago – due to greater flexibility of response – but it is not clear that our economy is more resilient to large shocks of the kind that produce depressions.

Marshal (Chapter 6) presents evidence of substantial robustness dividends from adopting polycentric rather than monocentric governance. He points out that Australian governments have been making tentative attempts to move in this direction since the 1970s but he suggests that vested interests and persistence of modernist beliefs pose formidable obstacles to this transformation. He argues that the transformation could be facilitated if politicians and officials began experimenting actively with polycentric arrangements, at scales that keep risks within comfortable limits, so that experience can be gained and confidence built. Cork (Chapter 15) identifies reluctance to address governance issues as a major factor preventing the lessons from resilience thinking being implemented in government environmental polices around Australia.

## Box 2.2   Attributes of governance systems and other institutional arrangements identified as being important for resilience by authors in the volume

- Leadership and statesmanship.
- Clear and agreed visions, objectives, roles, responsibilities and resourcing.
- Encouragement of diverse ideas and skills.
- Modularity of networks.
- Feedbacks that ensure rapid and effective detection of change, and the capture and sharing of relevant information.
- Capacity for, and encouragement of, self-organisation.
- Governance that spreads authority and responsibility more broadly across society, considering which people and organisations are best placed to detect and deal with change, to collect and disseminate information and to catalyse cooperative actions.
- Development and testing of suitable approaches to implementing polycentric governance.
- Processes that truly engage a wide range of Australian society in meaningful dialogue that informs them, listens to their views and involves them in the processes of detecting and responding to threatening *and* beneficial change.

The issues outlined by Marshal are echoed in most other chapters to some degree. In particular, Behm (Chapter 7), Douglas (Chapters 11 and 19), Burgess (Chapter 12), Lewis *et al.* (Chapter 14), Barratt *et al.* (Chapter 16), Nicholls (Chapter 20) and Citraningtyas (Chapter 21) discuss the importance of individuals, families and communities being able to feel involved, informed, resourced and listened to in critical decision-making processes and to feel a sense of control over their own destinies if they are to remain optimistic and motivated to prepare for uncertain futures and recover from set-backs, ranging from disasters to the challenges of growing up and ageing. These aspects of governance have often been overlooked by Australian governments (KPMG 2009) but hopefully the lessons of recent disasters will lead to improved harnessing of the substantial social and human capital that exists in communities.

Similarly, Buckley (Chapter 8) argues for reforms that give developing countries greater control over their own destinies as a way to remove undesirable resilience from the global financial systems and build desirable resilience in those countries.

Prowse (Chapter 18) observes that scientists work in an increasingly complex and technologically sophisticated environment and need to consider a wider range of factors than ever before if their work is to be effective and often do not know where to turn to for collaboration and information. He concludes that *'platforms for collaboration exist within specific research disciplines but numerous gaps inhibit them from operating effectively across disciplines'*. These conclusions are drawn with respect to biosecurity but they apply much more broadly across scientific and other communities that deal in knowledge. Prowse acknowledges, however, that substantial advances are being made with respect to biosecurity, which could provide models for other sectors.

### *Invest appropriate time and resources identifying what is resilient to what pressures*

Consider a typical definition of resilience: *'the capacity of a system to absorb disturbance and reorganise while undergoing change so as to still retain essentially the same function, structure, identity and feedbacks'*. Whether a system is considered to be resilient depends on who is doing the considering and what they value about the system. For example, a person who values agricultural industries might consider a regional social–ecological system to be resilient in a positive way if agriculture continues to thrive despite climatic and economic changes, but a person who values biodiversity might see the same system as being non-resilient with respect to retaining native species. A third person who would like to see major changes in land-use in the region might think the social–ecological system is undesirably resilient if it makes it hard to achieve those changes. Thus, in order to think seriously about resilience, and to take action, it is essential to identify what aspects of a system are retained because of its resilience, or might be retained if that resilience was enhanced, and who values what aspects of the system.

Gruen and Quiggin (Chapter 5) bring this issue into focus with respect to the resilience of Australia's economy. They argue that many major environmental problems might be expensive to Australian governments, businesses and individuals but that they are unlikely to threaten the resilience of the overall economy. This raises the question, 'what are the essential *function, structure, identity and feedbacks* of the Australian economy?' Some people might think that major problems in the agricultural sector represent a fundamental change to Australia's economy (and therefore that its resilience has been overcome) but others would argue that the economy is being resilient so long as GDP continues to grow. There is no right answer but it is important for these issues to be discussed or different stakeholders will be talking about different things when discussing resilience.

These issues emerge in some form in most chapters of this volume. Another example is Eckersley's assertion (Chapter 13) that *'to enhance Australia's resilience, we need to make 'better health' (in the broadest sense), not 'greater wealth', the nation's defining goal'.* The 'system' that Eckersley focuses on encompasses processes impinging on all aspects of human well-being. As Eckersley points out, however, others have argued that life has never been better, based on a narrower set of issues, such as life expectancy. For Eckersley, Australia is not resilient if it allows optimism, confidence and hope for the future to decline, whereas for others taking a narrower perspective Australia is resilient because we continue to live longer on average each year.

### *Whether in the government or other sectors, recognise that resilience is about more than good risk assessment and expand the scope of preparing for the future to include the ability to deal with the unexpected and unimaginable*

Parker (Chapter 4) makes this point strongly with respect to businesses – it is one that is easily overlooked. Resilience has become a hot topic in the business sector largely as a way to decrease the impacts of shocks like the global financial crisis. Traditional approaches to risk management and preparation for the future focus on predictable or imaginable events and trends ('specified resilience'). For example, presentations on business resilience frequently mention resilience of the supply chain and the risks of relying too heavily on single suppliers for critical components. This is consistent with the tendency in all walks of human life to focus on relatively certain and controllable aspects of the future (Figure 2.1) while avoiding uncertain and uncontrollable aspects (van der Heijden 1996; Peterson *et al.* 2003).

Many challenges and opportunities are neither predictable nor avoidable. Developing cultures that value awareness, anticipation, imagination, learning and other attributes that support 'strategic conversations' (Schwartz 1996, 2003) has given organisations and societies in the past the ability to detect change early, prepare and respond appropriately, and recover or transform in an orderly way (Diamond 2005). Most of the chapters in this volume focus on specified resilience, which is understandable given that the brief of the authors was to comment

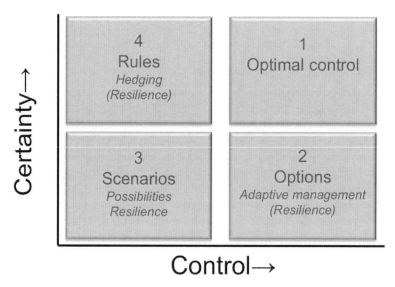

**Figure 2.1**   Different approaches to dealing with the future depending on controllability of actions and certainty about outcomes (modified from Peterson *et al.* 2003). Resilience thinking is particularly useful in quadrant 3 but also in 2 and 4.

on resilience in relation to specific issues. It is important, however, that the development of general resilience is not overlooked.

### *Recognise that resilience can be not only desirable but also undesirable*

The distinction between desirable and undesirable resilience is often not considered and yet it could be the difference between successful and failed policies and plans.

A system's resilience is desirable to stakeholders if it maintains functions, structures and identity that those stakeholders value, but resilience can be undesirable to stakeholders who want to change a system. This is an example of an insight that comes when we move from using resilience as a slogan and think more deeply about it.

Buckley (Chapter 8) and Burgess (Chapter 12) draw attention to the resilience of global financial governance and the health, education and early childhood development systems that make it difficult to bring about change. Most other chapters identify aspects of existing systems that they think should be changed and others that should be retained.

It is not a new idea to suggest that some aspects of a system might work against the changes one is trying to bring about (for example, this is what systems thinkers call reinforcing versus balancing loops) but it is an issue that can be overlooked in the enthusiasm of *building* resilience. Sometimes, our strategies might have to involve *breaking down* some resilience.

### *Address declining reserves: consider what levels of reserves of human and other resources and diversity of ideas and approaches are needed for a resilient Australia and take steps to increase these where levels are too low*

Adequate reserves are fundamental for resilience in any systems. The question is how much of any resource is needed and what level of reserves is required. As Cork (Chapter 15) points out, application of overly narrow approaches to efficiency have the potential to drastically reduce resilience by running down reserves. Examples of reserves that authors have suggested are in need of enhancement in Australia include national savings (Chapter 5) and skills in biosecurity (Chapter 18), pandemic preparedness (Chapter 19), strategic thinking (Chapters 3, 4, 8, 9, 15 and 16 in particular), environmental sciences (Chapter 15), education (Chapter 14) and communication skills and resources (Chapters 20 and 21). Most chapters also expressed concern about running down social capital, including people's goodwill, enthusiasm, optimism and altruism if Australia's leaders are unable to instil confidence about how the nation is preparing for the future.

### *Consider 'systems' at scales above and below the one under scrutiny*

Most authors in this volume have given examples of how resilience of a system can only be considered usefully if we also consider the larger systems that it sits within and the smaller systems within it. This is the concept of 'panarchy' from social–ecological research (Gunderson and Holling 2002). This relates to the discussion above about factors that work against building and maintaining desirable resilience – often these factors are operating at different scales to ones we are focusing on and can be overlooked unless we consider those different scales.

Grigg (Chapter 17) highlights the separation of actions from impacts as a common and significant barrier to resilience. As well as time and space, Grigg identifies a range of more subtle drivers of separation, including: the classification of knowledge into different disciplines; decision-making confined to narrow terms of reference; the interplay between individual and collective interests; and a focus on local efficiency. She proposes that shared global ethical principles are needed to negotiate this barrier.

Burgess (Chapter 12) illustrates how thinking beyond early childhood development systems to health and education at state, national and even global scales is vital to understand what needs to change in early childhood development and why it has been hard to make those changes.

Similarly, Buckley (Chapter 8) shows how processes within developed nations are responsible for undesirable resilience of global financial governance, making it difficult to simply change the 'rules' at a global level.

The issues of scales and thinking beyond the immediate system of interest have been emphasised for many years by systems thinkers and are at the heart of debates in the policy sciences about perverse policy outcomes.

### Develop a new approach to national security, prosperity and well-being

Most chapters argue for the rethinking of elements of how Australians perceive themselves and of the options available for dealing with future challenges and opportunities. Two chapters in particular challenge Australia to make fundamental changes. Eckersley (Chapter 13) argues that ' *we must reconceptualise health and healthcare, reorient education and set stricter standards for the corporate sector, especially in media and marketing … make 'better health' (in the broadest sense), not 'greater wealth', the nation's defining goal'*. Behm (Chapter 7) proposes that national security now '*has as much to do with clean water, reliable food supplies and individual and community wellbeing as with the ability of the state to protect its sovereignty against threats from other states*' and that '*in the 21st century, national security must transcend defence and law enforcement systems to include resilience and social inclusion, the protection of rights and the promotion of values*'. Apart from the assertion that some of Australia's values might be worth reconsidering, these two challenges are about taking holistic approaches to what Australia seeks to be and to achieve. Virtually all informed discussions about resilience in the literature make this same point – that retaining the core values of a country or any other system requires both encouraging dialogue about those values and considering how the many facets of life in that system interact to give it resilience.

Taking these two challenges together with others from throughout this volume, a new approach to national security, prosperity and well-being should include at least the following factors and the interactions among them: population health; social and economic implications of environmental change; allowing individuals to retain power in and over their circumstances while feeling supported by the system; genuine two-way communication between all sectors of society; capacity to respond as a society to disease and biosecurity challenges; maintenance of personal, family and community financial security; a strong focus on giving children a good start in life; developing an education system that supports diversity and originality of thinking while preparing people of all ages to deal with the world; helping Australians to understand the nature of global changes in power and attitudes and what role they can play in defending Australia's values while helping other countries to defend theirs; making best use of Australia's intellectual resources; removing barriers to cooperation between and within parts of Australian society, government and business; and considering and promoting national visions and narratives that give Australians hope and confidence while promoting quality of life for all.

### Develop nation-building response plans to address a number of interrelated challenges across all sectors of Australian society

Although not all authors in this volume express opinions about how urgent the need for action is in their area of expertise, these opinions probably would vary. In two areas – energy and climate change – urgency is emphasised very strongly. Dunlop (Chapter 9) argues that not only is action needed urgently to address the possibility of declining oil availability in the very near future but that *'Australian governments and business leaders should be honest and open about the real challenges we now face with respect to energy, climate change and unsustainable consumption of resources generally and development of a nation-building response plan to address the challenges across all sectors of society ... '*

Similarly, Barratt *et al.* (Chapter 16) observe that *'human experience is no guide to the magnitude and urgency of the climate-change issue'*. They argue that there is an urgent need to expand dialogue about climate change *'not only to changes in precipitation, temperature and weather patterns, but also to changes in our terms of trade, destruction of our tourist icons, changes in the social, economic and environmental circumstances of countries in our region and increasing demand upon the humanitarian capabilities of the Australian Defence Force and Australian non-government organisations'* and that *'uncertainty on this issue is not a reason for delaying decisions but flexibility can be maintained through application of a portfolio approach to energy options while national and international experience are developed'*.

### *Especially with respect to Australia's cities, take steps to achieve efficient energy and water use, carbon-neutrality, eco-efficiency, green productivity and satisfaction of human cultural and other social needs*

What is surprising in the media coverage of sustainability, carbon emissions, oil depletion and water use is the rarity of stories about the substantial knowledge and technology already available to address these issues, especially in the design of cities. Newman (Chapter 10) reviews progress and ideas about how cities can be made resilient to anticipated and unanticipated challenges and opportunities of the coming decades. Harking back to the discussions above, Newman illustrates how important it is to define what values we want to promote and retain in future cities, by identifying seven archetypes that emphasise different attributes. Perhaps there is merit in considering a set of resilient-Australia archetypes to guide dialogue about future nation-building?

## Conclusions

The insights from the authors in this volume accord well with the opinions expressed by participants in a workshop help by Australia21 in 2008 (Cork *et al.* 2008). These participants, from across Australian academic, business, health, education, defence, public administration and other sectors, were also concerned about declining diversity, dwindling reserves, inadequate national leadership and non-inclusive governance systems that do not address the scale and magnitude of current and future challenges and opportunities. While a lot of progress has been made in understanding resilience, assessment of Australia's resilience must still be based largely on opinion as the necessary data have not yet been collected in ways that support a more robust assessment. Australia21 hopes that the opinions expressed in this volume will generate dialogue that leads to further critical thinking and data collection so that Australia's future-preparedness can be considered more rigorously.

## References

Cabinet Office UK (2009) *UK Resilience Homepage*. Cabinet Office, London, <http://www.cabinetoffice.gov.uk/ukresilience.aspx>.

Cascio J (2009) The next big thing: Resilience. *Foreign Policy* **May/June 2009**, <http://www.foreignpolicy.com/story/cms.php?story_id=4851>.

Cork S (2009) 'Brighter prospects: Enhancing the resilience of Australia'. Australia21, Canberra, <www.australia21.org.au/pdf/A21%20Brighter%20Prospects%20Report.pdf>.

Cork S, Eckersley R and Walker B (2007) 'Rapid and surprising change in Australia's future – Anticipating and preparing for future challenges and opportunities on the way to a sustainable Australia'. Australia21, Canberra, <http://www.australia21.org.au/pdf/Tipping2007.pdf>.

Cork S, Walker B and Buckley R (2008) 'How resilient is Australia?' Australia21, Canberra, <http://www.australia21.org.au/pdf/Resilient08.pdf >.

Council of Australian Governments (2009) *Council of Australian Governments' Meeting - 7 December 2009*. Commonwealth of Australia, Canberra, <http://www.coag.gov.au/coag_meeting_outcomes/2009-12-07/index.cfm>.

Diamond J (2005) *Collapse: How Societies Choose to Fail or Succeed*. Viking Press, New York.

Gunderson L and Holling CS (editors) (2002) *Panarchy: understanding transformations in human and natural systems*. Island Press, Washington, DC.

International Resilience Project (2009) *The International Resilience Project*. The International Resilience Project (IRP), Halifax, Nova Scotia, <http://www.resilienceproject.org/index.cfm?fuseaction=text.&str_cmpID=227>.

KPMG (2009) 'Benchmarking Australian Government Administration Performance'. KPMG, Australia, <http://www.dpmc.gov.au/consultation/aga_reform/docs/benchmarking_australian_government_KPMG.pdf>.

McClelland R (2009) *Remarks at the Critical Infrastructure Advisory Council Meeting*. Office of the Attorney-General for Australia, Canberra, <http://www.attorneygeneral.gov.au/www/ministers/mcclelland.nsf/Page/Speeches_2009_FourthQuarter_9December2009-RemarksattheCriticalInfrastructureAdvisoryCouncilMeeting>.

Peterson GD, Cumming G and Carpenter SR (2003) Scenario planning: a tool for conservation in an uncertain world. *Conservation Biology* **17**, 358–366.

Resilient Organisations (2009) *Resilient Organisations*. Resilient Organisations, Christchurch, NZ, <http://www.resorgs.org.nz/index.shtml>.

Risk Management Institution of Australasia (2009) *Home page*. Risk Management Institution of Australasia, Carlton South, Victoria, Australia, <http://www.rmia.org.au/>.

Schwartz P (1996) *The Art of the Long View*. Currency Doubleday, New York.

Schwartz P (2003) *Inevitable Surprises: Thinking Ahead in a Time of Turbulence*. Gotham Books, New York.

Skandinaviska Enskilda Banken (2009) *Eastern European Outlook: Resilience is Eroding*. Skandinaviska Enskilda Banken AB, Stockholm, <http://www.seb.se/pow/wcp/index.asp?ss=/pow/wcp/templates/sebarticle.cfmc.asp%3FDUID%3DDUID_A52D488A7D0E9123C12574DC00328543%26sitekey%3Dseb.se%26lang%3Dse>.

Torrens Resilience Institute (2009) *Torrens Resilience Institute*. Torrens Resilience Institute, Adelaide, <http://torrensresilience.org/>.

Trusted Information Sharing Network (2007) *National Organisational Resilience Framework Workshop*. Commonwealth of Australia, Canberra, <http://www.tisn.gov.au/www/tisn/rwpattach.nsf/VAP/(99292794923AE8E7CBABC6FB71541EE1)~Resilience+FINAL+Workshop+Report.pdf/$file/Resilience+FINAL+Workshop+Report.pdf>.

Trusted Information Sharing Network (2009) *Resilience Community of Interest*. Commonwealth of Australia, Canberra, <http://www.tisn.gov.au/www/tisn/tisn.nsf/Page/AbouttheTISN_ResilienceCommunityofInterest>.

van der Heijden K (1996) *Scenarios. The Art of Strategic Conversation*. John Wiley & Sons, Chichester, UK.

# ORGANISATIONS AND ECONOMIES

# CHAPTER 3

# Organising to deliver resilience

Paul Barratt

## Abstract

Of fundamental importance in delivering resilience in any domain is ensuring that all organisations with a regulatory or functional contribution to make actually perform their intended purpose to the required standard. This means ensuring that they have a clear mission, are adequately resourced and adequately governed, have staff that is adequately trained and has appropriate authorities and resources, that there are clear relationships with other relevant organisations and that there are systems in place to ensure that the governing body and leadership are in control of the business at all times and have timely notice of any shortfalls in performance. After a case study illustrating the failures that can occur when these criteria are not met, a framework is presented outlining the accountability and performance management practices that are required.

## Introduction

*'Over the years, if imperfectly, socialists have had to learn that faith is not enough.*
*Things have to work. Frequently the best course is to rely pragmatically on the market.*
*Now ... the lesson for conservatives is equally clear. Faith in the universal efficiency and*
*beneficence of the market, however devout, is also not enough. Here, too, ideology is not a*
*substitute for thought' (Galbraith 1979).*

This book outlines the considerations that will determine the extent to which Australia is resilient in areas that are important to the nation's future. To ensure our resilience, we need to make effective arrangements to produce and protect it. This will typically consist of some mix of regulation, agencies to oversee compliance with the regulations and agencies to deliver services consistent with both the policy goals of the Government and the regulations designed to align action with those goals.

An appropriate framework for agency governance and managerial leadership is an important component of any system for delivering resilience, to ensure that organisations can reliably perform their functions across the full spectrum of the shocks they might be required to address. In other words, of fundamental importance to the achievement of resilience is ensuring that all organisations with a contribution to make are fit for purpose – they have a clear mission, they are adequately resourced and adequately governed, they have high quality leadership, their staff is adequately trained and has appropriate authorities and resources and their relationships with other relevant organisations are clear.

Consider the following examples:

- the United States Government has a Federal Emergency Management Agency but, as the case of Hurricane Katrina showed, if the Agency is not capable of performing its functions then the supposed capacity of the society to absorb a shock and continue to function turns out to be illusory.
- Australia was an enthusiastic supporter of sanctions against Saddam Hussein's Iraq and put customs regulations in place to implement them in accordance with United Nations resolutions, but the sanctions were totally ineffective and Australia distinguished itself by the volume of cash that was paid by way of kickbacks to the Saddam Hussein regime.
- the world's major ratings agencies gave AAA ratings to collateralised debt obligations and other paper that turned out to be worthless, thereby making a significant contribution to the global financial crisis.
- investors in funds controlled by Bernard Madoff (United States financier convicted in 2009 for fraud) were entitled to expect that they would be protected by the regulatory activities of the Securities and Exchange Commission and by the annual audits of the funds, but in both cases these protections turned out to be illusory. Those who invested indirectly through the wealth management activities of banks or other funds were entitled to rely also on both the due diligence of the fund managers and their professional prudence in spreading risk, but again they were not protected.

Fitness-for-purpose is to a very important degree ensured by the quality of an organisation's corporate governance. Corporate governance is, or ought to be, directed to ensuring that all aspects of the business of the organisation, be it a regulatory authority, a service delivery agency or a private business enterprise, are under control while the organisation goes about meeting the expectations of its legislation, clients or customers.

Having the organisation's business under control refers not only to being in control of the entity's functions and delivering the desired outcomes. It refers also to the systems in place to enable the governing body ('Board') and senior management to ensure that:

- the organisation is meeting all its responsibilities and acting within the boundaries of all applicable laws and regulations including those relating to public safety, occupational health and safety, environmental impacts, employment law, etc.
- all risks to the achievement by the entity of its corporate objectives (regulatory, service delivery, commercial or compliance) are, as far as possible, identified, assessed and controlled.
- there are systems in place to ensure the sustainability and continuity of the organisation's capabilities.
- there is in place an appropriate framework to ensure that the organisation's personnel at all levels are held accountable for delivering what is required of them and that they are suitably recognised when they do so.
- staff not only know what they should do but they also know what they should *never* do and understand the sanctions that will be applied for crimes and misdemeanours.
- the Board and senior management have timely notice of any shortfalls in performance in relation to any of the required parameters.
- the Board and senior management as appropriate can take timely and effective action to rectify such shortfalls and prevent their recurrence.

Achieving this state of affairs requires leadership of the highest order and sound management practice. The people appointed to lead the organisation must have the moral and intellectual authority to command respect throughout the organisation and credibly demand ethical behaviour from all staff. They must have the skills to select, motivate and reward executives who have appropriate skills and potential not only to carry out their assigned tasks, but to align, motivate and mentor their subordinates in accordance with the organisation's purpose. They must have the capacity and will to recognise quickly, and deal decisively with, underperformance, malpractice and inappropriate behaviour. The leadership must also have the management skills to design, roll out and operate the required systems and the domain knowledge for effective decision-making regarding organisational risks.

The role of the Chief Executive Officer (CEO) within this framework requires the CEO, under the policy direction of the governing body, to establish five managerial frameworks:

- a **client/customer framework,** which requires the organisation to deliver the required portfolio of goods and/or services to its clients or customers in a manner that meets their expectations in respect of all the attributes they would value: price, quality, performance, reliability, safety, security, etc.
- a **resource acquisition framework** that establishes the protocols by which the organisation obtains necessary funds, acquires physical inputs such as plant, equipment and infrastructure and acquires human resources and specialist skills such as IT skills, training and various forms of specialist advice.
- a **resource allocation framework** defining how financial resources, human resources, technical resources and physical assets are to be allocated having regard to competing claims and priorities.
- an **accountability framework,** which establishes who is accountable to whom, for what, by when, with what resources and to what standards. This framework must do more than define accountability within the chain of command; it must also define role relationships outside the chain of command, i.e. what duties individual managers and front-line staff owe to people who are not in direct supervisory positions over them and who has authority to decide upon matters upon which they cannot agree.
- a **control framework**, i.e. all the systems that enable the Board and higher management to monitor what is going on within the organisation and to take timely steps to intervene when corrective action is necessary.

Clearly achieving an appropriate degree of control over the business of the organisation requires a level of assurance about the behaviour of each and every person within the organisation and their alignment both with the purpose of the organisation and with its compliance obligations.

No organisation can hope to achieve the required level of assurance through attempts to micromanage the behaviour of individuals through ever more elaborate rules, regulations, codes of practice, etc. The assurance must be systemic; that is, part of the organisation's DNA. It can only be achieved by leadership which communicates clearly what is required of staff, motivates and resources them to deliver it and recognises them when they do.

There are several modern trends that are inimical to the standards of competence and governance that are required in order to provide the necessary assurance and deliver resilience. These include:

- 'mate-based' appointments; the practice of appointing Board members, CEOs and other senior officers on the basis of their known political allegiance, membership of some kind of 'inner circle', or being someone that the person to whom they will be reporting is 'comfortable with', rather than on the basis of a rigorous assessment of their knowledge, skills, experience and relevant personal attributes.
- the tendency of a number of Australia's top 100 companies to recycle the members of a small and remarkably narrow though well-remunerated elite – one that is not particularly distinguished by either competence or expertise – through their governing Boards may have been a significant contributor to the decline in shareholder value during the global financial crisis (GFC).

- the practice of populating government agencies with the politically aligned can hardly be said to have enhanced the quality of government policy-making or service delivery in recent years. Prior to the GFC, Australia experienced more than a decade of economic boom conditions, but there is widespread dissatisfaction with the state of the nation's infrastructure, education and medical services, to name just a few.
- the cult of the generalist; the notion that a person who is smart enough can do anything he/she turns his/her mind to, thereby discounting domain knowledge to zero. There have been countless disasters in the corporate, public sector and military realms perpetrated by people who were perhaps intelligent but lacked the requisite domain knowledge and experience. Wisdom is always a product of experience and knowledge, not intelligence.
- the illusion that all risks can be quantified and therefore can be regulated. This is often associated with the illusion that the past is a guide to the future. These two illusions have come together disastrously in the 'value at risk' approach to the management of financial market risk (e.g. Anonymous 2008).
- confused thinking about who owns various risks. State governments have assumed that when they privatise the electricity system or the public transport system they are passing all the risks to the private operator, but the public still holds the government accountable for the safe and reliable operation of the system. If the lights go out, or the trains are crowded or do not run on time, or privately owned and operated infrastructure costs much more than a traditional publicly owned infrastructure investment, governments soon find out that they are still carrying the political risk, even though they are not the ones managing the specific risks directly associated with operating the infrastructure.
- faith that outsourcing is synonymous with efficiency.
- an obsession with efficiency at the expense of effectiveness and resilience. There are two aspects of this:
  - especially in the military domain, laudable as efficiency is, effectiveness is usually the most important objective. When people are being put in harm's way, utilising equipment that is difficult or impossible to replace, the important thing is to maximise the prospects of victory, not to achieve some sort of trade-off which is a 'reasonable balance' between cost and prospects of success.
  - if the desired state of critically important organisations is that everyone works very hard all the time, where is the capacity to deal with peaks of activity? Why should we expect in those circumstances that hard-pressed regulators would spot unusual patterns of activity and have the time to reflect that there is something not quite right, something that should be investigated more closely? And if everyone is hard pressed, who would undertake that closer investigation? Should we be aggrieved if regulators, emergency responders and military personnel are not flat out all the time?

## Case study: the Waterfall rail accident

The findings of the Special Commission of Inquiry into the Waterfall Rail Accident present a striking case study of how corporate governance is not a dry-as-dust matter of who attends how many meetings and whether or not there is a nominations committee or a remuneration committee. It is a real-world matter of how those who are charged with the governance of an organisation make sure that their writ is followed and how ensuring that the organisation is effectively governed and led can literally be a matter of life and death.

Poor governance at the State Rail Authority of NSW (SRA) led directly to poor managerial leadership, a confused, ramshackle organisation, unclear lines of authority, no effective accountability, bizarre approaches to human resource management, decisions made with no regard for attendance to safety and a reactive rather than a systemic approach to risk.

The accident which was the subject of the inquiry occurred at approximately 7:14 am on 31 January 2003, when a southbound Outer Suburban Tangara passenger train designated 'G7' left the track at high speed and overturned approximately 1.9 kilometres south of Waterfall railway station. The train driver and six passengers were killed. The train guard and the remaining 41 passengers suffered injuries ranging from minor to severe (McInerney 2005, p.i).

In the Executive Summary of the Final Report of the Inquiry, the findings of the interim report on the proximate causes of the accident were summarised as follows (McInerney 2005, pp. iii–iv):

> *Investigation of the causes of the accident at Waterfall proved to be an extraordinarily difficult task. The cause of the accident was not apparent. The train driver was deceased and the guard claimed to have no recollection of events prior to the derailment. While G7 had been fitted with a data logger, it was not operating at the time. Consequently, there was no record of the actions of the deceased driver in the period immediately before the derailment.*
>
> *In the interim report of the Inquiry, the Commissioner concluded that the mechanism of the accident was a high speed rollover. G7 was travelling at approximately 117 km/h as it entered the curve on which it derailed. The speed limit at that point was 60 km/h.*
>
> *Extensive investigation and testing led to the conclusion that both the condition of the track and associated infrastructure and mechanical malfunction of G7 could be excluded as possible causes of the accident. Deliberate or reckless behaviour on the part of the driver could also be excluded.*
>
> *The train driver, Mr Zeides, had a number of risk factors for coronary heart disease. Post-mortem examination revealed that he had a 90 per cent blockage of the left anterior descending coronary artery. While this did not establish conclusively that he had a heart attack, the preponderance of evidence was that he was at considerable risk of an incapacitating cardiac event.*
>
> *Being able to exclude the possible causes mentioned above, the inference from the known state of Mr Zeides' health led the Commissioner to find that he suffered a sudden incapacitating heart attack at the controls of G7.*
>
> *That conclusion led the Commissioner to examine why, in those circumstances, there was a failure of the deadman system, which is supposed to prevent an accident of this kind if the driver has a sudden heart attack. The deadman system was designed to stop the train unless the train driver maintained continuous pressure either on a spring-loaded hand control or a foot pedal. The foot pedal was designed so that if too much or too little pressure was applied, the emergency brakes would be applied.*
>
> *Expert evidence before the Special Commission indicated that an incapacitated driver weighing more than 110 kilograms could, by the static weight of his legs, hold the foot pedal in the set position whilst G7 was in motion, preventing an emergency brake application. Mr Zeides weighed 118 kilograms at autopsy.*
>
> *The Commissioner was satisfied that Mr Zeides was using the foot pedal when he had a heart attack and that the foot pedal failed to operate as intended.*
>
> *It became apparent that the SRA had information for approximately 15 years that the deadman foot pedal in Tangara trains had the inherent deficiency that train drivers over a certain weight could set the pedal inadvertently if they became incapacitated. In attempting to determine why such a dangerous state of affairs had been allowed to exist*

*for such a long period, the Commissioner concluded that there were serious deficiencies in the way in which safety was managed by the SRA over that period of time.*

*Apart from the unsafe rolling stock, it was also necessary to understand why the train guard failed to take any action when it became apparent G7 was travelling at excessive speed sufficient to alarm the passengers and how the train driver, a person at considerable risk of a heart attack, could have passed the periodical medical assessments.*

*As well as these deficiencies, there were deficiencies in the way in which the safety regulatory system operated. The safety regulatory regime in place, which had as its purpose the prevention of incidents of this kind, failed to operate on this occasion. This must be regarded as one of the latent or indirect causes of the accident.*

The Commissioner's findings on the emergency response when the accident occurred are disturbing and give an idea of just how pervasive the safety problems of SRA were (McInerney 2005, p.xiii):

- the Rail Management Centre (RMC) did not trigger a major incident management response until 7:32 am, although information sufficient to do so was known 14 minutes earlier.
- power to the area was not isolated until 8:06 am; during the intervening period several attempts were made to reset the circuit breakers that had been tripped by the derailed carriages – fortunately these were not successful.
- valuable time was lost by police, fire brigade and ambulance officers as a result of inaccurate information as to the location of the accident and lack of knowledge about access gates and tracks.
- emergency response personnel were not aware of the external door release on Tangara carriages, which would have enabled passengers to be promptly evacuated.
- the train guard was not permitted to use the most efficient means of communicating critical information to the RMC, namely the Metronet radio in his cabin.
- there were other communications equipment deficiencies, including the lack of awareness of signal telephones by emergency response personnel and the fact that satellite telephones were not immediately available.
- there were deficiencies in communications procedures, including the fact that there was no single nominated person at the RMC and no compliance with any language protocol.
- the procedure for identifying a site controller in charge of the accident site was not followed.
- the emergency services were not operating under a coordinated response plan.
- there was no proper site control; there were unauthorised persons on the site and congestion on the access track caused by vehicles left empty and parked with the keys removed.
- the rail commander on site failed to perform the emergency response function intended for that role.

At a corporate governance level the Commissioner made the following findings with respect to successive Boards and Chief Executives of the State Rail Authority and its successor RailCorp (McInerney 2005, pp.liii–liv):

- they failed to implement a system by which each could quickly and readily obtain information as to the overall safety of the organisation.
- they failed to have clearly identified measures for determining the level of safety of each organisation and the safety performance of managerial staff.

- they failed to have clearly defined and appropriate safety responsibilities and accountabilities included in managerial position statements.
- they failed to have measurable criteria for assessing the safety performance of individuals in managerial positions.
- they failed to have adequate internal audit systems in place to test the adequacy of the safety management systems in place.
- they failed to use external auditors to test the adequacy of the safety management systems.

There were many more findings on the adequacy of the safety management systems applicable to the circumstances of the accident, 139 in all, covering emergency response, design and procurement of rolling stock, driver safety systems, risk management, data loggers, communications, train maintenance, medical examinations, safety document control, training, rail accident investigation, safety culture, occupational health and safety, passenger safety, corporate safety governance, RailCorp Safety Reform Agenda, safety regulation, integrated safety management and the independence of the regulators and the Rail Accident Investigation Board (McInerney 2005, pp. 318–332).

The Special Commission's report serves to illustrate just how thorough and comprehensive are the measures required to ensure that a large and complex organisation is in control of its affairs and delivers what is required of it, including when it is under stress.

Such organisations require a robust system of managerial accountability, something that was conspicuously lacking in the case of the State Rail Authority of NSW and would no doubt also be found to be lacking in the organisations that contributed to the failures mentioned at the beginning of this chapter.

Robust systems of managerial accountability do not occur by accident; they require thorough and interlocking systems of authority, training, staff selection, mentoring and resource allocation, to name some of the more important.

## The management accountability hierarchy

A well-known framework for effective leadership of the so-called Management Accountability Hierarchy in large organisations is that developed by Elliott Jaques over a long period of time from the 1970s and implemented in, amongst other organisations, CRA during the 1980s and 1990s (Jaques 1996).

The framework for establishing the 'Requisite Organisation' has five key themes:

- placing the right people in the right jobs – ensuring that the job descriptions throughout the organisation are properly constructed and that all of the people appointed to them are equipped, by way of personal qualities, qualifications and experience, to perform their duties to the requisite level of effectiveness.
- doing the right work at the right level – ensuring that all of the work that is done needs to be done (people not just doing things right, but doing the right things) and that it is done at the lowest level at which the individual to whom the work is assigned can reasonably be expected to perform it to the requisite standard.
- adding value at every level – no work should pass through a pair of hands that has no contribution to make. This only imposes delay and prevents the real players from dealing with each other directly.
- holding authorised managers accountable for their performance – ensuring that all managers have the authority (standing, skills, resources and authorisations) to undertake their assigned duties and that they are held to account not only for their own personal effectiveness but for the personal effectiveness of those whom they manage.

- establishing a culture of continuous improvement – holding all managers accountable for establishing continuous improvement arrangements for all programs and processes that they control.

Many organisations are reluctant to invest in their own capacity to improve, to change and to adapt. Realising these five themes requires re-skilling of the workforce, encouraging new ideas, rewarding initiative, training managers, developing leadership skills, investing in new technologies. All these forms of investment are critical to building resilience within organisations and to building organisations that are resilient. World's best practice is a laudable aim. But it cannot be achieved by complacently protecting mediocrity, or failing to find out what world's best practice is and where it is practised.

These objectives of the five key themes are realised by setting down a clear set of expectations for managers at every level, plus rules for induction and coaching, performance appraisal, establishing continuous improvement processes, responsibilities of supervisors of managers and protocols for staff selection and deselection.

The question of requisite organisational design is not a trivial one. To quote Elliott Jaques:

*'My view is that the way to get managerial leadership is through the development of the organization itself. Get the organization right and the people and the managers who give leadership to them will be enabled to work together in full collaboration and with constructive mutual trust. Given half a chance, people are keen to get on with their work and to have work to get on with. What is missing is an adequate organizational framework within which to work and cooperate with each other ' (Jaques 1996).*

This accords with my own experience of over 20 years at senior leadership levels in the Australian Public Service. The prime sources of inefficiency and conflict are not unwilling, unable or difficult people; they are poor organisational design and the poorly specified accountability and authority that almost inevitably go with it. A resilient organisation has none of these; neither do the organisations that effectively deliver or protect the resilience of our society and our environment.

*Paul Barratt AO is a Director of Australia21 and a Former Secretary of the Departments of Primary Industries and Energy, and Defence.*

## References

Anonymous (2008) Professionally gloomy: risk managers take a hard look at themselves. *The Economist*, **15 May 2008**, 6–8.

Jaques E (1996) *Requisite Organization: A Total System for Effective Managerial Leadership for the 20th Century.* Cason Hall & Co., Arlington, VA.

Galbraith JK (1979) Oil: A solution. New York Review of Books 26, <http://www.nybooks.com/articles/7689 >.

McInerney PA (2005) 'Special Commission of Inquiry into the Waterfall Rail Accident. Final report, Volume 1, January 2005'. Special Commission of Inquiry into the Waterfall Rail Accident, Sydney, Australia.

# CHAPTER 4

# Managing for resilience

Rita Parker

## Abstract

Today's complex global environment of enhanced communication, new security threats and unforseen events demands a level of organisational resilience that goes beyond traditional defensive management tools such as business continuity planning and risk minimisation.

Achieving an appropriate level of resilience requires a recognition of the interdependencies of vertical and horizontal operations and a hard look at organisational attributes including leadership and adaptive capability. This holistic approach by management leads an organisation on a path to resilience in the face of both anticipated and unforseen events.

The level of resilience and the attendant ability to work through and even benefit from crises, is directly related to the extent to which organisations adopt a holistic approach and address aspects such as core capabilities, vulnerabilities and critical assets. When conducted with sufficient commitment and rigour, the organisation can achieve a state of adaptive preparedness or offensive strategic resilience where disruption and risk-taking can have positive outcomes for reputation, effectiveness and morale.

The level of organisational resilience may be assessed through a review of key attributes leading to a ranking of the organisation within a model of organisational resilience maturity.

## Introduction

The 21st century has brought great challenges that have contributed to an uncertain and, at times, turbulent global environment. In this age of increasing globalisation and interconnectedness, threats, risks and challenges are more complex than ever before, with a wider range of unforeseen and indirect consequences (Australian Academy of Science 2006).

Today's challenges have drawn attention to vulnerabilities which were previously less evident. The changing environment means management and organisations are facing often unprecedented challenges and crises. Organisations need new thinking about how they currently operate so they can operate better in the future.

Resilience is important for management and for organisations. Today's business environment requires a robust and resilient enterprise approach to deal with unexpected crises and disruptive events. Corporate brand and reputation, as well as the trust and loyalty of personnel and stakeholders, are critical factors to allow organisations to survive and thrive in a changing environment. Increasingly, organisations are looking for integrated value-creation structures under which the risk profile of their activities is more clearly linked to the values and culture of the organisation and its leadership and decision-making processes to meet its strategic and operational objectives.

From a management and organisational perspective, resilience demands that we confront the limitations of workplace silos of expertise and address the issues associated with our increased global interconnectedness. Adopting a perspective of resilience assists management in developing the necessary adaptive capacity to set and deliver priorities.

Increasingly, management is appreciating and applying resilience concepts. This has led to a growing trend of appreciation of the value of a holistic management systems approach within organisations and this in turn is reflected in the development of standards for organisational resilience in Australia and around the globe.

## Disruption, risk and resilience

The management view of risk and disruptions and what we do about them in the 21st century, is changing. Disruptions are often unforeseen or unanticipated and Nassim Taleb (2007) has given us the theory about 'Black Swan' events. The black swan is a metaphor and refers to high impact, hard to predict and rare events beyond the realms of normal expectations. As the Federal Attorney-General, Robert McClelland, noted in September 2009: 'Resilience for an organisation is more than simply preventing a range of identifiable risks. It's about being able to continue to meet objectives in the face of significant, disruptive circumstances' (McClelland 2009).

By definition, disruptions are difficult to anticipate and hard to predict. These can be random, accidental or intentional. Often they begin to unfold before they are noticed and they can have unforeseen consequences. We are now more interconnected than ever before and that connectivity is largely conducted electronically. Most global financial transactions today are virtually instantaneous and electronic. There is greater connection between databases with data mining providing another dimension of connectivity. This speed and interconnection has added vast power to such systems; it also means much more risk if disruption occurs.

Imagine if the physical interconnection for financial transactions failed or the software failed through an accidental, natural or deliberate disruption. The implications and ramifications are both significant and diverse. Take for example the earthquake that struck the Japanese city of Kobe on 17 January 1995 and the indirect consequence of the collapse of the British Barings Bank (BBC 2009). One of Barings' derivative futures traders in Singapore, Nick Leeson, was engaged in risky trading that relied on stability in the Japanese stock market to avoid major losses. The Kobe earthquake, however, caused the Nikkei Index to drop by 7% in one week. The situation rapidly unravelled and Barings' losses escalated, reaching £1.3 billion. This example highlights an important aspect of resilience for management and organisations: the need to look at an organisation as a system in its entirety and in the context of its overall environment. This is central to the attributes and characteristics of resilient organisations.

It is increasingly evident that traditional management tools using scenario-based planning are not enough for an organisation today where there are many Black Swan events. The most recent global financial crisis has further focused on the need to look beyond traditional indicators and to take account of a broader range of factors. The recent crisis has seen an unprecedented trend of government intervention in the free market economy in Australia and elsewhere to ensure the financial system remains robust and resilient and does not follow the Barings example.

The term 'risk' generally has had a negative association and it is often linked to disasters, both potential and actual. This in turn has coloured management perceptions about how best to deal with the associated challenges. Slovic (1992) wrote that 'risk does not exist "out there", independent of our minds and culture, waiting to be measured. Human beings have invented the concept of "risk" to help them understand and cope with the dangers and uncertainties of life' (Slovic 1992).

Some organisations look only at limiting or minimising the downside of risk and not at its positive potential. From a corporate perspective, if management understands its risk profile and its risk bearing capacity, it can be a competitive resilience advantage. Risk can be a positive as well as a negative. As noted by Botterill and Mazur (2004), some risk behaviours can have positive outcomes. Kokinov and Raeva (2004) noted that, 'the whole economy depends on the willingness of people to risk, on their initiative and entrepreneurship'.

By looking through a different prism, one of building resilience in an organisation, management is better placed to look for, and take advantage of, opportunities including those presented by risks. By doing so, it reflects an ability to be alert, to anticipate and to adapt – that is, to be resilient.

Any disruption, intentional or otherwise, can add to the changing environment in which organisations and businesses operate and can have a severe impact on them and on the people involved if they have a low level of resilience maturity. Alternatively, disruption can lead to a positive outcome such as enhanced reputation, improved effectiveness and increased staff morale if the organisation is robust, reliable and resilient.

An integrated approach by management encourages the establishment of priorities that manage operational risks within an environment of natural, intentional or unintentional threats and hazards.

## Holistic management systems are on the increase

Resilience requires a holistic management systems process that recognises and benefits from the interrelationship of the different business practices and work units within an organisation. Business plans are essential for all organisations whether they are large or small, for-profit or not-for-profit, government or small business. From a management perspective, resilience does not replace these plans but provides the overall contextual framework for them to work within and enables organisations to move beyond the silos. Managing a resilient organisation requires willingness to access and share information from multiple sources and to avoid vested interests in the status quo of workplace silos.

A resilient organisation is better able to identify strategies and solutions that are relevant now and sufficiently flexible for the future. It does this through an understanding of its capabilities, vulnerabilities and interdependencies and the relationships between risks. Resilience provides management with the ability to leverage the perspectives, knowledge and capabilities of individuals in an organisation. Increasingly, Australian organisations appreciate the need to move beyond being reactive and recognise the benefits of being flexible and adaptive. The insurance industry has traditionally penalised risk with higher premiums but we are now starting to see the industry reward organisations that take steps to assist recovery from unforeseen events through staff training, crisis management exercises and simulations. These mechanisms provide tangible and immediate rewards for building resilience.

In today's environment, there is greater understanding that organisations are more than the sum of their separate components and must operate in an integrated and holistic way focused on systemic resilience. Frontline managers, recovery managers, business continuity, security and risk managers all need to work together and align their strategies to achieve common corporate goals. The key is to be sufficiently alert to the unexpected and adaptable to changing circumstances. These key members of staff need to have a level of strategic offensive resilience to ensure that business plans are integrated, current and relevant.

Alistair Mant (1999) gave us the story of the frog and the bicycle, a useful metaphor for the importance of adaptation and for adopting a management systems approach in the context of organisational resilience. Briefly, as Mant explains, the essential difference between a frog and a bicycle, when viewed as systems, is the relationship of the parts to the whole. You can take a bicycle completely apart and reassemble it, confident that it will work perfectly again – as a bicycle. The frog is different. You can, to a limited degree, take bits off the frog but once you remove a single part, the entire system is affected for the worse. If you continue to remove parts of the frog, it will make a series of subtle, but still unpredictable adjustments in order to survive, until it can do so no longer. The frog is then dead and it will not help to sew the parts back on. The point is that the frog is a complete, complex and interconnected organism – it is a system, similar to an organisation.

From an early age we are taught to take problems apart; to break them down into manageable pieces. This approach is sometimes described as the program approach, which lists what is needed and separates pieces of the puzzle. While this might make complex tasks more manageable, we run the risk of losing the intrinsic sense of connection to a larger whole and of losing sight of the consequences of our actions. When we then try to see the big picture, we attempt to reassemble the pieces in our minds. But the task is Sisyphean because it is similar to trying to reassemble the fragments of a broken mirror to see a true reflection. It will always be distorted.

The trend towards looking at the interrelationship of all components as a whole is a growing one and is essential to develop effective resilience. This is the systems approach, which puts the pieces of the puzzle together to look at the whole picture. The frog metaphor reinforces the point that most complex systems, and those containing and serving people, have natural properties and work best when all the parts are connected.

## Steps to build resilience

Organisational resilience requires a different way of management thinking. It is a transformation from reactive to proactive and on to adaptive. Therefore resilience is more than bouncing back to the same point after a disruptive event because that is when the organisation was vulnerable. Today, managers of resilient organisations recognise that where they were before a disruption may not be appropriate for the future. Instead, following a disruption, an organisation with a higher degree of resilience can use the event as an opportunity to improve its effectiveness, enhance its reputation and increase staff morale.

All organisations face some degree of uncertainty and risk. Each organisation has different imperatives and economic drivers for managing disruptive events. In some organisations management will focus their efforts on avoidance or reduction of risks prior to a disruptive event, others will emphasise the management of a crisis as the event unfolds, while others will focus on preparing for, and responding to, the impacts and consequences of a disruptive event (Seigel 2008). These approaches are valid and complementary rather than mutually exclusive perspectives and reflect where an organisation sits on the resilience continuum.

Organisations must have a flexible and adaptive system to manage their risks in order to ensure sustainability of operations to maintain resilience, performance and competitiveness. The challenge is to determine how much risk and uncertainty is acceptable and, from a cost perspective, to manage the risk and uncertainty effectively while at the same time meeting the organisation's strategic and operational objectives (Seigel 2008).

It is imperative that management has business-friendly tools to address any disruption. There is a view, however, that some business practices and programs have not achieved high levels of resilience for organisations. Starr *et al.* (2003) express the view that conventional models fail to account for interdependencies across vertical and horizontal operations. This can be overcome by recognising the limitations of scenario-based planning and embracing the distinctive attributes of a resilient organisation. These attributes can be grouped under five broad headings:

- leadership, management, values and culture
- business planning, strategies and processes
- personnel and stakeholder relationships
- key capabilities
- adaptive capacity and assurance levels

The values and culture of anticipation, alertness and adaptation are reflected in the leadership and management of a resilient organisation and are understood and demonstrated by all personnel. Secondly, the organisation's business planning and strategies reflect and reinforce the values and culture of the organisation. Thirdly, trusted partnerships with stakeholders and open communication with personnel are fundamental and reflect the organisation's reliability and commitment. Fourthly, a clear understanding of capability strengths and vulnerabilities is an integral aspect of a resilient organisation. Lastly, adaptive capacity refers to the organisation's understanding of its own capabilities and people together with knowledge about what is necessary to continue, even under duress, and if required, then to change its strategic goals. These attributes can be used to assess how resilient an organisation is now and can be used to track its overall resilience maturity.

In turn, each of these attributes has a number of distinctive characteristics. Each of the characteristics can help to discern and assess an organisation's individual resilience profile. These characteristics include the extent of alertness and anticipation, interdependence and connectivity, vulnerability awareness and interdependency and overall capability capacity within the organisation. The extent to which these attributes and characteristics are present can reveal the level of resilience maturity.

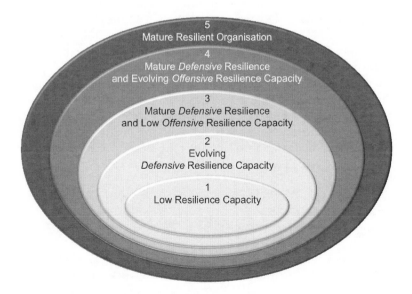

**Figure 4.1**   Organisational resilience maturity model

## Organisational resilience maturity model

Figure 4.1 shows a maturity model to assist organisations assess their level of resiliency.

Level one reflects a very low level of resilience where an organisation may have some business plans but little or no confidence in whether they are workable, reliable or effective. This level therefore has a low level of defensive resilience. Level two of the maturity model shows an evolving level of defensive resilience capability where there may be some scenario-based assessment or testing of existing plans. The third level of organisational resilience reflects a maturity level of defensive resilience and a low level of offensive resilience capability. An organisation achieving level four has started to view its activities from a holistic perspective and would demonstrate a mature level of defensive resilience and an evolving offensive resilience capability. The highest level, five, is appropriate for a mature resilient organisation, which combines defensive and offensive capabilities.

The model introduces the concepts of offensive strategic and defensive resilience for management to apply to their organisations. Briefly, defensive resilience includes traditional business practices such as conventional risk management, business continuity planning, governance, emergency management and security. They are integral to building resilience and they contribute to achieving a healthy bottom line. But they do not necessarily provide a competitive advantage or sufficient adaptive capacity to survive a major disruptive event. These practices form the defensive elements of resilience and rely on 'what if' planning and scenario-based threat models. These plans provide a basis on which to build a higher level of resilience by enabling identification of an organisation's core business capabilities and attendant vulnerabilities, critical assets and interdependencies. These business practices are important but they are insufficient to build a mature level of resilience in an organisation found at levels four and five.

To achieve a mature level of resiliency, organisations need to develop their offensive strategic resilience. This is essential to maintain reputation, customers, suppliers and market share and it is achieved by adopting a capability-based, anticipatory and adaptive approach.

Offensive resilience builds on existing activities, adopts a holistic approach and breaks down silos within an organisation. Glasgow Airport is an example of a highly adaptive, flexible and resilient organisation. After the bombing on 30 June 2007, the airport was up and running within 24 hours. To be precise, it was exactly 23 hours 59 minutes from the incident to operational recovery. It was able to enhance its good reputation and staff morale in the face of a significant and very public disruption.

By adopting an offensive strategic resilient posture, management has the flexibility to support the unique requirements of diverse business units and geographical regions in which organisations operate. The attributes and characteristics outlined enable an organisation to increase its level of resilience and to develop the necessary qualities to ensure the continued operation of the organisation in the face of any disruptive event – whether it was planned for or not. Offensive resilience is underpinned by high and reliable levels of alertness, anticipation and adaptation.

A resilient organisation effectively aligns its strategy, operations, management systems, governance structure and decision support capabilities so that it can uncover and adjust to continually changing risks, endure disruptions to its primary earnings drivers and create advantages over less adaptive competitors.

The complex global environment in which organisations operate today requires new thinking about how they function on a daily basis and how they will manage in the future. Increasingly, managers are recognising and acting upon the need to redefine their organisations and how they operate to be effective.

In the event of a major Black Swan disruption or catastrophic event in this changing environment, management needs to be able to restore material services quickly. Resilience provides management with a platform of operational excellence to do so and to mitigate the negative effects of disruption. Anticipation and adaptation are essential management tools and organisational traits to achieve resilience in these turbulent times. It takes effort and time, but it is a necessity for management in the 21st century to deal with future challenges.

*Rita Parker is Chief Executive of Innovative Solutions for Security and Resilience (ISSR) and a Visiting Fellow in the Defence and Security Applications Research Centre, the University of New South Wales at the Australian Defence Force Academy, Canberra.*

# References

Australian Academy of Science (2006) 'The changing risk environment: ideas for a new Australian policy framework for handling risks'. Australian Academy of Science, Canberra.

BBC (2009). Case closed: infamous crimes, Nick Leeson and Barings Bank. BBC, London, <www.bbc.co.uk/crime/caseclosed/nickleeson.shtml>.

Botterill L and Mazur N (2004) 'Risk and risk perception: a literature review'. Rural Industries Research and Development Corporation, Publication No. 04/043, Canberra.

Kokinov B and Raeva D (2004) Can an incidental picture make us more or less willing to risk? Unpublished paper for the First European Conference on Cognitive Economics, 22–24 September, Gif-sur-Yvette, France. Ecole Polytechnique, Paris, <http://ceco. polytechnique.fr/COLLOQUES/ECCE1/index2.htmhttp://ceco.polytechnique.fr/ COLLOQUES/ECCE1/index2.htm>.

Mant A (1999) *Intelligent Leadership*. Allen & Unwin, Crows Nest, NSW, Australia.

McClelland R (2009) Speech to Australian Security Industry Association, Security 2009 Conference, 24 August 2009, Sydney. Australian Security Industry Association, Sydney, <http://www.asial.com.au/Assets/1280/1/ SpeechbyAGASIALSecurity2009Conference24Aug09.PDF>.

Seigel M (2008) Societal Security Management System Standards. ASIS International, Alexandria, VA, USA, <http://www.asisonline.org/guidelines/Societal-Security-Management-System-Standards.pdf>.

Slovic P (1992) Perception of risk: reflections of the psychometric paradigm. In *Social Theories of Risk*. (Eds S Krinsky and D Golding) pp. 117–152. Praeger, Westport, Connecticut, USA.

Starr R, Newfrock J and Delurey M (2003) Enterprise resilience: Managing risk in the networked economy. Business + Strategy 30, <http://www.strategy-business.com/ article/8375?pg=0>.

Taleb NN (2007) *The Black Swan: The Impact of the Highly Improbable*. Random House, New York.

# CHAPTER 5

# Boiling frogs, black swans and the Lucky Country – how resilient is our economy and how could we improve its resilience?

Nicholas Gruen and John Quiggin

## Abstract

The Australian economy has become substantially more resilient to the 'normal' shocks of national economic life in the last generation as a result of policy changes and developments in the financial markets. On the other hand, it is not clear that such changes have made our economy more resilient to large shocks of the kind that produce depressions. Australia's greatly increased foreign indebtedness means that in the event of a global depression we could fare very badly indeed. The present crisis has taken on global proportions with frightening speed. One way of enhancing our economic resilience might be an increase in the level of compulsory savings through superannuation or through some means whereby citizens deposit some of their savings with governments, thereby creating a state-based financial institution that competes with the commercial banking system. It is sensible for governments in the current crisis to be protecting against illiquidity in financial markets.

## Introduction

The boiling frog has long been the standard cliché referring to the situation in which people – particularly groups – fail to notice danger because of the smooth small increments with which it advances on them. The frog, we are told, apparently falsely (Gibbons 2002), won't jump out of water as it is heated to boiling point if it is heated slowly enough.

In the context of resilience, the boiling frog metaphor may be seen as a warning that gradual adverse changes may not be noticed until the system in question has passed the point where a shift to a new and adverse state is irreversible.

The metaphor is of some use in thinking about modern management of risk, as is another that has become popular more recently, that of the black swan. Most formal theory of risk is developed from mathematics that takes as its context certain well-defined probability distributions. The mathematics elegantly investigates the implications of the information we have providing our notion of what kind of population the sample comes from is accurate. And we can never really know if it is accurate.

Every observation of swans, until the discovery of Australia, led English scientists to conclude that all swans are white. But as we now know, black swans do exist in Australia.

There is a nasty coalescence of phenomena by which much of the risk management apparatus we have set up, from the theory of risk management to the institutions of the financial market, is well equipped to deal with the risk involved in 'normal' states of the world but fails when unusual events occur.

Yet things as diverse as limited liability companies, bonuses linked to corporate performance and risk management protocols with undue reliance on 'mark to market' valuations all tend to reward behaviors like excessive leveraging which greatly increase returns in normal times – and often increase individual remuneration even more – at the cost of catastrophe in the event of some unusual 'black swan' event.

Shouldn't managing for 'black swan' events be at the heart of risk management? That is; shouldn't we be seeking to construct a system of economic management that is highly resilient in the face of extreme and unexpected shocks?

The task of divining the resilience of our economy to adverse shocks in the future – whether they come from within or beyond that economy – must begin and end with modesty. Physicist Niels Bohr's observation that prediction is always difficult, especially about the future, is often cited at economics conferences, and is even taken to heart at the better ones.

Advocating cautious preparation is particularly difficult in a 'lucky country' like Australia. This phrase is so embedded in our thinking that it is difficult to recall the sardonic intent with which its originator, Donald Horne, proposed it. He called Australia 'a lucky country run by second-rate people who share its luck'.

You don't have to share Horne's negative assessment of Australia's leadership to make the judgement that our remarkable immunity to the global economic shocks of the last 15 years, including the Asian crisis, the dotcom bubble and bust and the global financial crisis that began in 2007, owes at least as much to good luck as to good management. Arguably the biggest risk we face is the complacent assumption that our institutions have proved themselves immune to the failures that have beset the US, UK and many other countries in the past few years.

To discuss the Australian economy's resilience to future shocks sensibly, we need to consider both our capacity to absorb a series of mild shocks and the possibility of another major crisis, similar to the near-meltdown of late 2008, to which we may be more vulnerable. The Australian economy is likely to be substantially more resilient to a mild downturn, and it might be more resilient still to a sharper but still short-lived downturn.

The big risk, however, is the extent to which Australia has increased its foreign borrowing and the huge resulting increases in its foreign indebtedness. In some possible futures it would become evident that such borrowing had been unwise. In the event of a really severe and prolonged global economic downturn, Australia's borrowing is likely to see its economy perform very badly, not just absolutely, as most economies would do in such circumstances, but even relative to the poor performance of other economies. By contrast, and paradoxically, Australia's high levels of indebtedness and reliance on imports actually helped it to avoid the bad investments and export shocks that have caused other countries so much grief in the current crisis.

This chapter begins with a brief consideration of the economic implications of environmental damage. Without downplaying their environmental significance, it is concluded that these threats do not pose a threat to the resilience of Australia's economy, either now or in the future.

## Economic resilience and the environment

The economic dimension to past ecological degradation is this: Biodiversity loss, salinity, water and depletion of various natural resources have reduced the economy's productivity. While the past and future economic costs associated with environmental problems are large in absolute terms, they are small relative to the total volume of economic activity. For example, the past mismanagement of water resources will necessitate public expenditure of as much as AUS$5 billion a year on repurchase of over-allocated irrigation entitlements and on urban water infrastructure. That is a substantial sum. But it is less than 0.5% of GDP (or, more relevantly, national income), which in turn is less than the effect of a single quarter of negative economic growth.

Further, though there may be some local 'tipping points', the macroeconomic implications of all of these phenomena will assert themselves both slowly and in a way that markets are relatively well suited to dealing with – and to the extent that they are not, we have developed a range of collective institutions, such as community action groups and governments at all levels which will also assist markets to deal with the problems.

Climate change might, however, change this situation. Here, although effects will emerge relatively slowly, there are global tipping points that we are in danger of reaching because of the scale and magnitude of both environmental and social change and the damage associated with uncontrolled climate change has the potential to be catastrophic. Accordingly it is worth spending resources in order to mitigate global climate change. The scientific consensus suggests that not doing so exposes us to the risk of a loss that is greater – possibly much greater.

Even here, the costs of an efficient, price-based strategy for stabilising atmospheric concentrations of greenhouse gases will be a small proportion of national income, almost certainly less than 5%. Such a reduction, accruing over decades, will be dwarfed by the growth of knowledge.

This is not an argument against tackling any of our environmental problems –addressing them efficiently will yield net economic benefits. The strongest argument for preserving our natural environment, however, is its intrinsic value, whether this is considered in terms of an obligation of stewardship, or in terms of fundamental human need for a relationship with nature.

## Resilience to relatively minor shocks

Australia's economy is much more resilient to minor economic shocks than it was a generation ago. The Australia of the 1970s imposed heavy constraints on the flows of goods and capital and set wages centrally. While central wage-setting could conceivably improve the economy's capacity to absorb certain kinds of shock – as it arguably did in the mid 1980s – most of the time central wage-setting was dominated not by economic thinking but by the political attitudes embodied in the concept of 'comparative wage justice'. In these circumstances external shocks such as booms in our terms of trade were liable to set off boom-and-bust cycles in the economy. This occurred in the mid 1970s and again just a few years later.

In the Australia of the late 1990s, flows of foreign capital and goods had been liberalised, the exchange rate floated, monetary authorities were independently targeting low and stable inflation and wage setting had been decentralised. Of course we will need several more cycles to be really confident, but theoretical considerations suggest that the economy will handle such shocks much more flexibly and the empirical evidence we have thus far confirms this expectation.

In the Asian financial crisis of the late 1990s the exchange rate depreciated heavily yet inflation and wages remained moderate, providing Australia with a trajectory through the crisis that would be hard to fault. In macroeconomic terms this trajectory resembles a typical Keynesian response to a downturn, except that it was engineered by the market. Thus, where initially the shock was to the traded sector in the form of reduced demand for our exports and falling import prices, a substantial portion of that shock was passed on to the rest of the economy by the falling dollar. Likewise, external borrowing rose to enable Australians to smooth their consumption through the temporary downturn in external demand.

Likewise, in the current difficult economic circumstances, we are far from being out of the woods yet and a recession is quite possible. But so far the Australian economy appears to be weathering the various storms around it much better than it might be doing with the institutions of the 1970s. (It should be acknowledged that similar predictions of success were made in 1989 at what may prove to be a similar time of that cycle compared with the current one, but it would be better to wait before being too confident that we will make it through this cycle with a 'soft landing'.) It is notable, for instance, that our appreciating exchange rate since the early 2000s has moderated the inflationary impact that Australia's terms of trade boom would otherwise have had. Likewise, decentralised wage-bargaining and the credibility of independent monetary policy has prevented the current terms of trade boom from creating a wages boom (Gruen 2006). Note also that as a slowdown has approached, exchange rates have suddenly fallen – from a Trade Weighted Index of 73 in June 2008 to 64 in mid-September at the time of writing. Markets do not always behave so benignly but all of what we have described here is consistent with standard economic theory.

## Indebtedness domestic and foreign and the current account

Access to a global financial system has the potential to increase Australia's resilience to economic shocks whatever their source. By borrowing from overseas lenders, Australian households can smooth their aggregate consumption and firms can finance new investments even when domestic institutions are unwilling or unable to extend credit. This was evident during the Asian financial crisis, improving the resilience of our economy.

On the other hand, excessive reliance on overseas borrowing might reduce the resilience of the Australian economy, particularly to large external shocks, by increasing the risk of a foreign debt crisis. If large debts are incurred under favourable conditions, as has been the case in Australia, there is a risk that foreign creditors will be unwilling to extend additional credit if circumstances deteriorate.

Australia's actual experience yields only equivocal evidence on the question of how overseas borrowing might affect Australia's resilience. On the one hand, the Australian economy has exhibited a high degree of resilience since the severe recession of 1989–91. The expansion since that recession has been, according to some measures, the longest in our history. But contrary to the expectations of many, even a substantial improvement in our terms of trade has not produced sustained balance of trade surpluses or any significant reduction in the ratio of foreign debt to Gross Domestic Product (GDP). This is partly because investment has grown, particularly in mining, to raise production of increasingly valuable commodities. Interacting and counteracting factors such as these and others mean that whatever strategy Australia takes with respect to overseas borrowing we are taking a risk that our policies will yield unexpected results.

If all goes well, our increased indebtedness will have enabled us to finance greater invest-ment with minimal sacrifices in our own consumption, something that is to be welcomed. On the other hand, it is possible to envisage a scenario in which this course of action might look foolish in hindsight. It is not that difficult to imagine a situation in which the economies of the developing giants of China and India experience a slowdown, particularly as a result of reduced import demand from depressed Western economies and/or some domestic problem such as inflation and/or financial crises as occurred in Asia in 1997.

## Financial sector shocks

The Australian economy, like the global economy, has experienced spectacular growth in the volume and sophistication of financial transactions since the 1970s. A vast range of new finan-cial products, collectively referred to as derivatives, has emerged. These products include options, swaps and securitised obligations. The total volume of derivatives currently outstand-ing globally is well over US\$300 trillion or more than five times the annual value of world output.

Derivative contracts provide households, firms and governments with a range of flexible options to manage the risks they face. Regulators have devised a sophisticated framework to ensure that financial institutions use such options to achieve a sustainable allocation of risk rather than engaging in dangerous speculation that might create the possibility of bank failure or, worse, a failure of the entire system. Despite the difficulties that have affected a number of institutions in the last year, no such systemic failure has emerged in Australia.

By comparison with USA and European banks, the core of the Australian banking sector has suffered little damage from the current financial crisis. The rapid emergence of the finan-cial crisis in the USA, where only a year ago problems were thought to be restricted to the subprime sector of the home mortgage market, raises the concern that a similar crisis could still emerge here.

Astute observers, such as Ian MacFarlane, have concluded that much of our immunity was due to unintended byproducts of aspects of our system that are more likely to prove negative. First, the 'Four Pillars' policy, which precluded mergers between major banks, also discour-aged the kind of high-stakes rush for market share and market position seen in the USA. The cost of this policy, however, is a banking system with little competition, especially after the disappearance of most of the competitors who relied on the ability of financial markets to securitise loans.

Even more strikingly, MacFarlane argues that our foreign indebtedness pushed Australian banks into a primary role of borrowing from overseas and lending on to Australian borrowers. As a result, they were unable to invest on any large scale in subprime mortgages and the associ-ated derivatives.

In summary, the relative mildness of the downturn in Australia is the product of good luck as well as good management. As argued by a group of economists, including the authors of this chapter, we cannot count on being so lucky a second time. Only a full-scale independent com-mission on the financial system from top to bottom can put us on a path to continued stability and insulation against the unpredictable. Our relatively strong economic position offers an opportunity to review, investigate, consolidate and reform (if necessary). We need to take active steps to avoid the temptation of complacency and accept the lure of challenge.

# A global depression

Before the emergence of stagflation in the 1970s, many economists would have believed that we had essentially mastered economic management sufficiently to rule out another Great Depression. Again, by the early 2000s many were claiming that advances in monetary policy had produced a 'great moderation' in economic volatility. Such claims have proved false.

The financial crisis we are currently experiencing has been easily the most comprehensive since the Great Depression. And it has taken on global proportions with frightening speed. Of central importance is the extent to which the financial sector expanded beyond the structure for which we have developed reasonably comprehensive (though not error-proof) prudential supervision.

A number of governments, including those of Australia, China and the USA, responded to the crisis with large-scale fiscal stimuli, sufficient to soften the impact of the crisis. But in other countries a combination of ideological resistance and constraints on the borrowing capacity of governments precluded this response, resulting in depression-level losses in national income of more than 10% in a number of countries. A further round of economic shocks in a few years might see the US Government, now heavily indebted, unable to fund the necessary policy response.

Further, we are moving away from a world in which there was a dominant economy – the USA – that was both able and prepared to take a global leadership role in maintaining global aggregate demand and stabilising the global financial system. The Asian development model as pioneered by Japan, and then imitated throughout Asia, has emphasised export-led development. But countries seeking to increase net exports must do so with trading partners prepared or able to increase their net imports. And the importing countries have typically been the English-speaking developed counties. Most have run up sizeable foreign debts and so their capacity to continue on this path is likely to moderate. As Dani Rodrik put it recently, 'we are moving to a new world economy and one of the casualties of the transition could well be the East Asian export-led growth model' (Rodrik 2008).

It is possible, though not very likely, that this could lead to a situation in the developing economies where growth stalls and in such a situation it is also possible that those countries or some of them would encounter financial crises as Asia did in the late-90s. A coincidence of the kinds of 'bad news' outlined above could lead to a very severe and prolonged global downturn.

In this situation Australia's position would be unusually poor. Its terms of trade are amongst the most volatile in the world but, unlike commodity-importing countries, Australia's volatility tends to amplify the effect of the volatility in global growth rather than dampen it. Thus, our stock of foreign liabilities and our ongoing current account deficit would both tend to affect Australia's performance during such a difficult time.

# What could be done to improve Australia's resilience?

One way to improve Australia's economic resilience would be to increase national savings. Australia might use some of the dividends of the current windfall it is experiencing in its terms of trade to invest for the future. If it were to do so offshore this would diversify the investments held by Australians and so reduce risk in the future. The Norwegians have done this via a sovereign wealth fund with their own resources windfall from North Sea oil.

In this context, we note the benefits of compulsory superannuation. By increasing Australian savings and by channelling it overwhelmingly into professionally managed, relatively high return, portfolios of assets (including a substantial portion of offshore investments) this policy has also made Australia less reliant on foreign capital –something that will stand it in good stead should foreign investors become less favourably disposed to Australia in the future. The contrast with New Zealand is instructive. With no compulsory superannuation, New Zealand's firms have poorer access to capital and have accordingly invested less heavily in projects that would benefit the nation. New Zealand has invested far less capital per person in foreign assets and runs a higher current account than Australia. These things make its economy relatively less resilient to adverse shocks.

Increasing compulsory superannuation further would probably be sensible in this context. Under 'default' mechanisms, people's contributions would rise over time unless they made a conscious decision to opt out of such plans (Gruen 2005). Nevertheless, if this were done, steps should also be taken to reduce the regressiveness of the tax concession on saving within the superannuation system. The current system gives greater benefits to those on higher incomes.

But even with compulsory super and various other measures to increase national savings dating back to the Fitzgerald Report of the early 1990s, household savings have remained low or negative and national savings remain inadequate to produce a decline in the current account deficit.

A focus on resilience might, therefore, suggest the adoption of more conservative prudential policies for Australian financial institutions. The aim would be to ensure that aggregate borrowings from overseas were kept sufficiently low to reduce the risk of a systemic failure arising from a credit crisis. It might also make sense to try to facilitate a situation in which lenders took greater account of the cycle in their decisions about the creditworthiness of borrowers and the security of assets. One way this might be done would be to calibrate capital adequacy requirements and/or prudential rules on borrowing with greater sensitivity to the economic cycle. Thus, for instance, one might allow lenders to lend 75% of the value of residential property of a certain quality during booms and 85% during downturns before requirements for additional security – via mortgage insurance – was required. It would not be possible to 'fine tune' such a policy as regulators could only know approximately – but not precisely – where we are in the current cycle.

In the age of the internet, governments could provide a simple deposit-taking service that would give citizens a low cost and relatively easy way of placing their savings with government online in return for some reasonable interest payments as well as a means of making payments to others in the same system. This system could, for example, be done through existing governmental websites and could compete with the existing banking system (Gruen 2008a, b).

More generally, it has been accepted since the recovery from the Great Depression that governments have a central role in providing market-making facilities such as shoring up liquidity in critically important financial markets by being lender of last resort. In the wake of a generation of financial innovation, government intervention of last resort is playing 'catch up'. It seems both likely and sensible that the state will expand its operations to protect against illiquidity in financial markets beyond the core banking markets within which current central banks now operate. The difficulty will be in working out the details and the limits of this transition.

*Nicholas Gruen is trained in history, statistics, law, education and economics and has published internationally on a range of issues including economic liberalisation and fiscal policy architecture. He has been an advisor to two Federal Ministers, been appointed to the Productivity Commission where he completed five inquiries as an Associate and two as a Presiding Commissioner. He leads Lateral Economics and Peaches, a discount finance broker, is a substantial contributor to Australia's thriving blog scene, a board member of the government agency Sustainability Victoria and chairman of Online Opinion. He has a regular column in the* Australian Financial Review *and is occasionally published in the* Age, *the* Australian *and* Crikey.

*John Quiggin is a Federation Fellow in Economics and Political Science at the University of Queensland. He is prominent both as a research economist and as a commentator on Australian economic policy. He has produced over 1000 publications, including five books and over 300 journal articles and book chapters, in fields including environmental economics, risk analysis, production economics and the theory of economic growth. He has also written on policy topics including climate change, micro-economic reform, privatisation, employment policy and the management of the Murray–Darling river system.*

## References

Gibbons W (2002) The legend of the boiling frog is just a legend. Ecoviews **18 November**. University of Georgia, Savannah River Ecology Laboratory Outreach Program, Savannah, Georgia, USA. <http://www.uga.edu/srel/ecoviews/ecoview021118.htm>

Gruen D (2006) A Tale Of Two Terms-Of-Trade Booms. Address to Australian Industry Group, Economy 2006 Forum, Melbourne, <http://www.treasury.gov.au/contentitem. asp?NavId=016&ContentID=1077>.

Gruen N (2005) Designed defaults: how the backstop society can failsafe Australians' superannuation. <http://www.craigemersonmp.com/files/nicholas_gruen_designed_ defaults_how_the_backstop_society_can_failsafe_australians_superannuation.pdf>.

Gruen N (2008a) Govt could be net banker. Australian Financial Review 29th July.

Gruen N (2008b) Banking on the ATO. Online Opinion, 10 November, The National Forum, Australia <http://www.onlineopinion.com.au/view.asp?article=8133>.

Rodrik D (2008). Is export-led growth passe? Dani Rodrik's Weblog, September 13, <http:// rodrik.typepad.com/dani_rodriks_weblog/2008/09/is-export-led-growth-passe.html>.

Taleb NN (2007). *The Black Swan: The Impact of the Highly Improbable*. Allen Lane, Camberwell, Australia.

# GOVERNANCE AND SECURITY

# CHAPTER 6

# Governance for a surprising world

Graham R Marshall

## Abstract

Investment in the robustness of Australia's governance systems is required if they are to cope with an increasingly uncertain and surprising world. Attempts to transform these systems in response to the challenges faced since the 1970s have been constrained by persistent modernist beliefs encouraging a confidence in the predictability of social–ecological systems that can rarely be justified nowadays. A case is made in this chapter for making governance systems more robust by transforming them towards polycentric systems (i.e. comprising multiple centres and levels of decision-making that retain substantive autonomy from one another). The role of the principle of subsidiarity in guiding this transformation is highlighted. Although vested interests and 'locked-in' modernist beliefs pose formidable obstacles to this transformation, the time is long gone when resistance could plausibly be justified by the adage, 'if it ain't broke don't fix it'. Politicians and officials need to begin experimenting with polycentric arrangements of such scale and scope that the risks are affordable to them, the experiences gained provide the confidence and public trust they require for more ambitious experiments and the needed transformation can gain momentum. Further, we need to challenge outdated belief systems by inspiring the public imagination with ideas based on the best science available for the world we inhabit today.

## Introduction

Australians have been grappling with serious challenges to the robustness of their governance systems for at least four decades. Before proceeding to consider these challenges, it may be useful to consider what 'robustness' means and why it is used in this chapter instead of 'resilience'.

The term 'robustness' is now used frequently by institutional analysts in referring to governance systems that behave as complex adaptive systems. The term has been defined as 'the maintenance of some desired system characteristics despite fluctuations in the behaviour of its component parts or its environment' (Carlson and Doyle 2002, p. 2538). Applied to a governance system, therefore, it focuses on the capacity of the system to adapt in response to disturbances and thereby continue to deliver the outcomes desired from the system.

Robustness is similar to the concept of resilience, but this latter concept can be difficult to apply to systems like governance, in which some components are consciously designed (Carpenter *et al.* 2001). While the theory of resilience offers important insights, the robustness concept is more useful for guiding decisions concerning the degree to which adaptive capacity should be designed into a governance system. This is because investing in adaptive capacity often involves significant costs in terms of reduced short-term performance.

The robustness concept emphasises such trade-offs between longer-term benefits from adaptability and short-term costs and is therefore more appropriate than 'resilience' for studying governance and other systems consciously designed to cope with uncertainty (Anderies *et al.* 2004). Although 'resilience thinking' as popularised by Walker and Salt (2006) does emphasise these trade-offs, the concept of resilience is less useful than that of robustness as a guide to resolving them.

## Modernism and centralised governance

Various innovative governance designs have been tried in Australia, such as the regional delivery model for community-based natural resource management, in an attempt to address the mounting challenges to the robustness of this nation's governance systems. However, robustness in this sphere seems as elusive as ever. Recent insights from robustness and resilience scholarship reveal these attempts have been too much like 'business as usual'. Some core beliefs about the way governance works that served us well in earlier times will need to be questioned deeply if future attempts to bolster the robustness of our governance systems are to make more headway.

These core beliefs are those upon which the scientific and industrial revolutions contributed so monumentally to human knowledge and upon which the modern era was founded. Ongoing successes from applying these beliefs in solving scientific, technological and other social problems imbued these beliefs with scientific credibility. The first of these modernist beliefs is objectivism, namely that people can remain apart from the system they are seeking to understand and act upon. The second is universalism – a belief that the myriad phenomena of the world, and the relationships between them can be explained by relatively few universal principles. The third is mechanism, namely that all natural and social systems work like machines; i.e. behaving in regular, and therefore predictable, ways. The fourth is atomism, a belief that all systems can be understood completely as the sum of their parts. The last of these is monism – that there is a single best way of understanding any natural or social system (Norgaard 1994).

By the early 20th century in western societies, governance in the public sphere was striving to become scientific in modernist terms, in part to bolster citizens' trust in its competence by appealing to the hold of science on the public imagination. Objectivism led to a distinction in governance functions between the realms of 'politics' and 'administration'. The latter realm was to regard values and policy directions set in the political realm as externally determined and thus objective, and to pursue them efficiently on the basis of the other four modernist beliefs. Universalism, for instance, was reflected by the confidence of 'administrative rationalists' that phenomena widely dispersed in space and time could be understood by applying a few basic principles and that solutions to local problems could accordingly be devised from afar by a central authority. Centralised (or 'monocentric') government administration, with its decisions implemented through a single integrated command structure, thus came to be viewed as the most cost-effective governance arrangement across all areas of public policy (Marshall 2005).

# Doubts and critiques

The 20th century did not play out well for the administrative rationalist approach to public governance. Monism, or the belief that human conflict would fade away as ideological, religious and other 'divisive' ways of thinking converged steadily on scientific rationality, seemed contradicted by escalation in the human cost of war, terrorism and other forms of conflict (Nelson 1987). Administrative rationalism was revealed as lacking scientific rigour, its principles often contradictory platitudes (Simon 1946). Once the hero of the industrial revolution, the 'machine' had by virtue of an accumulation of wars, nuclear and chemical accidents and other tragedies, become a metaphor for social and ecological destruction (Ezrahi 1990). Consequences of public policy interventions were found increasingly harder to predict than expected on the basis of mechanism and atomism, and continuing intervention on this basis thus led to an accelerating accumulation of unexpected side effects (Norgaard 1994). Increasingly, these side effects emerged beyond the scale that individual national governments could address effectively by themselves (Dietz et al. 2003; Berkes et al. 2006; Berkes 2007).

Moreover, the scope for choosing interventions apolitically on the basis of science narrowed as the policy arena became influenced increasingly by sectional interests better able to act collectively, compared with the general public, in lobbying governments and influencing public opinion (Olson 1982). Aside from the specific factors already mentioned, the accumulated general effect of organising public governance according to modern beliefs (i.e. 'modernisation') was to distance public and private life to a degree historically unprecedented. Political crises arose because governments had 'come to be devoid of personal meaning and ... therefore viewed as unreal or even malignant' (Berger and Neuhaus 1977, p. 3).

# Centralised governance reconceived

By the 1970s, citizens' trust in administrative rationalist governance had eroded in Australia and many other nations to a point that the robustness of this governance model in gaining sufficient cooperation from citizens to implement its decisions was under threat. Governments looked towards new ways of operating. One main response was to acquiesce to the strong demands that had arisen for collaboration by communities in public decision-making. Aside from legislating rights for such collaboration in otherwise centralised decision-making processes, Australian governments from the 1980s onwards began decentralising responsibilities to community-based programs as a way of strengthening the public's ownership of, and cooperation with, public policy decisions. Advocates for such programs were influenced by community development, rural development and other disciplines that had demonstrated the contributions that community empowerment, supported by change agents, could make in solving otherwise intractable problems.

The other main response was to agree that the aspiration of achieving all public goals through direct administration was unrealistic and at the same time substitute the idea that these goals be attained through centralised manipulation of the 'market mechanism' (Nelson 1987). This response followed from mainstream economic arguments that the 'invisible hand' could achieve spontaneously what direct administration could not, provided that governments refocused their energies on remedying 'market failures' (e.g. externalities and monopolies).

This second response has been central to how the ideas of New Public Management (NPM), now the dominant paradigm for public governance around the world (McLaughlin and Osborne 2002), have come to be applied. This paradigm underpinned the Australian Government's commitment in the late 1990s to 'effective federalism' (Crowley 2001). It sees government as 'steering not rowing', using market and market-like instruments in delivering public services. A key outcome from adopting this viewpoint in Australia has been a marked shift towards governments 'purchasing' the production of public services from 'providers' (Carroll and Steane 2002). The dominance of this paradigm owes much to the far-reaching ideological sway of neo-liberalism since the 1980s. This is an ideology that advocates rolling back government and an increased reliance on markets.

So dominant have been NPM ideas that governments soon came to reinterpret their commitments to community-based programs through the prism of these ideas and particularly in terms of a purchaser–provider model where governments purchase public services (e.g. delivering social support or organising implementation of conservation works) from community-based organisations (e.g. charities or Landcare groups) as providers of these services. More particularly, this reinterpretation was via mainstream economic theory founded on the modernist belief in mechanism. Consequently, this theory justifies confidence by any government in its ability to predict all the key details of purchaser–provider contracts needed for the market's invisible hand to adequately deliver any chosen set of policy goals (Marshall 2008). Given this confidence, any government has little reason to treat citizen groups as true partners in so-called community-based arrangements and consequently to show as much accountability to them as it expects them to show it. Even so, many supporters of community-based approaches have been co-opted into what is mostly a top-down policy agenda. This is explained by the pervasive influence of neo-liberal ideas on the contemporary public imagination, governments' astute cloaking of these ideas in 'partnership rhetoric' (Lockwood *et al.* 2005) and also because the purchaser–provider payments on offer are often 'the only game in town'.

## Complexity, surprise and the value of robustness

Meanwhile, the problem for Australians of building governance systems robust in the face of the novel and immense challenges we will face this century awaits solutions unconstrained by beliefs that our reality has outgrown. Fortunately, an extensive international body of knowledge from institutional analyses conducted over at least two decades is available for us to draw upon (e.g. Berkes *et al.* 2003; Ostrom 2005; van Laerhoven and Ostrom 2007). This accumulated knowledge reveals the serious handicaps that modernist beliefs often place on efforts to understand and solve problems of governance. It demonstrates contemporary governance problems are normally better understood as complex adaptive systems rather than as systems that behave mechanistically (Anderies *et al.* 2004).

In contrast to a mechanistic system with unchanging relationships between unchanging parts, the parts of a complex adaptive system adapt continually to one another and to the state of the whole system as it changes in an emergent process. The positive-feedback dynamics driving this process amplify random events (e.g. chance meetings) and can thereby 'flip' a system into one of many possible paths. The timing of such a flip and its effect on the path taken are rarely predictable (Berkes 2002). A world of complex adaptive systems is therefore one characterised by high levels of uncertainty or 'surprise'. Confidence in monocentric efforts to devise universal solutions (e.g. purchaser–provider arrangements) effective for all governance settings is therefore unjustified. Science has moved on and the modern project needs to catch up.

This knowledge also demonstrates the folly of looking only to governments and markets as structures for addressing the complex governance challenges we face. It reveals community-based and other civil structures often have vital roles in shoring up the respective weaknesses of government and the market (Baland and Platteau 1996). Such structures are often well positioned to establish trust from both citizens and government, for instance. Thus, by acting as 'mediating structures', these structures can rekindle citizens' trust in governance arrangements (Berger and Neuhaus 1977).

We find also from this research that blending community and other civil structures into multi-layered governance systems often enhances their robustness in other ways too. This is true, however, only to the extent that this blending is sensitive to the respective comparative advantages of governments, markets and civil structures in each different setting. Government might be the dominant player in one setting, the market in another and civil society in yet another. In most cases, however, each will benefit substantially from support by the others. Moreover, inclusion of civil structures into governance systems will impart robustness only when these structures are allowed discretionary powers sufficient to adapt their modes of operation to the unique and evolving circumstances each inhabits.

## Subsidiarity and polycentric governance

There is a robustness dividend to be gained in complex problems, therefore, from effecting transformation to governance systems that are polycentric (i.e. comprising multiple centres and levels of decision-making that retain substantive autonomy from one another) rather than monocentric (Ostrom 1999). The dividend from the decentralised aspect of polycentric governance can include reduced costs of enforcing rules by strengthening their local legitimacy and by making it easier to craft rules that can be monitored affordably. There is evidence that polycentric arrangements, by bringing autonomous decision-making closer to the local level, can increase voluntary cooperation by citizens in implementing the decisions made and thus (given the high political and other transaction costs of coercing cooperation) reduce the risks of implementation failure (Marshall 2009).

Polycentric governance also enables 'multiple units [to experiment] with rules simultaneously, thereby reducing the probability of failure for an entire region' (Ostrom 1999, p. 526). Governance of this kind confers robustness also by complementing its decentralised aspect with more centralised levels of governance able to deal with problems exceeding the capacities of some lower-level units to solve alone (e.g. intercommunity conflict). The overlapping and redundancy of governance units in polycentric arrangements may itself contribute to robustness, by enabling information about innovations that have worked for one unit to be conveyed more easily to other units. Further, it means that 'when small systems fail, there are larger systems to call upon – and vice versa' (Ostrom 1999 p. 528). This benefit follows from the modular structure of a polycentric system; the substantive self-reliance of each of its components enables the overall system to keep performing when some components 'go off the rails'. This modular structure can also strengthen the adaptability and transformability of a governance system, and thereby its robustness, by making the governance system's 'building blocks' smaller and more autonomous than they would otherwise be. The smaller these building blocks, and the more autonomous they are, the less costly will it be to reconfigure the system over time to match our evolving understanding of the problems it seeks to solve (Walker and Salt 2006).

The increasing importance of strengthening the adaptability and transformability of our governance systems is highlighted by the finding of a recent assessment of the vulnerability of Australia's biodiversity to climate change that:

> ' even under the most modest climate change scenario ... [f]ormation of novel
> ecosystems, abrupt changes in ecosystem structure and functioning and surprising,
> counterintuitive outcomes will become more common. Coupled with the existing stressors
> on biodiversity, these climate-induced complications challenge the policy, management

*and governance communities to develop and implement innovative, adaptive and resilient (or transformative) regimes for the conservation of Australia's biodiversity under rapid change. Thus, investing in adaptation is not an 'optional extra' but is central to any strategy to minimise the impacts of climate change on Australia's biodiversity' (Steffen et al. 2009, p. 41).*

The key to reaping robustness dividends by effecting a transformation to polycentric systems of governance is the principle of subsidiarity: allocate each governance responsibility to the lowest level of governance with capacity to exercise it effectively (Marshall 2008). Higher-level governance structures are thus viewed as subsidiary to lower-level ones, assuming responsibilities only to the extent that lower levels cannot accomplish them alone.

## Obstacles and opportunities

Efforts to apply the principle of subsidiarity often confront formidable obstacles not only from vested interests but also from the continuing hold of universalism, mechanism and other modernist beliefs on the worldviews of many politicians, policy makers, community leaders and citizens more generally. Politicians and government officials, for instance, have vested interests in obstructing subsidiarity whenever this principle recommends decentralisation of responsibilities on which their power, status or remuneration depends. And policy advisers trained in mainstream economics, for example, are predisposed by the modernist beliefs underlying this training against recognising communities and other civil groups as competent to be anything more than 'providers' of services tightly specified from the top down (Marshall 2005). None of this is to deny that:

*'Politicians and government officers often have valid reasons for treading cautiously in pursuing the collaborative vision [by way of polycentric governance arrangements guided by subsidiarity]. It is understandable that they are half-hearted in decentralizing management tasks to community and other lower-level actors until they have established trust that institutional arrangements for collaborative environmental management can be designed and implemented that enable those tasks to be performed more successfully than is already the case' (Marshall 2005, pp. 146–147).*

The time is long gone when resistance to moves in this direction could plausibly be justified by the adage 'if it ain't broke don't fix it'. Politicians and government officers need to actively experiment with polycentric arrangements of such scale and scope that the risks are affordable to them, the experiences gained provide the trust they need for more ambitious experiments and a transformative process towards increasingly polycentric governance can gain real momentum. Moreover, we all, not just politicians and officials, need to open our eyes to what polycentric governance arrangements around the world are already achieving. One of many examples relates to the governance arrangements developed by water producers in various groundwater basins of southern California. Blomquist (1992 p. 360) found that these polycentric arrangements generated levels of innovation, and diffusion of innovation though learning and adaptation, that most likely would not have occurred 'if southern California groundwater management had been part of a 'comprehensive' program adopted in, and directed from, Sacramento'. Acknowledging that the governance arrangements were far from flawless, he concluded that the flaws were:

*' more than offset by the effectiveness of the polycentric arrangements in overcoming serious problems of groundwater depletion, halting saltwater intrusion along the coast, and resolving upstream–downstream conflicts in seven of the eight cases. ... The water*

*users prefer the 'chaos' of these arrangements, not because they harbor some perverse preference for uncoordinated and ineffective management, but because the diverse systems they designed work reasonably well, and because they would rather govern their basins and watersheds themselves than have someone else do it for them or tell them what to do' (Blomquist 1992, p. 358).*

The obstacles to transformation towards polycentric governance via the principle of subsidiarity would not seem so formidable but for two important sources of de facto power governments can draw from in resisting transformation to polycentric arrangements (Young 2002). The first of these is the 'fiscal dominance' governments can exercise over community-based and other civil groups that depend on government funding. The second of these is the continuing 'cognitive hegemony' of modernist ideas over the public imagination, which places governments at a significant advantage in defending monocentric governance arrangements against arguments that polycentric arrangements are superior.

Part of the solution to the Australian Government's fiscal dominance involves reminding both policy makers and citizens that the bulk of taxation powers were entrusted to it not because it is necessarily best equipped to decide how tax revenues should be invested, but due to the economies available from centralised collection. Another potential part of the solution is to explore and agitate for alternative means of resourcing the participation of civil groups in polycentric arrangements, thereby circumventing the restrictions of tied funding from government being 'the only game in town'.

The answer to government's second advantage ultimately requires inspiring the public imagination with ideas based on the best science available for the world we inhabit today. Homer-Dixon (2006, p. 282) observed: '[W]e can't hope to preserve at least some of what we hold dear ... unless we're open to radically new ways of thinking about our world ... We need to exercise our imaginations so that we can challenge the unchallengeable and conceive the inconceivable'. This task will necessarily be multi-faceted, including leadership at all levels of society, ongoing clear communication of 'resilience thinking' to laypeople, sponsorship of deliberative fora that encourage the 'surfacing' and respectful challenging of outmoded beliefs, rewriting the textbooks and curricula for school and university education and, perhaps most importantly, making the most of those opportunities that do arise to craft polycentric governance arrangements, learn from them and celebrate their accomplishments.

*Dr Graham Marshall is Program Leader – Economics, Environment and Institutions at the Institute for Rural Futures, University of New England. He is author of* Economics for Collaborative Environmental Management: Renegotiating the Commons *and various recent journal articles concerned with social–ecological resilience. His current research focus is on methods for establishing economic accountability under decentralised systems of collaborative environmental governance, such as found under Australia's regional delivery model for natural resource management.*

## Acknowledgements

Preparation of this chapter was supported by a grant from the Commonwealth Environmental Research Facilities (CERF) program for the project 'Improving economic accountability when using decentralised, collaborative approaches to environmental decisions'. Neither this program nor the Australian Government necessarily shares the views expressed in the chapter.

# References

Anderies JM, Janssen MA and Ostrom E (2004) A framework to analyze the robustness of social–ecological systems from an institutional perspective. *Ecology and Society* **9**, 18 <http://www.ecologyandsociety.org/vol9/iss1/art18>.

Baland J-M and Platteau JP (1996) *Halting Degradation of Natural Resources: Is There a Role for Rural Communities?* Clarendon Press, Oxford.

Berger PL and Neuhaus RJ (1977) *To Empower People: The Role of Mediating Structures in Public Policy.* American Enterprise Institute, Washington, DC.

Berkes F (2002) Cross-scale institutional linkages: Perspectives from the bottom up. In *The Drama of the Commons.* (Eds E Ostrom, T Dietz, N Dolšak, PC Stern, S Stovich and EU Weber) pp. 293–321. National Academy Press, Washington, DC.

Berkes F (2007) Community-based conservation in a globalized world. *Proceedings of the National Academy of Sciences of the USA* **104**, 15188–15193.

Berkes F, Colding J and Folke C (Eds) (2003) *Navigating Social–Ecological Systems: Building Resilience for Complexity and Change.* Cambridge University Press, New York.

Berkes F, Hughes TP, Steneck RS, Wilson, JA, Bellwood DR, Crona B, Folke C, Gunderson LH, Leslie HM, Norberg J, Nystrom M, Olsson P and Osterblom H (2006) Globalization, roving bandits and marine resources. *Science* **311**, 1557–1558.

Blomquist W (1992) *Dividing the Waters: Governing Groundwater in Southern California.* ICS, San Francisco.

Carlson JM and Doyle J (2002) Complexity and robustness. *Proceedings of the National Academy of Sciences* **9** (suppl.1), 2499–2545.

Carpenter S, Walker B, Anderies J and Abel N (2001) From metaphor to measurement: Resilience of what to what? *Ecosystems* **4**, 765–781.

Carroll P and Steane P (2002) Australia, the New Public Management and the new millennium. In *New Public Management: Current Trends and Future Prospects* (Eds K McLaughlin, SP Osborne and E Ferlie) pp. 195–209. Cambridge University Press, London.

Crowley K (2001) Effective environmental federalism? Australia's Natural Heritage Trust. *Journal of Environmental Policy and Planning* **3**, 255–272.

Dietz T, Ostrom E and Stern PC (2003) The struggle to govern the commons. *Science* **302**, 1907–12.

Ezrahi Y (1990) *The Descent of Icarus: Science and the Transformation of Contemporary Democracy.* Harvard University Press, Cambridge, Massachusetts.

Homer-Dixon T (2006) *The Upside of Down: Catastrophe, Creativity and the Renewal of Civilization.* Text Publishing, Melbourne.

Lockwood M, Curtis A and Davidson J (2005) Regional governance of natural resource management: The Australian experience. Paper presented at the International Symposium on Society and Resource Management, Ostersund, Sweden.

Marshall GR (2005) *Economics for Collaborative Environmental Management: Renegotiating the Commons.* Earthscan, London.

Marshall GR (2008) Nesting, subsidiarity and community-based environmental governance beyond the local level. *International Journal of the Commons* **2**, 75–97. <http://www.thecommonsjournal.org/index.php/ijc/article/viewFile/50/19>.

Marshall GR (2009) *Polycentricity, reciprocity and farmer adoption of conservation practices under community-based governance. Ecological Economics* **68**, 1507–1520.

McLaughlin K and Osborne SP (2002) Current trends and future prospects of new public management: A guide. In *New Public Management: Current Trends and Future Prospects.* (Eds K McLaughlin, SP Osborne and E Ferlie) pp.1–3. Routledge, London.

Nelson RH (1987) The economics profession and the making of public policy. *Journal of Economic Literature* **25**, 49–91.

Norgaard RB (1994) *Development Betrayed: The End of Progress and a Coevolutionary Revisioning of the Future.* Routledge, London.

Olson M (1982) The Rise and Decline of Nations. Yale University Press, New Haven.

Ostrom E (1999) Coping with tragedies of the commons. *Annual Review of Political Science* **2**, 493–535.

Ostrom E (2005) *Understanding Institutional Diversity.* Princeton University Press, Princeton.

Simon HA (1946) The proverbs of administration. *Public Administration Review* **6**, 53–67.

Steffen W, Burbidge AA, Hughes L, Kitching R, Lindenmayer D, Musgrave W, Stafford Smith M and Werner PA (2009) 'Australia's biodiversity and climate change: A strategic assessment of the vulnerability of Australia's biodiversity to climate change'. Technical synthesis of a report to the Natural Resource Management Ministerial Council commissioned by the Australian Government. Department of Climate Change, Canberra.

van Laerhoven F and Ostrom E (2007) Traditions and trends in the study of the commons. *International Journal of the Commons* **1**, 3–28. <http://www.thecommonsjournal.org/index.php/ijc/article/view/76>.

Walker B and Salt D (2006) *Resilience Thinking: Sustaining Ecosystems and People in a Changing World.* Island Press, Washington, DC.

Young OR (2002) *The Institutional Dimensions of Environmental Change: Fit, Interplay and Scale.* MIT Press, Cambridge.

# CHAPTER 7

# Security, prosperity and resilience

Allan Behm

## Abstract

The concept of security is changing. It now has as much to do with clean water, reliable food supplies and individual and community well-being as with the ability of the state to protect its sovereignty against threats from other states. Prosperity and security now go hand in hand and neither is achievable without the other. In the 21st century, national security must transcend defence and law enforcement systems to include resilience and social inclusion, the protection of rights and the promotion of values. To see terrorism as an attack on the state is to misconceive it: terrorism is really an attack on the values that unite the community in common purpose. A key resilience challenge for Australia is to build these changing concepts of security into our national governance.

## Introduction

Since Federation, 'security' and 'prosperity' have existed in entirely different chapters of the national political lexicon. The Treasurer, together with the industry ministers, have been responsible for delivering prosperity, while the Defence Minister, with the occasional assistance of the Foreign Minister and the Attorney-General, has been responsible for delivering security. And ne'er the twain have met, except to the extent that security makes prosperity possible and prosperity makes security affordable. Yet there is a growing realisation that security and prosperity are inextricably linked, since neither is achievable without the other.

## Australian security policy

For the most part, Australian security policy has reflected a concentration on the principles advocated by the so-called 'Realist' school of international relations, articulated principally by Hans Morgenthau (1967) in his monumental *Politics among Nations: The Struggle for Power and Peace*. While Morgenthau did not devote much time to a systematic consideration of security – he was much more preoccupied with 'power' – it is clear that the basic premise on which his analysis depends (apart, of course, from the assumption that there is always a rational basis on which international power relationships are struck) is the enduring nature of the Treaty of Westphalia in defining the relationships between states.

To the extent that he does refer to 'security', Morgenthau appears to accept that security means 'the defence of the frontiers as . . . established by peace treaties' (p. 299). This essentially defines security in terms of the absence of threat against the territory or the sovereignty of the state. In other words, security is the ability of the state to maintain its power. This remains the critical consideration in all Australian statements concerning national security.

## Broadening the scope of 'security'

It is becoming increasingly clear, however, that 'security' incorporates something far more fundamental and compelling than the ability of the state to protect its sovereignty against threats from other states – important though that is to the safety of the citizens. It is not, of course, for the state to squander the lives of its citizens in its own protection: it is for the state to maintain the legal consensus that underpins the protection of its citizens' rights and to provide the economic and social infrastructure that enables the community to generate social capital. Security has as much to do with clean water, reliable food supplies, opportunities for children, freedom from ethnic or racial violence, the ability to live a fulfilling life: in other words, individual and community well-being.

While, at one level, this emerging concept of security may be comprehended as freedom from threat, it actually has more to do with the creation of opportunity, prosperity, resilience and well-being. A critical consequence of this changed sense of security is that the majority of citizens in 21st century democracies want freedom from military service rather than freedom through military service.

## The beginnings of a paradigm shift (globally)

The past decade or so has seen the beginnings of a 'paradigm shift' in the global approach to security – a shift that is yet to be detected in Australian security policy. National security has begun to include more basic concepts of values and rights – concepts that have not thrown over the need for states to be able to protect themselves against aggression, but have rather expanded the basic connotation of security to accommodate human security concerns. Security as a function of the power of the state to protect itself has expanded progressively to incorporate the basic need for personal and community well-being in a world where threats from states are diminishing while threats from other sources are increasing.

This evolution was captured nicely by Francisco Aravena (2002) when he noted that 'a conceptual transition is taking place from a Cold War perspective that visualised an enemy expressed in strongly military actions carried out by a state, to a post-Cold War perspective in which threats are diffused, the weight of military factors has diminished and many of the threats appear not to be linked to state actors and even not to be linked to any particular territory'. Aravena went on to say that four substantial elements need to be emphasised in today's security landscape:

- international security extends beyond its military components;
- international security is transnational, global and interdependent;
- international security is produced by a plurality of actors, the state is no longer the exclusive actor; and
- international security in the 21st century has enlarged its agenda and demands that actors work together.

It would be wrong to suggest that Australia now needs to replace its traditional concept of security with one that focuses exclusively on values and rights. Rather, what Australia needs to do is to expand its understanding of security to include the management of pandemics, criminality, pollution and environmental degradation, the creation of human and social capital, the expansion of institutional and other arrangements that enhance social equity and the recognition that resilience and social inclusion are of greater significance in maintaining and enhancing national security than are defence and law enforcement systems.

In this context, it is important to recognise that social inclusion is eroded and community cohesion is undermined when the rule of law is in any way compromised. It is paradoxical that a scrupulous adherence to due process offers a better defence of social inclusion and community cohesion than does the creation of arbitrary exceptions in the name of 'national security'. In other words, adaptability, flexibility, resilience and legality are the new hallmarks of security, as they are of economic prosperity.

In the emerging world of the 21st century, prosperity and security go hand in hand. Security will not be guaranteed by a clinical preoccupation with military threat (and/or its absence) and freedom from crime while more devastating possibilities – with potentially greater costs in terms of human lives and national treasure – progressively dominate the national and international consciousness.

## Challenges for governments

For governments, this creates a new set of challenges. Whereas, during the 20th century, governments of all persuasions looked to 'hard power' (that is, military capabilities) to assert their authority, to protect the nation against attack and to promote their strategic interests, the demand of the 21st century will be to develop the appropriate forms of 'soft power' that at once realise the security aspirations of the community while constraining those circumstances in which 'hard power' might be required.

The so-called 'war against terrorism' offers a salutary lesson in this regard. The military capabilities and doctrines developed to ensure victory in any possible war against an aggressor state have already proved themselves to be largely irrelevant in the fight against those groups that resort to a form of asymmetric warfare (terrorism) to promote their cause. They do this either to penalise those states that pursue policies against the interests of such groups (for instance, the liberal democracies, whose basic support for the value and freedom of the human individual flies in the face of the theocratic absolutism of radicalised Islam) or to force concessions that would have the net effect of undermining liberal democracy itself. Random acts of violence and terror simply cannot be prevented by air strike, tanks and prolonged military occupation. Indeed, all that these measures seem to succeed in doing is to sap the strength and resolve of the nation that deploys forces and to provide the rich, sludgy soup of anarchy that offers the perfect incubator for terrorism. As modified US tactics have begun to demonstrate in Iraq, 'search and destroy' has to be matched with 'hearts and minds': negotiation with the enemy is just as important as the annihilation of the enemy's hard core.

The basic problem is that, like security, the very concept of terrorism is misconceived. It is seen as an attack on the state when it transparently is not: it is an attack on the values that unite the community in common purpose and joint endeavour. It is hardly surprising, then, that a misconception of the nature of terrorism invokes an entirely inappropriate form of response – military force. This is, after all, the old security paradigm: where armed violence is employed against the state, the state retaliates with armed force, because it is the only entity that is constitutionally empowered to do so. But the response actually exacerbates the problem, because the aim of the terrorism is to provoke an over-reaction, thereby eroding whatever support the community might have for legitimate military force.

As Philip Bobbitt (2008, p. 182) has noted in his most recent essay on the subject, since the emergence of modern states during the Renaissance, the world has been divided into states of consent and states of terror. States of consent derived their legitimacy from the consent of the community given freely and renewed frequently – consent that can be withdrawn. States of terror govern through oppression of the people and their regimes do not cede power freely. Terrorism is the weapon of choice when the aim is to prevent states from operating on the basis of popular consent. Consequently, as Bobbitt notes, 'the threats we will soon face are such that we cannot afford to lose, yet to win we must reconceive victory; now that war must aim at victory newly conceived, we must change our ideas of what counts as war: the new warfare attacks innocent civilians because it challenges rights and opportunities, not nationhood or wealth or territory; finally, war is changing because states go to war on behalf of their legitimacy and the basis for legitimacy is changing' (Bobbitt 2008, p. 236).

## Positioning Australia

For Australia to position itself both to shape the emergent strategic environment and to deal with the stresses of the coming decades, it will need a 'whole of nation' approach that posits security in terms of national prosperity and vice versa. To this end, government will need to give policy expression to what it understands 'national security' to be. And, for its part, the community needs to understand the nature of the attack on values and needs to accept that an appropriate response is not to apologise for what Australia stands for but to promote those values. To achieve this, it also needs a 'whole-of-government' approach to security policy that integrates 'soft' power initiatives with 'hard' power capabilities and recognises that the drivers of national prosperity – education, infrastructure investment, health and the growth of social capital – are central to any evolved concept of national security.

This will demand a high degree of convergence within the Australian community on what constitutes 'security'. The inclusion of a rights- and values-based approach to security, going beyond traditional preoccupations with sovereignty and territorial integrity, means that, in addition to the traditional functions of law, defence and foreign relations, critical government functions such as economic management, health, education and community services have a legitimate place at the national security policy table. This imposes some exciting demands on governments. The traditional silos between the departments of state must be demolished. To advance competing defence and foreign policy agendas, for instance, is as self-defeating as it is delusional and wasteful. Yet, such has been the Australian practice for the past three decades or so. But if the barriers between departments are counterproductive, so also are the barriers within departments. These need to be radically overhauled if government is to be in a position to offer holistic security policies.

Central to that overhaul must be the establishment of processes that recognise a single point of accountability – wherever that is best situated bureaucratically. It would be the responsibility of that position to consult all who should be consulted, to canvass all the issues fairly, dispassionately and professionally and to produce clear recommendations that can be implemented and are the personal responsibility of the official preparing the advice.

The complexity of modern government might suggest a significantly more radical approach. It is imperative that Governments generate the kinds of analytical and policy tools necessary to deal with the sorts of discontinuities that will characterise the emerging national security environment (everything from pandemics and global warming to political chaos and social instability in neighbouring states). Such discontinuities have an immediate effect on national prosperity. To this end, governments need to consider how best to liberate the considerable intellectual resources that reside in universities, industry, business and the corporate world, as well as the public services. This is not simply about the 'outsourcing' of policy advice (an action not likely to be recommended by the current generation of public service leaders). It is about increasing the number of parties to the national security conversation – providing not only 'contestability' but also, and more importantly, creativity and imagination. This is a big 'ask', though the Rudd Government's 2020 Summit was at least a partial recognition of the problem.

Government must also invest in its capacity for long-term strategic thinking. This is an area in which Australia's performance has been woeful, part of a chronic underinvestment in intellectual capacity that distinguishes the Australian economy as a whole. The current professional development fads – with their emphasis on MBAs and Company Directors' courses to improve public sector 'management' (to the extent that it is not an oxymoron!) – fail to come to grips with the desperate need for expertise in the substance of public policy, not just the management of program and project delivery.

As the traditional approach to national security expands from a concentration on the power of the state to include the rights of its citizens to live rewarding, fulfilling and prosperous lives, so national security policy becomes an artefact of a successful, inclusive state built around the growth of social capital and national well-being. This, in turn, poses another basic challenge: the development of a robust framework for national governance that supports the national security and prosperity programs but remains independent of the cyclical changes of government.

The first Rudd Government has a unique opportunity to reformulate a national security policy. The challenge is to develop a new security logic that addresses the emergent strategic discontinuities, the huge shifts in power balance and the new threats to national well-being that reside in the complex cocktail of nationalism, ideological competition, terrorism, pandemics, global warming and the growing prospects of a global competition for energy and water. National prosperity is the key to a sound national security policy.

*At the time of writing this essay, Allan Behm was an independent consultant advising on strategic and political risk and was leading the Australia21 project on 'Security and Prosperity'. He currently holds an advisory position within the Australian Government. Allan has published frequently in academic and professional journals and has been a highly respected commentator on defence and security affairs in both the electronic and print media. He has lectured on strategy and security policy in a number of tertiary institutions in Australia and New Zealand. His career has included diplomatic postings in Kuala Lumpur and Geneva and Senior Executive Service appointments in the Department of Defence and the Commonwealth Attorney-General's Department.*

## References

Aravena F (2002) 'Human security: emerging concept of security in the twenty-first century'. Disarmament Forum 2, United Nations Institute for Disarmament Research, Geneva.

Bobbitt P (2008) *Terror and Consent: The Wars for the Twenty-First Century.* Allen Lane, New York.

Morgenthau HJ (1967) *Politics Among Nations: The Struggle for Power and Peace.* Alfred A Knopf, New York.

# CHAPTER 8

# Resilience and global financial governance

Ross Buckley

## Abstract

Resilience is generally seen as a positive attribute that should be enhanced. When a system is dysfunctional and needs to change its structure and identity, however, resilience can be a negative. As this chapter illustrates, our system of global financial governance works to benefit the elites in international banks and developing countries at the direct expense of the common people in those countries. The system is deeply unfair and dysfunctional and displays great negative resilience. This chapter analyses ways in which this negative resilience could be reduced.

## Introduction

A range of concepts is commonly used in analysing the global financial system, including stability, volatility, efficiency and others. Resilience is not among them. Yet we have a very resilient global financial system. It is unstable, volatile, narrowly efficient and highly resilient, principally in the negative sense of being resistant to change.

Resilience is the capacity of a system to withstand external shocks and retain its essential characteristics; its identity. Generally resilience is a positive feature. But when a system needs to change fundamentally and be restructured, resilience can be a marked negative. The global financial system is somewhat functional from the perspective of OECD nations and the international commercial banks, and quite dysfunctional from the perspective of developing countries. It displays a high degree of negative resilience.

Even the global financial crisis (GFC) has so far led to little substantive change in the system that produced it. The GFC has led to higher capital requirements, particularly for trading, tighter liquidity controls, closer supervision and restrictions on bankers' bonuses, but none of these changes are fundamental. If one considers how profoundly different the global financial system is today from what it was 30 or 40 years ago, these changes are merely cosmetic. Even the macro-prudential regulatory function in which systemic risk across the financial system is to be assessed and monitored, which is to be carried out by institutions such as the new European Systemic Risk Board, is but a belated example of regulation beginning to catch up with market changes that are decades old.

The only real change to the system as a result of the GFC has been the handover of economic coordinating authority from the G7 to the G20 nations. Comprising 19 nations and the European Union, the G20 represents 85% of global gross domestic product (GDP), 80% of world trade and two-thirds of the world's people. In addition to the G7 nations, it includes Brazil, China, India, Indonesia, Turkey, Australia, South Africa and others. This is an important change. Brazil, China and India not having a voice in economic policy coordination was becoming increasingly ridiculous.

This change, however, is yet to result in any fundamental changes to the system, in part because the G20 is merely a gathering of national leaders; it is not a formally constituted international organisation and lacks the capacity to enforce its decisions.

So why is a system that, for so many of its participants, is deeply dysfunctional so resilient? The answer lies in whom the current system serves and the general paucity of knowledge, outside those it serves, about how it works and its effects.

## The strong negative resilience of the global financial governance system

Resilience science teaches us that strongly resilient systems have strong feedback loops. This concept of feedback loops, developed in analysing systems, explains much of the resilience of our global financial system. The feedback loops in global financial governance show that the system tends to reward the international commercial banks and the elites in developing countries at the expense of the common people in the debtor countries. A few examples will suffice.

After the debt crisis struck in 1982 a way was needed to allow many hundreds of creditors to negotiate with many hundreds of debtors in each debtor nation. The commercial banks appointed steering committees comprising representatives from six to eight banks to represent all creditors and persuaded the sovereign debtor to also represent all other debtors within its jurisdiction (including state governments, state-owned industries and private corporations). This was sensible. The banks, however, went further and persuaded the debtor nations to bring all debt incurred by all entities within their jurisdiction under their sovereign guarantee. This was completely unnecessary and, from the perspective of the common people in the debtor nations, appalling. The inevitable, massive shortfall between what the sovereign now owed the bank creditors and what it could recover from the original debtors became a charge on government revenues. The people paid in reduced services so that the foreign banks could receive a free credit upgrade on most of their assets.

Likewise in Indonesia after the Asian economic crisis, the International Monetary Fund (IMF) and the foreign commercial banks insisted that the Republic of Indonesia assume the obligations of the local banks to foreign lenders and then seek to recover the funds from the local banks; by selling their assets if necessary. This again proved a difficult task and only about 28% of the total liabilities assumed have been recovered (Asian Development Bank 2009). Almost three-quarters of the cost of repaying those foreign loans has thus been borne by the Indonesian people. Yet there was no reason for Indonesia to assume responsibility for these loans. The market mechanism, if left to work, would have seen many of these Indonesian banks placed into bankruptcy by their Western creditors who would have received a proportion, presumably in the order of 28%, of their claims in the bankruptcy proceedings. Instead, insolvent local banks were put into bankruptcy by Indonesia, the creditors were repaid in full and the Indonesian people bore most of the cost of that repayment. The funds to repay the creditors came from the long-term loans organised by the IMF and invariably were described as bail outs of the debtor nations. Yet these loans were required to be used to repay outstanding indebtedness; so the bail outs were of the foreign banks. In Indonesia, the IMF coordinated a restructuring that socialised massive amounts of private sector debt (Buckley 2002).

Similarly, the centrepiece of the G20 response to the GFC in April 2009 was a US$500 billion additional credit facility for debtor nations. The conditions required to be eligible for these loans, however, exclude virtually all African and most Latin American nations. While it is not apparent on the face of the conditions, they are carefully crafted so that most of these loans will go to their intended destination; the East European countries. The German banks are heavily over-exposed to these countries. So this additional credit facility, in large measure, is designed to bail out the German banks. The funds lent come from the G20 nations, which know they will be repaid; official credit always is. The loss will fall on the people of these Eastern European nations, who will labour under massive debt burdens for decades to come. Once again normal market processes, which in Eastern Europe would have led to German banks incurring large losses on their ill-judged, excessive lending to the region, are abrogated to prefer foreign banks at the direct expense of the people of the poorer nations.

The benefits of our system of global financial governance to the commercial banks are thus manifestly clear. The market is given full rein when yielding large profits to the banks, but is interfered with when it would yield large losses.

The benefits to the elites in developing countries are far less obvious, but are often very substantial and are the reason that voices well placed to argue against the current system are rarely raised against it. An example is in the restructuring of Indonesia's indebtedness after the Asian crisis. When the assets of the insolvent local banks were sold, who was best placed to bid for those assets? Who knew everything about the assets and precisely what they were worth? The families who owned them and were the principal shareholders of the banks. So, in effect, these families were able to regain control of the assets they had owned before the crisis with their foreign debts discharged by their government, all for an average cost of 28%. Who would speak out against such extraordinary largesse? Would you if, somehow, you could repay your home mortgage for one-fourth of the debt owing? Our system of financial governance neatly transferred the real cost of the crisis, which should have been borne by borrowers and lenders that had engaged in imprudent borrowing and lending, onto the people of the debtor nations who had done nothing.

As Professor Luis Carlos Bresser Pereria, former Finance Minister of Brazil, testified before a US House Committee in the aftermath of the debt crisis, the elites in the debtor nations often profited from that crisis (Pereira 1990). Periods of great volatility and forced asset sales offer huge opportunities to those with access to better information, power and financial resources.

Overall, the system of global financial governance has displayed a quite remarkable degree of resilience. When one analyses whom it serves, this is unsurprising. Any system that rewards the powerful at the expense of the powerless is likely to prosper.

Yet the system was not designed to do this. Its architects were Keynes and White at Bretton Woods in 1944. Their primary goal was the promotion of global trade. Fixed exchange rates were to facilitate that trade. The IMF was established to provide short-term loans and technical advice to nations to facilitate their management of these fixed rates. This fixed exchange-rate system ended in the 1970s as the US went off the gold standard and floated its currency and other developed nations followed suit. During the 1970s, the IMF's core mission ended.

Global institutions are, however, notoriously hard to kill. Witness the Bank for International Settlements, which Keynes and White had intended be closed but which lived on to become the most significant global banking regulatory institution.

So the IMF continued on until the debt crisis of 1982 gave it a new role. The commercial banks needed to keep lending to the sovereign debtors so they could service their debts, but they didn't want to advance more funds without changes to the policies that had led these nations to the brink of insolvency. Yet it was politically impossible for a Bank of America or J.P. Morgan to be dictating economic policy to a Brazil or Argentina. The IMF stepped in. As a supposedly independent international financial institution it was well positioned to play the role of crisis manager of nations in trouble. It was well positioned for the role but not staffed or equipped to discharge it. So the IMF performed poorly, with disastrous consequences for the human rights of poor people in poor nations. Yet it has continued to fulfil this function, with substantially unchanged policies, for over a quarter of a century – talk about negative resilience! Over time, as its litany of policy failures began to mount, the Fund attracted sustained, unrelenting criticism from both sides of politics in the US and from developing countries and it was allowed to shrink in size from a total staff approaching 3000 to about 1700 (Vines and Gilbert 2004, Meltzer 2000).

Yet in 2009, another crisis rescued the Fund. The GFC meant the G20 needed an organisation through which it could channel most of its US$1.1 trillion funding package, a bill the IMF fitted. And so, today, the credibility of the IMF has been somewhat restored by having a new role and its staffing levels are again climbing.

The IMF continues to exert control over the economic policies of developing countries in crisis some 35 years after the role for which it was established ended. It has proven to be a remarkably resilient institution, to the detriment of a substantial proportion of the people on the planet.

## Why such an unjust and dysfunctional system is not remedied

So why do the normal checks and balances of democratic systems not rein in and redirect the system of global financial governance if it so often implements ends that serve the rich at the expense of the poor? Part of the answer is that voters in rich countries cannot understand how international finance works and care far less about the problems of people in poor countries than they do about their own backyards. This lack of understanding is promoted by the media, which does a poor job of covering global financial governance. The media typically focuses on the most recent development and reports it, shorn of context. Its coverage is often inaccurate, promoted by the closeness with which information is guarded in this sector. The poverty of the media coverage means the powerful can continue to use the system in ways that suit them free from countervailing pressures from civil society and democratic voters.

Two examples follow, although there are many others. In late 1997 the IMF-organised bail outs of Indonesia, Korea and Thailand were reported widely as if they were grants, not loans. Furthermore, the purpose for which the bail out funds could be applied was not reported in the media at all, as that was only to be found in the fine print which was not generally available. Yet the loans could only be applied to debt then due, which was mostly short-term debt. So the bail outs were essentially bail outs of Western banks, not East Asian nations and the bail outs rewarded the lenders who advanced the most destabilising form of loans – short-term ones – at the expense of those who had advanced less-volatile, longer term debt. Thus was perpetrated a disastrous policy that received no critical media coverage until it was old news, many years later.

In 2009 the G20's principal response to the GFC was a US$1.1 trillion dollar funding package. US$100 billion was additional concessional financing for poor nations. US$250 billion was to support trade finance, financing for which had been severely limited by the GFC. Another US$250 billion was an increase in Special Drawing Rights, the IMF quasi reserve-capital. And the final US$500 billion was the additional credit facility. The first two tranches are readily understandable. The last two are not. Special Drawing Rights (SDRs) are based on a basket of four currencies – the US dollar, the pound Sterling, the euro and the yen – and are the ways nations make their contributions to the IMF. They are an excellent source of funding for poorer nations and the increase in them is a laudable response to the GFC. However, SDRs can only be drawn down in proportion to a nation's quota. Accordingly, nearly two-thirds of the increase in SDRs is available to OECD nations, leaving US$100 billion to developing countries, within which only US$19 billion is available for low-income nations (Oxfam 2009; IMF 2009). So reporting the US$250 billion increase in SDRs as a measure to assist poor countries, as was often the case, was quite misleading.

The US$500 billion is, as we have seen, even more opaque. The principal destination of these funds is intended initially to be the Eastern European nations and ultimately the repayment of their loans to the German banks. The media has not, to my knowledge, reported the destination of the US$500 billion additional credit facility because it cannot be divined from the terms of the facility. It is quite simply beyond the capacity of the media to cover such developments accurately, a state with which the powerful players are content.

So if the system exhibits such strong negative resilience, how might that resilience be lessened so that needed changes come about?

## Steps needed to reduce undesirable resilience

Perhaps the initial principal step that needs to be undertaken to reduce the undesirable resilience of our system of global financial governance is to return the IMF to its original mandate, or what is left of its original mandate. The skills required to turn around poorly performing economies are utterly different from those typically held by central bankers and PhD graduates in macroeconomics; the two most common backgrounds of IMF staffers. The IMF is the wrong organisation to set economic policy for nations in crisis. Because the IMF is not equipped for the role it stumbled into, it has been open to capture by the powerful in the international financial community and the poor countries and it should be removed from this role. If an international financial institution is required to play this role, a new one, with staff equipped with the right skills and attitudes and with the right culture needs to be established. This change would limit the IMF to data collection, technical surveillance and advisory roles.

The next step is to reform the governance of the IMF and the World Bank. There have been tiny reforms in the past two years but, essentially, most votes are in the hands of the US and the leading European countries. So these institutions, whose clients are the world's poorer countries, do the bidding of the richest countries. This is absurd. The principal clients of these institutions need a real voice in their governance.

The third step is to applaud the move from the G7 to the G20 and to strengthen further the G20. This could be done by increasing its size slightly by the addition of some regional representatives. While it will be difficult to remove the seat of any current nation, logically Italy should lose its seat, Argentina's seat should go to a regional grouping for Latin America, Saudi Arabia's to a regional grouping for North Africa and the Middle East and a seat should be given to a sub-Saharan African grouping. If the G20 were then expanded to a G22 and regional seats added for ASEAN and South Asia, the organisation would directly or indirectly represent the great majority of countries.

The final and most significant step to reduce negative resilience, or resistance to change, is to diminish the strength of the current feedback loops. The best way to do this is to make the system more fair and balanced. The strength of the feedback loops arise because of the degree to which the system currently favours the powerful among banks and within developing nations. The system needs to change in fundamental ways and this is not likely to occur without these feedback loops being first weakened.

The UN established the Stiglitz Commission as part of its response to the GFC and the best way to disempower many of the feedback loops would be for the G20 to implement some of the Commission's recommendations. The Commission's three recommendations most ready for implementation are that: (i) new financial mechanisms be introduced to mitigate risk, including international institutions lending in local currencies; (ii) highly indebted countries be given a moratorium or partial cancellation of debt; and (iii) new mechanisms be introduced for handling sovereign debt restructuring, such as a sovereign bankruptcy regime. The commission also recommended that the US dollar be replaced as the global reserve currency. There were other recommendations, but I will focus upon these four.

There are strong reasons why all reschedulings of rich country to poor country loans should be in local currency, as should all lending by international financial institutions such as the IMF and World Bank (Buckley and Dirou 2006). Our current system places the currency risk on the party least able to bear it; the borrower. This is illogical. Lending in local currency puts the currency risk on those best able to bear it and hedge against it, the lenders.

Likewise there are strong arguments for debt relief for more countries than currently receive it and for an orderly, rules-based approach to sovereign insolvencies (Buckley 2009).

A new reserve currency is needed because when one nation's currency serves as the global reserve currency the extra liquidity required to meet the global liquidity needs inevitably puts downward pressure on the currency's value thereby making it more volatile and less attractive as a reserve currency. This is known as the Triffin dilemma. It has required the US to run consistently massive trade deficits so as to inject sufficient dollars into the global system, which is not sustainable. Premier Wen Jiabao has said he is worried that China holds most of its reserves in dollars and well he might be, as the decline of the dollar in recent years has cost China a fortune. Twice in 2009 the governor of China's central bank called for a new reserve currency regime focused on Special Drawing Rights. China Inc. doesn't make such comments without careful consideration and is hard at work researching alternatives, such as denominating and settling its trade with Brazil in real and renminbi, not the US dollar.

## Conclusion

The greatest reduction in negative resilience in global financial governance would be achieved if we were to promote lending to developing countries in their own currencies, grant more debt relief to more poor countries, stop the socialisation of private sector debt in debt restructurings, introduce a fair and independent arbitration process for sovereign bankruptcy and move towards a different global reserve currency, perhaps an instrument crafted from a basket of currencies. These changes would go a long way to making the global financial system fairer, reduce the extent to which it favours the powerful and therefore disempower the feedback loops that make the current system so resistant to change. Of course, the negative resilience of the system means that these changes will be strongly resisted by the system's powerful participants.

*Ross Buckley is Professor of International Finance Law at the University of New South Wales, a Fellow at the Asian Institute of International Financial Law, University of Hong Kong and an Australia21 Fellow.*

## References

Asian Development Bank (2009) Lessons from the Asian Development Bank's Response to Financial Crises. Asian Development Bank, Manila, <http://www.adb.org/Documents/Evaluation/Information-Briefs/EIB-2009-02.pdf>.

Buckley RP (2009) The bankruptcy of nations: an idea whose time has come. *The International Lawyer* **43**, 1189–1216.

Buckley RP and Dirou P (2006) How to strengthen the international financial system by improving sovereign balance sheet structures. *Annals of Economics and Finance* **2**, 257–269.

Buckley RP (2002) The fatal flaw in international finance: The rich borrow and the poor repay. *World Policy Journal* **19**, 59–64.

International Monetary Fund (2009) IMF Resources and the G20 Summit. International Monetary Fund, Washington, DC, <http://www.imf.org/external/np/exr/faq/sdrfaqs.htm#q7>.

Meltzer A (2000) Report of the International Financial Institution Advisory Commission. United States House of Representatives, Washington, DC, <http://www.house.gov/jec/imf/meltzer.pdf>.

Oxfam (2009) G20 Media Brief, Money for Nothing: Three Ways the G20 Could Deliver up to US$280 Billion for Poor Countries. Oxfam, Oxford, UK, <http://www.oxfam.org.uk/resources/policy/debt_aid/money-for-nothing-g20.html>.

Pereira LCB (1990) Solving the debt crisis: Debt relief and adjustment. *Revista de Economia Política* **10**, 147–154, <http://www.rep.org.br/pdf/38-10.pdf>.

Stiglitz J (2009) Report of the Commission of Experts of the President of the United Nations General Assembly on Reforms of the International Monetary and Financial System. United Nations, New York, <http://www.un.org/ga/econcrisissummit/docs/FinalReport_CoE.pdf>.

Vines S and Gilbert C (2004) *The IMF and its Critics: Reform of Global Financial Architecture.* Cambridge University Press, Cambridge, UK.

# ENERGY AND SETTLEMENTS

# CHAPTER 9

# Peak oil – catalyst for a resilient, sustainable society

Ian T Dunlop

## Abstract

The peaking of the world's oil supply will probably be the catalyst that forces the world to address global warming and global sustainability. Yet peak oil continues to be ignored by successive Australian governments despite our acute vulnerability to it. A resilience approach to this problem will require honest public acknowledgement by government and business leaders of the real challenges we now face; urgent education campaigns and an emergency nation-building response that will focus on energy conservation and efficiency, large-scale conversion to renewable energy and possibly new generation nuclear power, major changes in urban design and our transport system, phasing out of high carbon emission facilities, introduction of high speed broadband, investment in low emission technology and rapid reform of the tax system. Can our current form of government rise to this unprecedented challenge?. Our failure to face up to the risks of global warming thus far does not engender confidence, but we cannot waste the great opportunity that is now before us; to place the world on a genuinely sustainable footing.

## Introduction

Since oil prices receded from their July 2008 (US$147/bbl) peak as the Global Financial Crisis (GFC) destroyed demand, there has been an inevitable tendency to assume the oil "problem" is fixed and move on to the next issue. Unfortunately nothing could be further from the truth. We have been given a warning, which we should heed, as the problem is certainly not fixed. The peaking of global oil supply, peak oil, will probably be the catalyst that forces the world to address the related questions of global warming and, beyond that global sustainability, seriously and far more rapidly than we are expecting. In short, peak oil is a good thing, provided you are well prepared; it is likely to have even greater impact than global warming in the short term!

It is the issue our political leaders still seem determined to ignore, although an increasing number of international oil company Chief Executive Officers (CEOs) are quietly acknowledging the reality we now face. Having built our prosperity on cheap energy from fossil fuels, particularly oil, it is perhaps understandable that we are reluctant to admit that business-as-usual is over as that cheap energy disappears.

## What is peak oil?

Peak oil takes its name from the bell-shaped curve that typifies the production profile of any oilfield. Once an oilfield is discovered, oilwells are drilled and production rises until drilling saturation is reached, whereupon production levels off at the peak. Production then drops, along the declining segment of the bell-shape, until the reservoir is exhausted. This production profile applies to an individual oilfield, to all oilfields in a region and conceptually to the globe, although it gets distorted along the way by, for example, geopolitics.

At the peak, oil does not run out as roughly half of the ultimately available oil remains to be produced. It is the point, globally, at which further expansion of oil production becomes impossible because production from new oilfields is more than offset by the decline of production from existing oilfields. It may be a sharp peak if, for example, some of the giant fields start to decline rapidly, or it may be an undulating plateau spread over a number of years if, for example, oil demand is destroyed as a result of recession or countries are no longer able to afford high oil prices. Once demand begins to exceed supply, oil prices rise, as they were doing in the lead up to the GFC; the bigger the gap, the higher the price. Arguably, the oil price spike was one of the main triggers of the GFC, being the last straw that broke the financial back of debt-laden, gasoline-dependent consumers on the periphery of cities in the USA.

## Changing views on peak oil

The 'official view' until 2006, from organisations like the International Energy Agency (IEA), the energy watchdog of the developed world, was that we had abundant oil resources available from both conventional and unconventional sources, which would meet rapidly expanding global demand as China and subsequently India became large consumers. The economists took comfort as the oil price rose, on the grounds higher prices would stimulate additional production so that supply eventually balanced demand and forced the price down in the classical mode. As Brian Fisher, the former head of ABARE, colourfully put it: 'if the price of eggs is high enough, even the roosters will start laying!' (Holmes 2006).

Maybe so, but this is primarily a technical, rather than an economic, issue. It is one thing to have theoretical oil resources in the ground; it is quite another to convert those resources into practical oil flows to the market. It now seems that there are unexpected problems in so doing, to the extent that we probably are approaching the peak of global supply. We may have already passed the peak, or it may be some years ahead, but the exact date is less important than accepting the principle and taking action to prepare for it.

The 'official view' since 2006 is still scrambling to catch up with reality. Cracks in the optimism began to appear in 2007; in November, the Chief Economist of the IEA commented, ' putting these two things together, the short term and medium term security of our oil markets, plus the climate change consequences of this energy use, my message is that, if we don't do anything very quickly, and in a bold manner, the wheels may fall off. Our energy system's wheels may fall off – within the next seven years' (Crooks and Blas 2007). In May 2008, urging OECD governments to rapidly change policy from 'business-as-usual', he commented that 'we must leave oil before it leaves us' (Birol 2008).

His concerns were echoed shortly afterwards by Mohamed El Baradei, Director-General of the International Atomic Energy Agency, in calling for a global energy organisation 'to take action on the energy crisis that is taking shape before our eyes. … We need to act before crisis turns into catastrophe' (El Baradei 2008).

Sheikh Yamani, the former Saudi and OPEC Oil Minister, anticipated it long ago with the observation that 'the Stone Age did not end for lack of stones and the Oil Age will end long before the world runs out of oil' (Economist 2003).

## The need for an energy revolution

The reasons supply is not expanding are:

- new oilfields are not being discovered quickly enough and certainly no giant fields are being discovered;
- data on existing fields is suspect, particularly in the Middle East, so we may not have as much oil as we thought;
- production from many existing oilfields is declining, as part of the natural process, often more quickly than admitted officially;
- unconventional oil resources, such as deep water and tar sands, are proving more difficult to develop, technically and economically, even with higher oil prices – there also are major environmental problems associated with these sources, such as high carbon emissions and high demand for water and energy, to the point where, in some cases, almost as much energy is needed to produce the oil as is ultimately recovered; and
- oil-producing countries are using more oil domestically and are less prepared to export it.

Given the absolute dependence of modern societies on oil and gas, price hikes and supply shortages will be traumatic, as evidenced by the 2008 unrest in Europe, and protests in the Middle East and Asia as oil subsidies were withdrawn. Peak oil was ignored by the previous Federal Government and is barely acknowledged by the Rudd government; but it is arguably the biggest issue Australia will have to contend with in the next decade.

Oil prices dropped as the GFC destroyed demand and are now gradually recovering. It is possible that increased oil discoveries will result from the exploration triggered by the earlier higher prices, and a number have been announced recently, but new production will take time to materialise. Further, we are witnessing rapid depletion in some of the world's major oil reservoirs, such that new production will struggle to offset the decline in existing production. Some forecasters suggest that we may see a net oil supply decline of around 50% by 2030 (Energy Watch Group 2007). Others maintain there will be no problem for some years ahead even with rapidly increasing demand (Jackson 2007). Suffice it to say the IEA, having been optimistic, undertook an urgent review of world oil supply, published in its 2008 World Energy Outlook, and ran up the warning flag: 'The world's energy system is at a crossroads. Current global trends in energy supply and consumption are patently unsustainable – environmentally, economically, socially … What is needed is nothing short of an energy revolution' (International Energy Agency 2008). The IEA Chief Economist continues to express concern: 'the oil on which modern civilisation depends is running out faster than previously predicted and global production is likely to peak in about ten years – at least a decade earlier than most governments had estimated' (Connor 2009). Those warnings are reiterated in the IEA's 2009 World Energy Outlook (IEA 2009). To many, the IEA view, while an improvement, is still overly optimistic.

The general oil price trend is most probably upwards, subject to the speed of recovery from the GFC. So any respite from high oil prices is likely to be temporary and it is misleading to pretend otherwise. We should be preparing for that eventuality now, not playing King Canute in futile attempts to turn back the global tide with fuel excise or GST adjustments as proposed in 2008 – although King Canute was wiser than we often give him credit for; he sat on the beach to demonstrate to his courtiers the nonsense of the policies they were advocating!

We actually need higher oil prices to wean us off our dependence on oil and to encourage alternatives. This may seem hard but, unless we face up to this reality quickly, the problem will become far worse. There is certainly a case for assisting those most exposed, to ease the transition to a world of expensive energy, but it should be via specific targeted measures, not with across-the-board attempts to drop petrol prices, which are miniscule in relation to the size of the problem.

Passing the peak raises the question of who gets the available oil. Solutions range from:

- letting the market take its course – the preferred route of most economists – which conveniently skirts around the traumatic societal impact of recession or depression arising from high energy prices, the potential for the creation of failed states as developing, and possibly some developed, countries may be increasingly forced out of the market;
- the 'Washington Consensus' of sending in the marines to secure supply (recent experience in Iraq suggests this is hardly a sustainable alternative); to
- a global mechanism for equitable sharing of available oil, for example an Oil Depletion Protocol, akin to the Kyoto Protocol for carbon emissions. Indeed, the IEA was created in 1973 for exactly this purpose; to assist the OECD countries in allocating oil during the first oil shock. This time the problem is far greater, but we have handled similar situations in the past and we will probably have to resort to allocation mechanisms again despite the protests of the market economists!

Australia is particularly vulnerable. We are approximately 50% self-sufficient in oil, declining rapidly unless new discoveries are made. We rely on long supply lines from Asian refineries for around 85% of our daily use, offset by high exports. We do not comply with the requirements of IEA membership to maintain a 90-day net import strategic petroleum reserve, relying instead on operational stocks and just-in-time delivery. The cost of our oil and gas imports is now close to twice our oil and gas exports, with high coal exports compensating for some of this cost.

But, as if peak oil was not enough, there is another problem; the rapidly escalating risks of global warming and the need to radically reduce our carbon emissions from fossil fuel use far more than is being admitted politically (probably to completely decarbonise the economy by 2050). This will itself raise fossil fuel energy prices as carbon is properly priced, via mechanisms such as emissions trading, to reflect its environmental cost.

## What might appropriate policy responses look like?

There are solutions to these converging issues, but they take time to implement and we should have been planning for them years ago. We did not do so and now we face the consequences. Some obvious responses, for example increased coal consumption, or coal conversion to liquids, which Martin Ferguson continues to advocate, are carbon emission-intensive and, in the absence of carbon capture and storage, which is still unproven for large-scale application, would be extremely detrimental to addressing global warming. The two issues – energy supply and global warming – are inextricably linked; hence the need for consistent and holistic policy to address the integrated problem.

So what would that policy look like?

- an honest, public acknowledgment by Australian governments and business leaders of the real challenges we now face;

- immediate education campaigns to inform the community and gain support for the hard decisions ahead; and
- an emergency, nation-building response plan established to place the economy on a low-carbon footing, minimising the consumption of oil, akin to a 21st century version of the 1950's Snowy Hydro Scheme, but much bigger and broader, or the Marshall Plan which financed reconstruction of Europe after World War 2.

The components would be:

- a major focus on energy conservation and energy efficiency;
- large-scale conversion to renewable energy and possibly new-generation nuclear power;
- major investment in efficient public transport, rail, bus, cycling, etc. and an immediate halt to investment in freeway and airport expansion;
- a rapid phasing out of high carbon emission facilities such as coal-fired power stations unless safe carbon capture and storage can be introduced within 10 years;
- urgent introduction of high-speed broadband to minimise travel and improve communication efficiency;
- continued investment in low-emission technology;
- a focus on biological, as well as geological, carbon sequestration; and
- a rapid reform of the tax system to remove perverse incentives that encourage oil use and carbon emissions.

Australians and others face major changes to their lifestyles. It is not just high oil prices and global warming, but the very question of the sustainability of humanity on the planet as population rises from 6.7 billion people today to a projected 9 billion in 2050, all aspiring to an improved quality of life. New technology will undoubtedly come to our aid but that will not be enough; our values must also change. Conventional economic growth in the developed world will have to be set aside in favour of a steady-state, resilient economy where the emphasis is on non-consumption and the quality of life rather than the quantity of things.

There will be far more focus on local food production, opening up new opportunities for rural areas. Cities will be redesigned using high-density sustainability principles to avoid urban sprawl and integrated with public transport to minimise energy consumption. Work centres will be decentralised. Rail, powered by renewable energy, will become a major transport mode for both freight and high-speed passenger traffic. Air travel will reduce unless new technology develops jet fuel from, for example, bio-sources and even then, emission constraints may limit its use. The internal combustion engine will disappear in favour of electric vehicles for many applications. Cycling and walking will become major activities for both work and pleasure – obesity and diabetes will decline!

The challenge is enormous but, rather than view this as a disaster, it is the greatest opportunity we have ever had to place the world on a sustainable footing, for what we are currently doing is not sustainable. We must not waste the opportunity, but it needs far bolder and broader thinking than we are seeing at present. In particular, we need to understand the resilience of our economy and society to major shocks; we may well have to fundamentally restructure our energy system and economy in the face of acute oil shortages.

This raises the question of the ability of our democratic system of government to implement such change. It will require statesmanship of the highest order, a quality sadly lacking nationally and globally, demonstrated only too clearly by our current failure to face up to the risks of global warming. Debate is urgently needed on alternative forms of government to ease our transition to a resilient and sustainable future.

*Ian Dunlop was formerly an international oil, gas and coal industry executive. He chaired the Australian Coal Association in 1987–88, chaired the Australian Greenhouse Office Experts Group on Emissions Trading from 1998–2000 and was CEO of the Australian Institute of Company Directors from 1997–2001. He is a Director of Australia 21, Chairman of Safe Climate Australia, Deputy Convenor of the Australian Association for the Study of Peak Oil and a Member of the Club of Rome.*

## References

Birol F (2008) Outside View: We can't cling to crude: we should leave oil before it leaves us. *The Independent*, London, 2 March, <http://www.independent.co.uk/news/business/comment/outside-view-%20we-cant-cling-to-crude-we-should-leave-oil-before-it-leaves-us-790178.html>.

Connor S (2009) Warning: Oil supplies are running out fast. *The Independent*, London, 3 August, <http://www.independent.co.uk/news/science/warning-oil-supplies-are-running-out-fast%C2%AD1766585.html>.

Crooks E and Blas J (2007) Transcript: Interview with the IEA Chief Economist. *Financial Times*, London, 7 November, <http://www.ft.com/cms/s/0/3c8940ca-8d46-11dc-a398-0000779fd2ac.html>.

El Baradei M (2008) A Global Agency is Needed for the Energy Crisis. 23 July. *Financial Times*, London, <http://www.ft.com/cms/s/0/b3630dd0-58b5-11dd-a093-000077b07658.html?nclick_check=1>.

Energy Watch Group (2007) Crude Oil – The Supply Outlook, Report to the Energy Watch Group, EWG–Series No 3/2007. Energy Watch Group, Berlin, <http://www.energywatchgroup.org/fileadmin/global/pdf/EWG_Oilreport_10–2007.pdf>.

Holmes J (reporter) (2006) Peak Oil? ABC Four Corners Transcript 10 July, Australian Broadcasting Commission, Sydney, <http://www.abc.net.au/4corners/content/2006/s1683060.htm>.

International Energy Agency (2008/9) 'World Energy Outlook, Nov. 2008 & Nov. 2009'. International Energy Agency, Paris.

Jackson PM (2007) Peak Oil Theory Could Distort Energy Policy and Debate. *Journal of Petroleum Technology* **59**, [online] <http://www.spe.org/spe-app/spe/jpt/2007/02/guest_ed.htm>.

*The Economist*, 'The End of the Oil Age, 23 October 2003, <http://www.economist.com/opinion/displaystory.cfm?story_id=E1_NTVVSTS>

CHAPTER 10

# Resilient cities

Peter Newman

## Abstract

In order to create resilience in cities, in Australia and around the world, there will need to be: renewable energy strategies showing how to progressively tap local resources; carbon-neutral strategies that can enforce energy efficiency, integrate with the renewables strategy and direct the carbon offsets into the bioregion; distributed infrastructure strategies that enable small-scale energy and water systems to flourish; biophilic or green infrastructure strategies that include the photosynthetic resources of the city and which can enhance the green agenda across the city through food, fibre, biodiversity and recreation pursuits locally; eco-efficiency strategies linking industries to achieve fundamental changes in the metabolism of cities; sense-of-place strategies to ensure the human dimension is driving all the other strategies; and sustainable transport strategies. This chapter explores how elements of these requirements have been achieved nationally and internationally and what more needs to be done to achieve resilient cities in Australia.

## Introduction

Resilience is increasingly being used as a way to describe human activities that are smart, secure and sustainable. They are smart in that they are able to adapt to the new technologies of the 21st century, secure in that they have built-in systems that enable them to respond to extreme events as well as being built to last, and sustainable in that they are part of the solution to the big questions of sustainability such as climate change, peak oil and biodiversity. Resilience thinking has been applied mostly to regions and natural resource management systems (Walker and Salt 2006) but can also be applied to cities (Newman *et al.* 2009).

The question of what kind of infrastructure helps cities to be more resilient is the focus of this chapter. Seven characteristics are outlined to help define these features and they are illustrated by examples from around the world. These are then applied briefly to Australian cities.

## Innovations in resilient infrastructure cities

Globally, there are seven features of resilience that are emerging in infrastructure. These are described as seven archetypal cities:

- the 'renewable energy city';
- the 'carbon-neutral city';

- the 'distributed city';
- the 'biophilic city';
- the 'eco-efficient city';
- the 'place-based city'; and
- the 'sustainable transport city'.

These city types are obviously overlapping in their approaches and outcomes, but each provides a perspective on how attempts to improve the resilience of a city can be achieved.

While no one city has shown innovation in all seven areas, some are quite advanced in one or two. The challenge for urban planners is to apply all of these approaches together, to generate a sense of purpose through a combination of new technology, city design and community-based innovation in resilient infrastructure.

## The 'renewable energy city'

There are now a number of urban areas that are partly powered by renewable energy techniques and technologies, from the region to the building level. Renewable energy enables a city to reduce its ecological footprint and, if using biological fuels, can be part of a city's enhanced ecological functions.

Renewable energy production can and should occur within cities, integrated into their land use and built form and comprising a significant and important element of the urban economy. Cities are not simply consumers of energy, but catalysts for more sustainable energy paths and they can increasingly become a part of the earth's solar cycle.

While some solar city projects are underway (including Treasure Island in San Francisco), there are presently no major cities in the world that are powered entirely by renewable energy. Movement towards a renewable-energy future will require much greater commitment from cities themselves at all levels, including the local and the metropolitan.

Masdar City in the United Arab Emirates is an important first example of a city built from scratch with 100% renewable energy and zero car use (in theory). It is being built with a 60 megawatts solar photovoltaic plant to power all construction and will eventually have a 130 MW solar photovoltaic plant for ongoing power as well as a 20 MW wind farm and geothermal heat pumps for cooling buildings. Electric automatic pod cars running on an elevated structure will be the basis of the transport. Masdar has begun to be built.

North Port Quay in Western Australia is planned to host 10 000 households and is designed to be 100% renewable through solar photovoltaic, small wind turbines called wind pods and a nearby wave power system. The development will be dense and walkable with an all-electric public and private transport system, linked to renewable power through battery storage in vehicles. The concept has had a mixed response and will be several years in its planning phase as such developments are not easy to slot into town planning schemes designed around fossil-fuel based development.

Urban planning is necessary to create the infrastructure needed to support solar and wind power at the scale necessary to help power a city. While finding locations for large wind farms near urban areas has been controversial, there are significant opportunities to harness solar and wind power. Studies are also now showing that wind, like photovoltaic solar, can be integrated into cities and their buildings.

The shift in the direction to the renewable city can occur through many actions: demonstration solar or low-energy homes created to show architects, developers and citizens that green can be appealing; procurement actions that source regionally produced wind and other renewable energy to power municipal transit, lights and buildings; and green building stand-ards and requirements for all new public as well as private buildings.

Freiburg in Germany has incorporated solar energy in all major new development areas including Resielfeld and Vauban, which are new compact green growth areas in the city. Both active and passive solar techniques are employed in these projects and the city also mandates a stringent energy standard for all new homes. In Vauban, some 5000 zero-energy homes – homes that produce at least as much energy as they need – have been built and a zero-energy office complex was added in 2006, along with two solar garages where photovoltaic panels cover the roof of the only allowable parking in the area (Scheurer and Newman 2008).

Adelaide envisions itself as a renewable city, as part of its larger green city initiative. It has designated solar precincts for the installation of photovoltaic panels on the rooftops of build-ings, including Parliament House. There is a solar schools initiative, with the goal of 250 solar schools (schools with rooftop installations that incorporate solar and renewable energy). This idea has since been taken up by the Australian Government for application in every school in the country. Most creatively, the city has been installing grid-connected photovoltaic street lamps that produce some six times the energy needed for the lighting. These new lights are designed in a distinctive shape of a local mallee tree. This is one of the few examples of solar art or solar 'place' projects.

Along with incentives (financial and otherwise), solar cities recognise the need to set minimum regulatory standards. Barcelona has a solar ordinance, which requires new build-ings and substantial retrofits of existing buildings to obtain a minimum of 60% of hot water needs from solar. This has already led to a significant growth of solar thermal installations in that city.

Transport can also be a major part of the renewables challenge. The more public transport moves to electric power, the more it can be part of a renewable city. Calgary Transit's creative initiative called 'Ride the Wind' provides all the power needed for its light rail system from wind turbines in the south of Alberta, Canada. Private transport can now also be part of this transition through a combination of electric vehicles and new battery storage technology, together called 'Renewable Transport' (Went *et al.* 2008; Curtin University Sustainability Policy Institute 2009). Not only can electric vehicles use renewable electricity to power their propulsion, they can also be plugged in during the day and, through their batteries, provide storage for intermittent renewable energy as their power systems store four times their con-sumption. Thus they can play a critical role in enabling renewables to satisfy a much higher proportion of the urban energy demand.

Renewable power enables cities to create healthy and liveable environments while minimis-ing the use and impact of fossil fuels. But, by itself, this will not be enough to ensure resilient urban development.

## The 'carbon-neutral city'

Carbon-neutral can become the goal for all urban development, just as it has become for some businesses and households. This will require a three-step process:

- reducing energy use wherever possible – especially in the building and transportation sectors;
- adding as much renewable energy as possible, while being careful that the production of the renewable energy is not contributing significantly to greenhouse gases; and
- offsetting any $CO_2$ emitted through purchasing carbon credits, particularly through tree planting.

In 2007, Rupert Murdoch announced that News Corporation would be going carbon-neutral. This has led to some remarkable innovations within the company as it approached uncharted territory in aspiring to become a global leader in energy efficiency, renewable energy and carbon offsets (News Corporation 2009).

Many businesses, universities and households are now committing to minimising their carbon footprint and even becoming carbon-neutral. But can it become a feature of whole neighbourhoods and even complete cities? There are those who suggest it is essential if the world is to move to 'post-carbon cities' (Lerch 2007).

There are a number of initiatives that focus on helping cities to reach these goals, including ICLEI–Local Governments for Sustainability's 'Cities for Climate Change', 'Architecture 2030', The Clinton Foundation's 'C–40 Climate Change Initiative' and UN–Habitat's 'Cities for Climate Change Initiative' (CCCI). As mentioned earlier, many municipalities have started to offer incentives and/or require that new buildings meet certain green-building standards. Minimising carbon at the building level has momentum, as it is easier to integrate the technology into new buildings and the benefits have been proven – not just in energy savings but in increased productivity and fewer sick days taken by staff in green office buildings.

In Sydney, the BASIX programme has mandated that new homes must now be designed to produce 40% fewer greenhouse gas emissions compared with an existing house (after initially requiring 20% and finding it was relatively easy to achieve) as well as 40% less water use. The programme aims to reduce $CO_2$ emissions by 8 million tonnes and water use by 287 billion litres in ten years (Farrelly 2005). This is an important role for urban planning, through the assessment process, which can help to set up carbon-neutral suburbs. The next phase of this project is called 'Precinx' and seeks to establish the statutory planning governance for carbon-neutral neighbourhoods and subdivisions.

The United Kingdom has decided that all urban development will be carbon-neutral by 2016, with phasing in from 2009. The 'Beddington Zero Energy Development' initiative is the first carbon-neutral community in the UK. It has extended the concept to include building materials and, as it is a social housing development, it has shown how to integrate the carbon-neutral agenda with other sustainability goals, making it a more resilient demonstration.

Malmo in Sweden, has stated that it has already become a carbon-neutral city; Vaxja, Sweden, has declared its intention to become a fossil-fuel-free city and Newcastle in the UK, and Adelaide in Australia, also aspire to be carbon-neutral. Each has taken important steps in the direction of renewable energy.

Vancouver's new Winter Olympic Village was built as a model North American demonstration in carbon-neutral urban development.

The link to the green agenda of a city is very direct with respect to the carbon-neutral approach of bioregional tree-planting schemes. By committing to be carbon-neutral, cities can direct their offsets to bioregional tree planting, as part of the biodiversity agenda as well as climate change.

In all Australian cities, the carbon and greenhouse gas emissions associated with many municipal motor pools are being offset through innovative tree-planting initiatives and through organisations such as Green Fleet, which has recently planted its second millionth tree. Firms such as airlines, offer carbon-neutral services and schools as well as many businesses are committed to being carbon-neutral. The carbon-offsetting is accredited through a Federal Government scheme called 'Greenhouse Friendly' and provides a strong legal backing to ensure that tree planting does occur, is related to the money committed and is guaranteed for at least 100 years as required by the Kyoto Convention. Many of the carbon-offsetting programmes are directed towards biodiversity plantations that are regenerating a bioregional ecology around cities. A particular example is the 'Gondwana Links' project, which is regenerating an ecological link over 3000 km between the coastal ecosystems of the Karri forest to the inland woodlands by joining up various reserves across the whole southern coast of Western Australia. The project is driven by many big firms using their carbon offsets from energy use to create this biodiversity-based tree planting (Newman and Jennings 2008).

All these are good programmes, but none are committed yet to a comprehensive city-wide carbon-neutral approach that can link tree planting to a broader biodiversity cause. If this is done, cities can raise urban and bioregional reforestation to a new level and contribute to reducing the impact of climate change, simultaneously addressing local and regional green agenda issues.

The carbon-neutral city will receive a big boost when a global agreement on carbon trading can be achieved as this will enable the voluntary carbon-trading market to become mainstream.

## The 'distributed city'

The development of distributed power and water systems aims to achieve a shift from large centralised power and water systems to small-scale and neighbourhood-based systems within cities. The distributed use of power and water can enable a city to reduce its ecological foot-print, as power and water can be more efficiently provided using the benefits of electronic control systems and community-oriented utility governance.

Most power and water systems for cities over the past 100 years have become bigger and more centralised. While newer forms of power and water are increasingly smaller in scale, they are often still fitted into cities as though they were large. The movement that tries to see how these new technologies can be fitted into cities and decentralised across grids is called 'distributed power and distributed water systems' (Droege 2006).

The distributed water system approach is often called 'water sensitive urban design'. It includes using the complete water cycle (i.e. using rain and local water sources like groundwater to feed into the system and then to recycle grey water locally and black water regionally), thus ensuring that there are significant reductions in water used. This system can enable the green agenda to become central to the infrastructure management of a city, as stormwater recycling can involve swales and artificial wetlands that can become important habitats in the city. Grey water recycling can similarly be used to irrigate parks and gardens and regional black water recycling can be tied into regional ecosystems. All these initiatives require 'smart' control systems to fit them into a city grid and also require new skills among town planners and engineers, who are so far used to water and energy management being a centralised function rather than being a local planning issue (Benedict and McMahon 2006).

In large cities, the traditional engineering approach to providing energy has been through large centralised production facilities and extensive distribution systems that transport power relatively long distances. This is wasteful because of line losses, but also because large base-load power systems cannot be turned on and off easily, so there is considerable power shedding when the load does not meet the need. Renewable, low-carbon cities, however, aim at developing more decentralised energy production systems, where production is more on a neighbourhood scale and both line losses and power-shedding can be avoided. Whether from a wind turbine, small biomass combined heat and power plant (as in London's new distributed energy model) or a rooftop photovoltaic system, renewable energy is produced closer to where it is consumed and, indeed, often directly by those who consume it. This distributed generation offers a number of benefits, including energy savings, given the ability to better control the power production, lower vulnerability and greater resilience in the face of natural and human-made disaster (including terrorist attacks). Clever integration of these small systems into a grid can be achieved with new technology control systems that balance the whole system in its demand and supply from a range of sources as they rise and fall and link it to storage, especially vehicle batteries through vehicle-to-grid, or 'V2G', technology. A number of such small-scale energy systems are being developed to make cities more resilient in the future (Sawin and Hughes 2007).

Distributed power and water provision in cities needs community support. In Toronto, communities began forming 'buying-cooperatives' in which they pooled their buying power to negotiate special reduced prices from local photovoltaic companies that had offered an incentive to buy solar photovoltaic panels. The first co-op was the 'Riverdale Initiative for Solar Energy'. In this initiative, 75 residents joined together to purchase rooftop photovoltaic systems, resulting in savings of about 15% in their purchase cost. This then spread across the city. The Toronto example suggests the merits of combining bottom–up neighbourhood approaches with top–down incentives and encouragement. This support for small-scale distributed production – offered through what are commonly referred to as standard offer contracts (often referred to as 'feed-in tariffs' in Europe) – has been extremely successful in Europe where they are now common. The same can be done with new technologies for water and waste, such as rainwater tanks and grey water recycling.

One other example is the redevelopment of the Western Harbour in Malmö, Sweden. Here the goal was to achieve distributed power and water systems from local sources. This urban district now has 100% renewable power from rooftop solar panels and an innovative storm water management system that recycles water into green courtyards and green rooftops. The project involves local government in the management and demonstrates that a clear plan helps to drive innovations in distributed systems (City of Malmo 2005). Sydney is pursuing the distributed city idea through its Green Transformers program and the City of Stirling in Perth wants to develop a new city centre using distributed infrastructure.

Distributed infrastructure is beginning to be demonstrated in cities across the globe. Utilities will need to develop models with city planners of how they can carry out local energy and water planning through community-based approaches and local management.

## The 'biophilic city'

Biophilic cities are using natural processes as part of infrastructure. Growing energy and providing food and materials locally is therefore becoming part of urban infrastructure development. The use of photosynthetic processes in cities reduces their ecological impact by replacing fossil fuels and can bring substantial ecological benefits through emphasis on natural systems.

There has been a positive trend in planning in the direction of an expanded notion of urban infrastructure that includes the idea of 'green infrastructure' based on photosynthetic processes. Green infrastructure refers to the many green and ecological features and systems, from wetlands to urban forests, that provide a host of benefits to cities and urban residents – clean water, stormwater collection and management, climate moderation and cleansing of urban air, among others. This understanding of green infrastructure as part of the working landscape of cities and metropolitan areas has been extended to include the photosynthetic sources of renewable energy, local food and fibre.

Renewable energy can be tapped from the sun and wind and geothermal sources using small-scale decentralised technology, as described in the previous section; however, renewable energy can also be grown through biofuels. The transition to growing fuels is drawing on crops and forests that can feed into new ways of fuelling buildings and vehicles. Farms and open areas around cities are being developed as the source of renewable energy, especially the production of biofuels. However, biofuels are also being produced as part of improving the urban environment. This means more intensive greening of the lower density parts of cities and their peri-urban regions with intensive food-growing, renewable-energy crops and forests, but greening the high-density parts of cities as well.

The City of Vaxja in Sweden has developed a locally based renewable energy strategy that takes full advantage of its working landscapes, in this case the abundant forests that exist within close proximity of the city. Vaxja's main power plant, formerly fuelled by oil, now depends on biomass almost entirely from wood chips, most of which are a by-product of the commercial logging in the region. The wood, more specifically, comes from the branches, bark and tops of trees and is derived from within a 100 km radius of the power plant. This 'Combined Heat and Power' plant (Sandvik II) provides the entire town's heating needs and much of its electricity needs. Its conversion to using biomass as a fuel has been a key element in the city's aspiration to become an oil-free city. Clearly, each city can develop its own mix of local renewable sources, but Vaxja has demonstrated that it can transition from an oil-based power system to a completely renewable system without losing its economic edge. Indeed, cities that develop such resilience early are likely to have an edge as oil resources decline.

Green roofs and green walls draped across buildings and linked to open space greenery, especially on water-courses, can help create a more sustainable city. Dressing up high-density areas with biodiversity-enhancing green infrastructure helps restrain a city's sprawl as well as contributing to the regeneration of its local biodiversity. This has been the goal of Singapore in recent years, and grants are now awarded for sky gardens with some spectacular results.

One of the most important potential biofuel sources of the future will be blue-green algae that can be grown intensively on roof tops. Blue-green algae can photosynthesise, so all that it requires is sunlight, water and nutrients. The output from blue-green algae is 10 times faster than most other biomass sources, so it can be continuously cropped and fed into a process for producing biofuels or small-scale electricity. Most importantly, city buildings can all utilise their roofs to tap solar energy and use it for local purposes without the distribution or transport losses so apparent in most cities today. According to one advocate of this approach, 'every roof should be photosynthetic', meaning a green roof for biodiversity purposes, water collection, photovoltaic collectors or biofuel-algal collectors. This can become a solar ordinance set by town planners as part of local government policy.

Few cities have done much to take stock of their photosynthetic energy potential. Municipal comprehensive plans typically document and describe a host of natural and economic resources found within the boundaries of a city – from mineral sites, through historic buildings, to biodiversity – but estimating incoming renewable energy (sun, wind, wave, biomass or geothermal) is usually not included. In advancing the renewable energy agenda in Barcelona, the city took the interesting step of calculating incoming solar gain. As a former sustainable city counsellor noted, this amounted to '10 times more than the energy the city consumes or 28 times more than the electricity the city is consuming' (Puig 2008). The issue is how to tap into this across the city.

As well as renewable fuel, cities can incorporate food in this more holistic solar and post-oil view of the future. Food, in the globalised market place, increasingly travels great distances – apples from New Zealand, grapes from Chile, wine from South Australia, vegetables from China. 'Food miles' are rising everywhere and already food in the US travels on average a distance of between 1500 and 2500 miles from where it is grown to where it is consumed. Any exotic sources of food come at a high-energy cost. The growing, processing and delivering of food in the US consumes vast amounts of energy on par with the energy required to power homes or fuel cars (Starrs 2005).

After the collapse of the USSR in the late 1980s, Cuba lost Soviet aid, which had provided the country with modern agricultural chemicals. Thus 1 300 000 tons of chemical fertilisers, 17 000 tons of herbicides and 10 000 tons of pesticides could no longer be imported. Urban agriculture was one of Cuba's responses to the shock, intensifying the previously established 'National Food Programme', which aimed at taking thousands of poorly utilised areas – mainly around Havana – and converting them into intensive vegetable gardens. Planting in the city instead of only in the countryside decreased the need for transportation, refrigeration and other scarce resources. By 1998, over 8000 urban farms and community gardens had been established, run by over 30 000 people in and around Havana. Today, food from the urban farms is grown almost completely with active organic methods. Havana has banned the use of chemical pesticides in agriculture within city boundaries (Murphy 1999).

Cities need to find creative ways to promote urban farming where it is feasible, without creating tension with redevelopment for reduced car dependence through increased density. This may mean that a city can utilise the many vacant lots for commercial and community farms in areas that have been blighted (for example, the estimated 70 000 vacant lots in Chicago). If these areas are well served with good transit and other infrastructure, then such uses should be seen as temporary and, indeed, can be part of the rehabilitation of an area, leading to the development of eco-villages that are car-free and models of solar building, as in Vauban. Many cities have embarked on some form of effort to examine community food security and to promote more sustainable local and regional food production. These can be integrated into ecologically sustainable urban and regional rehabilitation projects (Beatley 2005) and can utilise the intensive possibilities of urban spaces, as in urban permaculture (see Newman and Jennings 2008).

In Madison, Wisconsin, a model urban garden called 'Troy Gardens' has emerged from excess land owned by a state-owned mental hospital. Dubbed the 'Accidental Eco-village' by those involved in its transformation, the land was being sold in 1995 when the community who used it as a garden and park stepped in and formed an association to try and buy the land. Through partnerships with other NGOs and the University of Madison Department of Urban and Regional Planning, the 'Friends of Troy Gardens' was able to create a diversity of uses that enabled the money to be found. Thus on the site now is a mixed income co-housing project involving 30 housing units, a community garden with 320 allotments, an intensive urban farm using traditional Hmong agricultural techniques for a community-supported agriculture enterprise and a prairie restoration scheme which is regenerating local biodiversity (Campbell and Salus 2003).

Progress in moving away from fossil fuels also requires serious localising and local sourcing of building materials. This, in turn, provides new opportunities to build more photosynthetic economies. The value of emphasising the local is many fold and the essential benefits are usually clear. Dramatic reductions in the energy consumed as part of making these materials is, of course, the primary benefit. It is also about strengthening local economies and helping them to become more resilient in the face of global economic forces and it is also about re-forming lost connections to place.

At the Beddington Zero Energy Development project in London, more than half of the building materials for the project came from within a 35-mile radius and the wood used in construction, as well as a fuel in the neighbourhood's combined heat and power plant, comes from local council forests. A biophilic approach to urban use of fibre will mean an added reduction in fibre miles as well as potential to help re-grow bioregions.

## The 'eco-efficient city'

In an effort to improve eco-efficiency, cities and regions are moving from linear to circular or closed-loop systems, where substantial amounts of their energy and material needs are provided from waste streams. Eco-efficient cities reduce their ecological footprint by reducing wastes and resource requirements and can also incorporate green-agenda issues in the process.

A more integrated notion of energy and water entails seeing cities as complex metabolic systems (not unlike a human body) with flows and cycles and where, ideally, the things that have traditionally been viewed as negative outputs (e.g. solid waste, wastewater) are re-envisioned as productive inputs to satisfy other urban needs, including energy. The sustainability movement has been advocating for some time for this shift away from the current view of cities as linear resource-extracting machines. This is often described as the eco-efficiency agenda (Girardet 2000).

The eco-efficiency agenda has been taken up by the United Nations and the World Business Council on Sustainable Development, with a high target for industrialised countries of a 10-fold reduction in consumption of resources by 2040, along with rapid transfers of knowledge and technology to developing countries. While this eco-efficiency agenda is a huge challenge, it is important to remember that throughout the industrial revolution of the past 200 years, human productivity has increased by 20 000%. The next wave of innovation has a lot of potential to create the kind of eco-efficiency gains that are required (Hawken *et al.* 1999; Hargrove and Smith 2006).

The urban eco-efficiency agenda includes the 'cradle to cradle' concept for the design of all new products and new systems like industrial ecology, where industries share resources and wastes like an ecosystem (McDonaugh and Braungart 2002). Good examples exist in Kalundborg in Germany, and Kwinana in Australia (Jennings and Newman 2008).

The view of cities as a complex set of metabolic flows might also help to guide cities dealing with situations (especially in the shorter term) where considerable reliance on resources and energy from other regions and parts of the world still occurs. Policies can include sustainable sourcing agreements, region-to-region trade agreements, urban procurement systems based on green certification systems, among others. Embracing a metabolic view of cities and metropolitan areas takes global governance in some interesting and potentially very useful directions.

This new paradigm of sustainable urban metabolism (seeing them as complex systems of metabolic flows) requires profound changes in the way cities and metropolitan regions are conceptualised as well as in the ways they are planned and managed. New forms of cooperation and collaboration between municipal agencies and various urban actors and stakeholder groups will be required. Municipal departments will need to formulate and implement integrated resource flow strategies. New organisational and governance structures will be necessary, as well as new planning tools and methods. For example, municipal authorities that map the resource flows of their city and region will need to see how this new data can be part of a comprehensive plan for integrating the green and brown agendas.

Toronto has a 'trash-to-can' programme, which allows the city to capture methane from waste to generate electricity. This not only reuses waste and provides an inexpensive energy source but also captures a significant amount of methane that would otherwise be released into the air. Before it reached capacity in its operation, it is estimated that Toronto's Keele Valley landfill generated three to four million dollars annually and provided enough power for approximately 24 000 homes (Clinton Climate Initiative 2009).

One extremely powerful example of how this eco-efficiency view can manifest in a new approach to urban design and building can be seen in the dense urban neighbourhood of Hammarby Sjöstad in Stockholm. Here, from the beginning of the planning of this new district, an effort was made to think holistically to understand the inputs, outputs and resources that would be required and that would result. For instance, about 1000 flats in Hammarby Sjöstad are equipped with stoves that utilise biogas extracted from wastewater generated in the community. Biogas also provides fuel for buses that serve the area. Organic waste from the community is returned to the neighbourhood in the form of district heating and cooling. There are many other important energy features in the design as well. The neighbourhood's proximity to central Stockholm and the installation (from the beginning) of a high-frequency light rail system have made it truly possible to live without a private automobile (there are also 30 car-sharing vehicles in the neighbourhood). While not a perfect example, it represents a new and valuable way of seeing cities and requires a degree of interdisciplinary and inter-sectoral collaboration in the planning system that is unusual in most cities (Newman *et al.* 2008).

## The 'place-based city'

Cities and regions are beginning to understand sustainability more generally as a way of not only reducing their footprint but also nurturing a high quality of life through building local economies and adding a strong commitment to community through a unique and special sense of place. The more place-oriented and locally self-sufficient a city's economy is, the more it will reduce its ecological footprint and the more it will ensure that its valuable ecological features are enhanced.

Local economic development has many advantages in the context of sustainable development, including the ability of people to travel less as their work becomes local. Finding ways to help facilitate local enterprises becomes a major achievement for cities in moving towards a reduced ecological footprint. Initiatives designed to help small towns in the US to create their own jobs have been developed (Sirolli 1999). What the pioneers of these initiatives have found, time and time again, is that place really matters. When people belong and feel an affinity with their town or city, they want to put down their roots and create local enterprise.

Local economic development is a first priority for most cities. As part of this, many cities are placing increasing emphasis on local place identity, as social capital has been found to be one of the best ways to predict wealth in a community (Putnam 1993). Thus when communities relate strongly to the local environment, the city's heritage and its unique culture, they develop a strong social capital of networks and trust that forms the basis of a robust urban economy.

This approach to economic development, which emphasises place-based social capital, has many supporters but very few relate this to the sustainability agenda in cities. For example, energy expenditures – by municipalities, companies and individuals – represent a significant economic drain, as they often leave the community and region. Producing power from solar, wind or biomass in the locality or region is very much an economic development strategy that can generate local jobs and economic revenue from land (farmland) that might otherwise be economically marginal, in the process recirculating money, with an important economic multiplier effect. Energy efficiency can also be an economic development strategy. For example, research on renewable energy and the creation of related products have developed into a strong part of the economy in Freiburg.

All the efforts at localising energy, food, materials and economic development remain dependent on the strength of the local community. The Beddington Zero Energy Development project shows the importance of thinking beyond the design of buildings and seeing urban development through a more holistic community-oriented design lens. However impressive the passive solar design and smaller energy demands of this project are (300 mm insulation, an innovative ventilation and heat recovery system, for instance), much of the sustainability gains will come from how residents actually live in these places. Here, residents are being challenged to rethink their consumption and mobility decisions – there is a car-sharing club on site, for example, a food buying club and a community of residents helping each other to think creatively about reducing their ecological impacts and footprints is emerging. This is actually a hallmark of European green projects and an important lesson for projects elsewhere.

A study that examined a range of European urban ecology innovations concluded that when the innovations came from a close and committed community they became ingrained in people's lifestyles, giving the next generation a real opportunity to gain from them. Many architect-designed innovations that were imposed on residents without their involvement, however, tended to fall into neglect or were actively removed (Scheurer 2003).

Sense of place is about generating pride in the city about all aspects of the economy, the environment and the culture of the city. The 'Magic Eyes' project in Bangkok has illustrated how a solid waste project can be facilitated through sense of place. This project ran a media campaign on the importance of not littering or dropping solid waste into the rivers of Bangkok with a large set of eyes (representing the spirit of the river) looking down at people from many sites (UN Habitat 2009).

Sense of place in a city requires paying attention to people and community development in the process of change – a major part of the urban planning agenda for many decades. This localised approach will be critical to creating a resilient city. It creates the necessary innovations as people dialogue through options to reduce their ecological footprint, which in turn creates social capital that is the basis for ongoing community life and economic development (Beatley and Manning 1997; Beatley 2005). City dwellers in many countries already increasingly want to know where their food is grown, where their wine comes from and where the materials that make up their furniture come from. This can increasingly move towards every element of the built environment. Thus, as well as a slow movement for local foods, a slow fibre and slow materials movement for local fabric and building purposes can also help create a sense of place and make a more resilient city.

City economies in the past had their own currencies and it has been argued that national currencies often fail to express the true value of a city and its bioregion (Jacobs 1984). Transforming urban economies towards a more bioregional focus has been assisted in some places by adopting complementary currencies that provide an alternative to national currencies and by establishing local financial institutions. It has been argued that a complementary local currency not only facilitates change but also creates a community with a mutual interest in productive exchange among its members in the bioregion (Korten 1999). In this way, a community affirms its identity and creates a natural preference for its own products. Over a thousand communities around the world have issued their own local currencies to encourage local commerce. How this has been related to urban planning is set out in Newman and Jennings (2008) using the example of Curitiba in Brazil, where the planning system gave special bonuses to environmental performance and innovation.

Most developed cities have created development bonuses similar to Curitiba's that are part of the non-monetary economy of the city. For example, in Vancouver, the city requires that 5% of the value of a development be directed towards social infrastructure. This is worked out by the developer and council in discussion with the local community who may want more landscaped streetscapes, more areas set aside for pedestrian use only, or a community meeting space, even an arthouse cinema. Social housing is worked out on the basis of receiving a density bonus for more development rights. The more Vancouver exercises these complementary currency requests, the more the development process works to create better public spaces to go with the private spaces developed by the market. Thus sustainability can be made to mean something at a very local level through the planning system.

All cities have the opportunity through their planning systems to create their own currencies that work in a parallel but complementary way with normal money. These 'sustainability credits' are not owned by the developer or by the city but they are in fact, owned by the community, as it is their values that are expressed in the development bonuses granted. Thus cities can create community banks of sustainability credit through their planning systems. Most cities in developing countries do not have much to invest in their public spaces hence the whole city economy suffers. Curitiba showed how cities could break that mould. Through the planning system, cities can create their own sustainability currencies for what they most need as determined by their local citizens – they just need to define them as 'development rights'. These new 'sustainable development rights' could be related to biodiversity credits, greenhouse reduction credits, salinity reduction credits, affordable housing credits or anything else that a community can create a 'market' for in their city and its bioregion.

## The 'sustainable transport city'

Transport is the most fundamental infrastructure for a city, as it creates the primary form of the city (Newman and Kenworthy 1999). Cities, neighbourhoods and regions are increasingly being designed to use energy sparingly by offering walkable, transit-oriented options, more recently supplemented by vehicles powered by renewable energy (Went *et al.* 2008). Cities with more sustainable transport systems have been able to increase their resilience by reducing their use of fossil fuels, as well as through reduced urban sprawl and reduced dependence on car-based infrastructure..

The agenda for large cities now is to have more sustainable transport options so as to reduce traffic while reducing greenhouse gases by 50% by at least 2050, in line with the global agenda set through the International Panel on Climate Change. For many cities, the reduction of car use is not yet on the agenda, apart from seeing it as an ideal to which they aspire. Unfortunately, for most cities, traffic growth has been continuous and appears to be unstoppable, though the first reductions in car growth have been set for US and Australian cities which have shown five years of per capita declines in car use (Puentes and Tomer 2009; Stanley and Barrett 2010). To reduce a city's ecological footprint and enhance its liveability, it is necessary to manage the growth of cars and trucks and their associated fossil-fuel consumption through sustainable transport innovations such as quality public transport, transit-oriented development, non-motorised transport priorities, plug-in electric vehicle infrastructure and urban growth boundaries (Newman *et al.* 2009).

## Urban planning for resilient urban infrastructure development

The above seven resilient city types suggest that in order to create resilience in cities, there will need to be:

- renewable energy strategies showing how to progressively tap local resources (such strategies should involve recognition of renewable resources in and around a city as part of the capital base of the city and establishing ordinances on buildings that facilitate the application of renewable energy);
- carbon-neutral strategies that can enforce energy efficiency, integrate with the renewables strategy and direct the carbon offsets into the bioregion (this can be enforced through planning schemes that mandate standards for significant reductions in carbon and water in all development, that prevent the loss of arable and natural land in the bioregion and direct planting to areas that are most in need of revegetation);
- distributed infrastructure strategies that enable small-scale energy and water systems to flourish (this can be built into the requirements for urban development and can be facilitated by providing incentive packages with new buildings for technologies such as

photovoltaic cells, grey water systems and water tanks, local plans for the governance of community-based systems and region-wide strategies for recycling sewage);

- biophilic or green infrastructure strategies that include the photosynthetic resources of the city and which can enhance the green agenda across the city through food, fibre, biodiversity and recreation pursuits locally (this can be achieved through development controls that focus on how the roof-tops (and walls) of buildings can be used for photosynthetic purposes as well as zoning areas for urban photosynthetic activity, including growing bio-fuels, food and fibre and biodiversity in and around the city);

- eco-efficiency strategies linking industries to achieve fundamental changes in the metabolism of cities (this can be done by taking an audit of all the wastes of the city and seeing how they can be re-used through stakeholder participation and government facilitation)

- sense-of-place strategies to ensure the human dimension is driving all the other strategies (this can be assisted by local economic development strategies, by place-based engagement approaches to all planning and development processes and by the innovative use of 'sustainability credits', or complementary currencies, to implement local sustainability innovations as development bonuses); and

- sustainable transport strategies incorporating: (i) quality transit down each main corridor which is faster than traffic; (ii) dense transit-oriented developments (TOD) built around each station; (iii) pedestrian and bicycle strategies for each centre and TOD with cycle links across the city; (iv) plug-in infrastructure for electric vehicles as they emerge; (v) cycling and pedestrian infrastructure as part of all street planning; and (vi) a green-wall growth boundary around the city preventing further urban encroachment.

## Application to Australian cities

The ideas discussed above apply to Australian cities in a range of ways:

- renewable energy strategies in Australian cities are not well developed with no clear plan yet for how they will address the national goal of 20% by 2020. Wind power, solar and wave technologies will be needed as the focus with some geothermal possibilities.

- carbon-neutral strategies that can enforce energy efficiency are beginning to be created though no city-wide attempt has yet been made to direct carbon offsets into the bioregion. A carbon plan is needed for each Australian city.

- distributed infrastructure strategies that enable small-scale energy and water systems to flourish have rarely been considered because Australian cities are almost fully sewered and have a fully reticulated water supply system and complete grid for electricity covering all buildings. As the small-scale systems for water, energy and waste become more mature it will be possible to put these back into the city while retaining the central grids for back-up. Only Sydney and the City of Stirling in Perth have begun to consider such a plan.

- biophilic or green infrastructure strategies are starting to be considered to supplement biodiversity strategies but no Australian city yet has a biophilic strategy. An urban agriculture strategy is not yet in place anywhere either despite good examples of community gardens in a number of inner city councils.

- an eco-efficiency strategy has been developed in Kwinana and in Gladstone. Few other examples of industrial ecology are obvious.

- sense-of-place strategies to ensure the human dimension of resilience is part of the policy mix are now apparent in most Australian cities. Urban design and development is constantly being re-evaluated in terms of their cultural relevance but how this relates to the sustainability agenda is not clear in most cities.

• sustainable transport strategies are now firmly on the agenda in all Australian cities with plans for doubling rail capacity in most cities and Federal funding for the first time being directed to this goal. Walkability and cycling agendas are also being pursued though often still have to fight for funds when roads are more easily funded. Dense TODs are suggested to be built around each station in Australian cities but few are happening as local planning schemes are not adapted to this agenda. Plug-in infrastructure for electric vehicles has begun to be considered and the Australian Government is promoting demonstrations of the 'Smart Grid Smart City'. This is an obvious next step for each city's innovation and resilience. A growth boundary around each Australian city preventing further urban encroachment is constantly on the agenda and rarely is able to be achieved leaving a legacy of non-resilience for the future in the areas developed on the old sprawl model.

*Peter Newman is the Professor of Sustainability at Curtin University and is on the Board of Infrastructure Australia that is funding infrastructure for the long-term sustainability of Australian cities. His two new books,* Resilient Cities: Responding to Peak Oil and Climate Change *and* Green Urbanism Down Under, *were both written with Tim Beatley. Peter invented the term 'automobile dependence' to describe how we have created cities where we have to drive everywhere. For 30 years since he attended Stanford University during the first oil crisis he has been warning cities about preparing for peak oil. Peter's book with Jeff Kenworthy,* Sustainability and Cities: Overcoming Automobile Dependence, *was launched in the White House in 1999. He was a Councillor in the City of Fremantle from 1976-80 where he still lives.*

## References

Beatley T (2005) *Native to Nowhere*. Island Press, Washington, DC.

Beatley T and Manning K (1997) *The Ecology of Place*. Island Press, Washington, DC.

Benedict M and MacMahon E (2006) *Green Infrastructure: Linking Landscapes and Communities*. Island Press, Washington, DC.

Campbell MC and Salus DA (2003) Community and Conservation Land Trusts as unlikely partners? The case of Troy Gardens, Madison, Wisconsin. *Land Use Policy* **20**, 169–180.

City of Malmö (2005) 'Sustainable city of tomorrow: Experiences of a Swedish housing exposition'. Swedish Research Council for Environment, Agricultural Sciences and Spatial Planning, Stockholm.

Clinton Climate Initiative (2009) C40 Cities. Waste. Toronto, Canada. Clinton Climate Initiative, London, UK, <http://www.c40cities.org/bestpractices/waste/toronto_organic.jsp>.

Curtin University Sustainability Policy Institute (2009) Renewable Transport. Curtin University, Curtin, Western Australia, <http://sustainability.curtin.edu.au/research_publications/renewable_transport.cfm>.

Droege P (2006) *The Renewable City*. Wiley, Chichester.

Farrelly E (2005) Attack of common sense hits planners. *Sydney Morning Herald* 26 April.

Girardet H (2000) *The Gaia Atlas of Cities*. Gaia Books, London.

Hargrove C and Smith M (2006) *The Natural Advantage of Nations*. Earthscan, London.

Hawken P, Lovins A and Lovins H (1999) *Natural Capitalism: The Next Industrial Revolution*. Earthscan, London.

Jacobs J (1984) Cities and the Wealth of Nations. Random House, New York.

Korten D (1999) The Post-Corporate World: Life after Capitalism. Berret-Koehler Publishers, San Francisco.

Lerch D (2007) *Post Carbon Cities: Planning for Energy and Climate Uncertainty*. Post Carbon Press, Portland, Oregon.

McDonough W and Braungart M (2002) Cradle to Cradle: Remaking the Way We Make Things. North Point Press, New York 2002.

Murphy C (1999) 'Cultivating Havana: Urban Agriculture and Food Security in the Years of Crisis'. Development Report No. 12, Food First, Institute for Food and Development Policy, Oakland.

Newman P and Jennings I (2008) *Cities as Sustainable Ecosystems*. Island Press, Washington, DC.

Newman P, Beatley T and Boyer H (2009) *Resilient Cities: Responding to Peak Oil and Climate Change*. Island Press, Washington, DC.

Newman P and Kenworthy J (1999) *Sustainability and Cities: Overcoming Automobile Dependence*. Island Press, Washington, DC.

News Corporation (2009) News Corporation Annual Report 2009. News Corporation, <http://www.newscorp.com/Report2009/html/energy.html>.

Puentes R and Tomer A (2009) *The Road Less Travelled: An Analysis of Vehicle Miles Traveled Trends in the U.S.* Metropolitan Infrastructure Initiative Series Brookings Institution, Washington DC.

Puig J (2008) Energy efficient cities: Political will, capacity building and peoples' participation. The Barcelona Solar Ordinance: A case study about how the impossible became reality. In *Urban Energy Transition*. (Ed P Droege) pp. 433–350. Elsevier, Oxford UK.

Putnam R (1993) *Making Democracy Work: Civic Traditions of Modern Italy*. Princeton Architectural Press, Princeton NJ.

Sawin JL and Hughes K (2007) Energizing cities. In *State of the World 2007*. *(Worldwatch Institute)*, pp. 90–107. Worldwatch Institute, Washington, DC.

Scheurer J (2003) *Urban ecology, innovations in housing policy and the future of cities: Towards sustainability in neighbourhood communities*. PhD Thesis. Murdoch University, Western Australia.

Scheurer J and Newman P (2008) *Vauban: A Case Study in Public Community Partnerships*. UN–Habitat Global Review of Human Settlements, Nairobi, Kenya. (Also available at <http://www.sustainability.curtin.edu.au>).

Sirolli E (1999) *Ripples from the Zambezi: Passion, Entrepreneurship and the Rebirth of Local Economies*. New Society Publishers, Vancouver BC. (See also <http://www.sirolli.com>).

Stanley J and Barrett S (2010) 'Moving people: Solutions for a growing Australia'. ARA, BIC, UITP, Canberra. <www.ara.net.au>

Starrs T (2005) The SUV in our pantry. *Solar Today* July/August.

UN–Habitat (2009). UN–Habitat. For a Better Urban Future. UN–Habitat, Nairobi, Kenya, <http://www.unhabitat.org/>.

Walker B and Salt D (2006) Resilience Thinking: Sustaining Ecosystems and People in a Changing World. Island Press, Washington, DC.

Went A, James W and Newman P (2008) 'Renewable transport: How renewable energy and electric vehicles using vehicle to grid technology can make carbon free urban development'. CUSP discussion paper 2008/1, Fremantle Western Australia.

# HEALTH AND EDUCATION

# CHAPTER 11

# Why are some people more resilient to health problems than others?

Bob Douglas

## Abstract

Modern medical practice builds from reductionist and linear thinking to arrive at precise causal links between hypothetical risk factors and disease and between treatments and outcomes. People like Ian Gawler and Lance Armstrong delight and surprise us at their ability to adapt to malignancies that are lethal in most others. Perhaps these outliers are telling us something about issues quite unrelated to the treatment given and are more related to modulation of complex systems by external modifying factors. A consideration of such outliers and of a Whitehall study of British civil servants suggests the possibility that 'sense of control' might play an important role here. I suggest a way to explore these possibilities further.

## System complexity applied to health

*'In biology, the Cartesian view of living organisms as machines, constructed from separate parts, still provides the dominant conceptual framework... the belief that all aspects of living organisms can be understood by reducing them to their smallest constituents, and studying the mechanisms through which these interact, lies at the very basis of most contemporary biological thinking. What is needed, is a new paradigm; a new dimension of concepts transcending the Cartesian view. It is likely that the systems view of life will form the conceptual background of this new biology' (Capra 1982).*

Resilience thinking is systems thinking (Walker and Salt 2006; Cork *et al.* 2008) in which we recognise that the world consists of billions of discrete complex adaptive systems, each with positive and negative feedback loops. Individual systems interact with systems above, below and around them. Through these interconnections and interacting feedback loops, the flap of a butterfly's wings in Brazil can conceivably set off a tornado in Texas (Lorenz 1972).

Each human body is a complex adaptive system, comprising thousands of sub-systems within, above and around it. Each physiological system (cardiovascular, respiratory, neurological, etc.) operates in harmony with the other systems and comprises multiple organs and specialised cellular systems that themselves contain other functioning systems. Above and surrounding each human body is a further set of social and environmental systems that are also complex and adaptive.

Health is a very complex construct that for each individual is a product of these billions of intersecting and interacting systems. According to the World Health Organization (WHO) definition, a completely healthy person is one who is not only free of disease but who is experiencing complete physical, mental and social well-being. Measuring health precisely in these terms is impossible; we necessarily depend upon surrogate indicators like life expectancy, morbidity rates and well-being surveys to help us decide who is healthy and who is not and whether a health care system is contributing beneficially to a healthy society or not.

But we need to remember that these proxy indicators of health are imperfect shorthand for the net operation of this vast array of natural and man-made systems.

By contrast with these systemic constructs, medical researchers still tend to operate in a reductionist Cartesian paradigm, seeking simple causal relationships between identifiable risk factors and disease and between treatments and outcomes. The systems are taken as givens and we tend to work with variables that represent tiny parts of the system. At the heart of our statistical approach to these relationships is the normal 'top hat' distribution curve.

Using statistical assumptions based upon this curve, we use linear models to assess the probability that risk factor 'a' causes disease 'b', controlling for confounding factors 'c', 'd' and 'e', or that disease 'f' responds to treatment 'g', controlling for confounding factors 'h', 'i' and 'j'. Clinical practice is built around evidence derived from these kinds of simple causal studies and we seek certainty about the utility of new treatments by calculating the 95% or 99% probability of the relationship being true.

But the normal distribution curve also reminds us that some people will respond much more rapidly or completely to a treatment than others and some will be less responsive. Every now and again, someone comes along who surprises us with a dramatic response that exceeds our expectations. These are the people in the very outer tails of the normal distribution curve.

When we come to apply the resilience lens to our understanding of the health and well-being of individuals, we enter a field ripe for new exploratory research. It raises the question: are there key factors operating in the complex of human and social systems that can modulate and help to push them over the threshold from normal function to disease or from well-being to malaise? Examining the outer tails of the normal distribution curve for people's response to treatment is a good place to begin trying to understand what makes some people more resilient than others.

## System modulators

A now classic Whitehall longitudinal study of civil servants in the United Kingdom (Marmot *et al.* 1984) set out to ask the questions: 'why are some people healthy and others not', and, 'are there systemic factors that modulate risk factors and the likelihood of developing chronic disease?' These studies have produced a rich stream of evidence, indicating that those with low 'sense of job control' experienced two-and-a-half times higher incidence of heart disease, controlling for all other known risk factors, than those with a high sense of job control. The same studies have also shown that women with a low 'sense of control at home' had four times higher risk of heart disease than women with a 'high sense of control at home'.

The present chapter has been stimulated by admiration for my colleague, Michael Ward, whose resilience during the past five years in the face of overwhelming health adversity has been a source of inspiration to his many friends. Those of us who have read his irregular emails, entitled 'Tumor Times' (Michael Ward, pers. comm. 2005–2009), over several years have watched in agony and admiration as he has openly and bloody-mindedly dealt with cancer, its management and its complications. From the day of his diagnosis he resolutely took control of his own body and the medical team that was caring for him. His experience as a former spokesperson for the NSW public health system gave him insights into its fallibility and he knew his way around the system. He knew how to exercise control over his care. He saw the seriousness of his situation and almost certainly willed his body to make the best of it. Michael Ward unquestionably occupies the outer tail of the normal distribution curve of resilience.

We need to discover whether people like Ward have common attributes and, especially, attributes that those of us who do not possess them could acquire. I am suggesting, on the basis of what I have said already about Michael and about the Whitehall studies, that a 'sense of control' could perhaps be a key variable that modulates a broad range of human biological systems.

This possibility has led me to explore the attributes of four other cancer outliers whose stories are in the public domain: Ian Gawler (Allenby 2008); Michael Milton (Milton 2009); Michael Rennie (Rennie 2008); and Lance Armstrong . All, like Michael Ward, contracted life-threatening cancer at a relatively young age and each responded to this assault on their person in ways that conventional medical science did not expect. All have displayed stunning single-minded determination to control their management and their lives.

All of the five men tried conventional medical treatment for their condition and looked elsewhere as well, adding meditation, dietary change and sometimes outlandish alternative remedies in their determined efforts to stave off what seemed like certain death. Of course, this is a carefully selected case series, which can do no more than raise possible questions and hypotheses for further testing. The question I am raising here is whether a sense of control might turn out to be a very important variable across a whole range of human biological systems including the general ability to adapt to cancer insult.

## Personal psychological resilience and learned helplessness

There is considerable attention in the literature to the issue of personal psychological resilience (Reivich and Schatte 2003). Resilient individuals have been found to have high expectations, a strong sense that their lives had meaning, goals, personal agency (which I take to be equivalent to a sense of control) and interpersonal problem-solving skills.

At the other end of the spectrum of personal resilience is the notion of learned helplessness. It has been found that animals receiving electric shocks that they had no ability to prevent or avoid were unable to act in subsequent situations where avoidance or escape was possible. Extending the ramifications of these findings to humans, Martin Seligman and his colleagues found that human motivation to initiate responses is also undermined by a lack of control over one's surroundings. Further, it has been found that this learned helplessness disrupts normal development and learning and contributes to emotional disturbances and depression (Peterson *et al.* 1993).

Our healthcare system is itself a large number of interacting man-made complex systems, each with feedback loops and thresholds that determine day-to-day functionality. It is capable of reinforcing patients' sense of control, or of promoting learned helplessness, and there is undoubtedly a tendency for it to promote the latter if the patient does not insist otherwise.

So we need to ask which elements of the health system promote and which inhibit resilience in those who use its services. We also need to explore whether the system promotes a sense of control or whether it promotes learned helplessness. Further, if my hypothesis were shown to be true, we would need to ask how the health system could be adapted in ways that actively promote a sense of control.

Sense of control is a variable that has already been extensively studied and has already been shown to influence disease incidence. I am proposing here that sense of control perhaps also influences resilience or adaptation to disease events in individuals. But systems thinking also requires that we ask other questions: what might be the disadvantages of a sense of control? If

I am correct that sense of control has a positive influence on a range of systems, is it always a good thing? Could it also push some systems to undesirable thresholds, not only at the individual level but at the health system level as well?

## How might these questions be answered?

One way to test the effect of control on the resilience of health outcomes would be to follow the health outcomes over time of four groups of newly diagnosed sufferers from cancer of the breast and cancer of the prostate, stratified into four groups at the time of diagnosis by a simple question about their sense of control over their life circumstances. The study could be undertaken in collaboration with a pathology laboratory that receives biopsy specimens of newly diagnosed cancer patients. This would ensure that a broad range of patients and medical carers would be involved in the study, which of course would require informed consent and ethical approval for the follow up over time of this cohort of patients.

The question is of more than academic interest. If the hypothesis were found to be true it would have significant implications for the way we structure health systems and health services. Developing a package of interventions that assist newly diagnosed patients to take greater control of their care and testing its impact in a randomised control trial model would be a logical next step.

## Conclusion

Introducing issues of resilience, learned helplessness and control into our thinking about health and health care could result in significant changes in the way health services are managed. Conventionally, doctors have maintained control of the system and information flows. Patients are not generally encouraged to manage their care and, in the present context, most would feel uncomfortable doing so. If control can be shown to be an important modulating factor in relation to health outcomes, this could lead to new pressures and approaches to reform.

I suggest that the predominantly mechanistic and reductionist approach to health and medicine needs to be heavily peppered with this type of systems and resilience thinking. The link between health and individual resilience demands innovative research approaches that could have implications not only for the way doctors deal with individual patients but also for the way health systems are structured in the future.

*Emeritus Professor Bob Douglas, AO, MD, FRACP, FRACGP, FAFPHM, is a Visiting Fellow at the National Centre for Epidemiology and Population Health at The Australian National University, where he was the founding director. He is the current Chair of the Board of Australia21.*

## References

Allenby G (2008) *Ian Gawler: The Dragon's Blessing*. Allen and Unwin, Crows Nest, NSW, Australia.

Capra F (1982) *The Turning Point*. Simon and Schuster, New York.

Cork S, Walker B and Buckley R (2008) 'How resilient is Australia?' Australia21, Canberra, <www.australia21.org.au>.

Hilborn RC (1972) Sea gulls, butterflies and grasshoppers: A brief history of the butterfly effect in nonlinear dynamics. *American Journal of Physics* **72**, 425–427.

Marmot MG, Shipley MJ and Rose G (1984) Inequalities in death – Specific explanations of a general pattern? *Lancet* **323**, 1003–1006.

Milton M (2009). *Michael Milton*. Michael Milton, Canberra, <http://www.michaelmilton.com/Home.aspx>.

Peterson C, Maier SF and Seligman MEP (1993) *Learned Helplessness: A Theory for the Age of Personal Control*. Oxford University Press, Oxford.

Reivich K and Schatte A (2003). *The Resilience Factor: 7 Keys to Discovering Your Inner Strength and Overcoming Life's Hurdles*. Random House, New York.

Rennie M (2008) Integrating Head and Heart. New Paradigm Newswire, Wordpress.com, <http://newparadigmnewswire.wordpress.com/2008/02/15/a-valentine's-day-launch-for-new-paradigm-newswire's-first-blog/>.

Walker B and Salt D (2006) *Resilience Thinking: Sustaining Ecosystems and People in a Changing World*. Island Press, Washington, DC.

# CHAPTER 12

# Reforming Australia's early childhood development systems – the role of resilience theory

Teresa Burgess

## Abstract

Many of our key bureaucratic systems are currently in need of transformation and significant change is proposed for the systems that look after early childhood development (ECD) – health, education, childcare and child protection. Most importantly, a newly structured early childhood development system must have the child and family at its operational centre. For any new system to be effective there needs to be integration of activity to avoid duplication, to ensure there are no gaps, ensure equity of care and access, minimise financial waste, reduce stress on families and improve early childhood outcomes. To-date however, there are very few data available on how the existing, disparate early childhood development systems affect the child and family and thus it is very difficult to identify exactly where and how to reform them.

Resilience theory has been proposed as offering a practical and constructive framework for allowing organisational change and adaptation to new roles and functions. Any new early childhood development system will require substantial changes in current legislation, information systems, workforce, monitoring and funding mechanisms. Analysing how a system is functioning using resilience theory can provide a way to identify barriers and harness positive drivers of change and use their influence to develop strategies and interventions that will allow the child and family to be truly at the centre of an integrated early childhood development system.

## Introduction

*'Children everywhere have the right to survival, to develop to the fullest, to protection from harmful influences, abuse and exploitation and to participate fully in family, cultural and social life' (UNICEF 2008).*

So states the United Nations Convention on the Rights of the Child. Governments around the world are recognising the importance of nurturing and supporting our children in their early years. There is a growing recognition, however, that the political and administrative structures that provide the services and supports for young children and their families may no longer be capable of meeting their needs in the 21st century.

In Australia, since the election of the Rudd Labor Government in 2007, there have been a number of new national and state policies and frameworks proposed around early childhood development. Their implementation, however, requires that multiple systems that have traditionally had little interaction work closely together to ensure that outcomes can be achieved. Realistically, Australia cannot totally restructure the systems involved in the delivery of early childhood development, so how can the existing systems adapt and change to accommodate the new requirements of the proposed policies and frameworks?

Resilience theory has been proposed as offering a practical and constructive framework for introducing organisational change and adaptation to new roles and functions. Although there is a growing recognition of the role that personal resilience plays in the lives of people, the role of resilience in systems is not so well understood. Over recent years, as a society, we have become much more familiar with the concept of personal resilience, or what has been often been called 'being able to cope' or 'inner strength'. Personal resilience has been looked at in a variety of settings and in a variety of populations such as grieving people (Bonanno *et al.* 2002), refugees (Schweizer *et al.* 2007) and Indigenous communities (Mooney-Summers and Maher 2009). More recently, there has been growing attention paid to how we might foster personal resilience in the early childhood years, as resilience in early childhood has been shown to improve psychological well-being and behaviour, school attendance and academic performance in children and adolescents (Challen *et al.* 2009; Earvolino-Ramirez 2007).

Resilience theory however, looks at resilience much more broadly than the personal level, examining the resilience of social–ecological systems at a range of scales that include personal resilience but also resilience of societies and institutions and the environmental systems that link them. In these contexts, resilience has been defined as:

> *'the ability to absorb disturbances, to be changed and then to re-organise and still have the same identity (retain the same basic structure and ways of functioning). It includes the ability to learn from the disturbance. A resilient system is forgiving of external shocks. As resilience declines the magnitude of a shock from which it cannot recover gets smaller and smaller. Resilience shifts attention from purely growth and efficiency to needed recovery and flexibility. Growth and efficiency alone can often lead ecological systems, businesses and societies into fragile rigidities, exposing them to turbulent transformation. Learning, recovery and flexibility open eyes to novelty and new worlds of opportunity'* (Resilience Alliance 2009).

There is a growing body of work around the role of resilience in social–ecological systems; however, the role resilience theory can play in helping us to understand and transform bureaucratic systems has not yet been explored in such detail. While the definition above refers to social–ecological systems, it can be seen that the concepts can be applied equally to bureaucratic systems and the emphasis on identifying flexibilities, system blocks and the cycles on which systems function can be very useful when attempting to bring different systems together.

It is widely acknowledged that many key Australian bureaucratic systems need transformation – a blueprint for a reformed health system was released in July 2009 (National Health and Hospitals Reform Commission 2009), and significant changes to the education and childcare systems have been proposed, with the release of policies such as the 'Early Childhood Development Strategy' (Council of Australian Governments 2009), 'The Early Years Learning Framework for Australia' (Australian Government Department of Education, Employment and Workplace Relations 2008) and the 'Development of Australia's First National Curriculum' (Gillard 2008). Child protection systems have reached breaking point. They no longer protect the most vulnerable members of society (Australian Research Alliance for Children and Youth 2008), and no systems have adequately addressed the needs of the Australian Indigenous population (Australian Government Department of Families, Housing, Community Services and Indigenous Affairs 2008).

## Australia's early childhood development system

There are four major Australian bureaucracies that intersect to form Australia's early childhood development system – health, education, childcare and child protection. These bureaucracies are increasingly being required to adapt to significant change to function effectively in support of the reform of early childhood development in Australia.

The health system has responsibility for children from well before they are born, providing antenatal care and education for parents. It is then responsible for nurturing and maintaining the health of the infant and child from birth as well as the overall well-being of the family. Early identification and intervention in areas such as vision, hearing, speech, fine and gross motor development and developmental delay all fall within the remit of the health system, as does laying the foundations for a healthy lifestyle. Unless the health system provides the bedrock from which children can develop, sub-optimal outcomes will result.

Education and childcare nurture children and support their development intellectually, emotionally and socially while no child can develop to their full potential in the presence of physical, sexual or emotional abuse and neglect.

A number of other systems are also key players in ECD, not least of which are Treasury, Finance and Community Services, but the four systems noted above are the four pillars on which ECD is built. They therefore can provide a useful example of how and why resilience theory might help make the required transformations to systems that will meet the needs of the Australian population in the 21st century.

## Why does it matter whether systems that support ECD are resilient?

There is now wide recognition of the central importance of care in early childhood as a contributor to long-term good health and education outcomes and to the resilience of society, as well as personal resilience. Worldwide, governments are recognising the critical importance of learning and good health in the very early years of life and the need to reorganise existing services and introduce new ones in ways that will enhance the physical, intellectual and social attributes and personal resilience of tomorrow's citizens.

The Commonwealth Government has stated that 'Investing in the health, education, development and care of our children benefits children and their families, our communities and the economy and is critical to lifting workforce participation and delivering the Government's productivity agenda' (Department of Education, Employment and Workplace Relations 2008). While investment is the starting point of an early childhood development system, the other pillar is integration – integration of the systems and services that directly and/or indirectly affect the family and child.

If we are to achieve the vision of the National Early Childhood Development Strategy released in July 2009 – i.e. 'By 2020 all children have the best start in life to create a better future for themselves and for the nation' (Council of Australian Governments 2009) – then systems have to be able to work together as an integrated whole to ensure that the ambitious goals and targets outlined in the strategy can be achieved. Health, education, childcare and child protection have historically worked in their own particular silos with little interaction. The Commonwealth/State divide in funding and administration of these services has also worked to produce rigid and non-responsive services that often do not meet the needs of the populations they are aimed at.

The issue of a system functioning to support the system rather than meet the needs of the population it is intended to serve is an ongoing one. The 2008 Garling Report into Acute Care Services in NSW provided example after example of a health system working to maintain itself rather than the patients it was designed to serve. The report's many examples included:

'A skilled workforce spread too thinly and too poorly supported in the dozens of administrative tasks which take them away from their patients.

Were senior specialists to do their ward rounds before 10 o'clock in the morning and thus discharge their patients before noon and free up each of those beds for another patient, the hospital would save many, many bed days and shorten the waiting time for patients to get a bed' (Garling 2008, p.3).

Justice Wood, in his 2009 report on Child Protection in NSW noted that:

'Too many reports are being made to DoCS which do not warrant the exercise of its considerable statutory powers. As a result, much effort and cost is expended in managing these reports, as a result of which the children and young people the subject of them receive little in the way of subsequent assistance, while others who do require attention from DoCS may have their cases closed because of competing demands on the system' (Wood 2008, p. iii).

Within our education system, Australia's extremely complex school-funding systems serve to entrench inequalities, promote duplication and interfere with efficient planning and quality improvement processes (Angus 2007; Dowling 2007). The recent problems with ABC Child-care could be considered to have been caused by the fostering of, and support for, the private sector in childcare systems and services in Australia becoming more important than the need to ensure that the services provided were sustainable and appropriate in assuring early child-hood development.

There is general awareness of the many failings in our systems, but how can they be effec-tively addressed? First and foremost, it is increasingly evident that what has worked (or hasn't worked) in the past can no longer be tinkered with around the edges. The changes called for by Mr Garling, Justice Woods and the recent Health and Hospitals Reform Commission are almost revolutionary for both the culture and the functioning of these systems. It should also not be forgotten that while four bureaucracies have been noted above, there are actually 36; one of each of the four in every State and Territory and the Commonwealth!

Most importantly, in terms of reforming early childhood development systems, a key outcome must be the placing of the child and family at the centre of the system. The 'National Early Childhood Development Strategy' (Council of Australian Governments 2009, p. 16) states that: 'An effective early childhood development system recognises the primary role of families in the lives of young children. It has strong leadership, coordinates policy direction, uses collaborative and inclusive approaches and forges strong links within and across services, professionals and communities'. How then can the Federal and State Governments ensure that early childhood development systems can interface effectively, particularly as there is currently little clarity about what comprises an 'integrated' early childhood development system? It is agreed that the education, childcare and health systems contribute core components but, inter-estingly, while there are significant reforms being suggested for child protection systems, there is no consensus that child protection should be included in an integrated ECD system, as has happened in the UK (United Kingdom Government Department for Children, Schools and Families 2009).

Why do early childhood development systems need to be integrated? Integration can prevent duplication of services, more effectively ensure there are no gaps in services, ensure equity of care and access, minimise financial waste, reduce stress on families and improve early childhood outcomes. While there is no established definition of integration, or indeed agreement on whether integration is an outcome or a process, there is a general understanding that integration means some form of communication and linkage, which may range across a continuum from collaboration through partnerships to fully integrated management and services.

It is not practical (or necessary) to integrate the whole of the systems contributing to early childhood development. In order to integrate relevant sections of systems, it must first be determined exactly which parts are relevant, what they do and how they may interact. Currently, each system is a silo, with families and children attempting to gain entry to each one individually and with each one requiring a different set of access criteria. If a child and family are to be at the centre of an early childhood development system, then the system must function to support the family, not to provide ongoing barriers to access and services.

## How can resilience theory assist us in transforming these systems?

For effective, integrated services that will meet the 21st century needs of families and children, the four nominated systems need to work much more collaboratively and provide their services in new and perhaps unfamiliar ways – i.e. they must adapt and change in significant ways. As previously noted, resilience is the ability of complex systems to maintain their general structure and functions (their broad 'identity') even though they must adapt and change in various ways within that broad identity. Resilience theory also acknowledges that resilience is not always 'good' (e.g. a system's structures and functions may be producing undesirable outcomes) and that resilience must not be considered in isolation from adaptation (the ability to change within a broad identity) or transformation (the ability to change to a new identity if the old one is not appropriate) (Walker *et al.* 2002). A key question raised by resilience theory is how much these changes require building desirable resilience of the current systems (so they can function better) and how much they require breaking down undesirable resilience (so they can be transformed).

There are few chances to implement systemic change and so the current opportunities should not be squandered. It is therefore important to understand all the variables that will affect the change processes required to transform our early childhood development systems so that policies and procedures that will enhance rather than impede their adaptability and resilience can be developed. There has, to-date, been no systematic assessment of the ability of the nominated systems to change and adapt to shifting circumstance – in fact there is evidence that they are relatively inflexible and unable to change.

Understanding the structure and functioning of each of the four systems involved in ECD is vital if these systems are to function effectively together. Each of these systems has their own distinct and separate workforce, funding mechanisms, governance, services and, perhaps most importantly, their own organisational cultures. Understanding and identifying whether resilience in these key components of organisational functioning is likely to impede or promote change is vital if change is to be facilitated. While some required changes will be structural and legislative, in many ways these are the easiest as they are tangible activities – it is when professional boundaries and organisational cultures are required to change that a particularly complex picture starts to arise.

Thus, the issue of complexity is raised and these are indeed a complex series of systems! The health system, in particular, is increasingly being recognised as a 'complex adaptive system', i.e. a system that is made up of many different parts that interact in a variety of ways through complex patterns of relationships. These relationships form feedback loops that may interact in unknown and unforeseeable ways with each other. With its myriad of professions, a requirement to deal with all people across the lifespan, multiple sub-systems (acute care, chronic care, allied health) and extensive range of services, the health system is 'more than just the sum of its parts' (Sturmberg and Martin 2009, p.543).

Although perhaps not quite as complex as the health system, the education and childcare systems are also complex bureaucratic systems, with multiple levels of administration, service delivery and providers. The child protection system, while not encompassing as broad a range of services and providers, faces its own particular challenges, with a number of high-profile cases in a number of states highlighting the fact that, as with health, 19th century solutions do not address 21st problems. Identifying strategies and procedures that will facilitate integration of these complex systems has proven difficult in the past and it is timely to look to alternative theories to assist in this important change process. Recent change theory sees change as a dynamic and complex process that must consider the historical, cultural, political and organisational context in which it occurs (Iles and Sutherland 2001) and resilience theory provides a comprehensive framework to allow just such an organisational review.

Resilience theory says we need to look to the broader systems in which any system is embedded and to smaller, local systems that are embedded in the system being examined. This is particularly relevant for systems such as health and education operating at Commonwealth, State and local levels, with multiple services embedded in them. It is also important to identify the cycles and feedback loops (both positive and negative) on which systems function. Resilience is a major factor in organisations and systems that can either impede or allow change management activities to be undertaken and to achieve success.

Resilience derives from many sources, including trust and cooperation among people and the capacity of people and social institutions to examine future possibilities to generate and use knowledge to find solutions to new challenges, work collaboratively and learn from experience. Working together requires flexible and responsive systems that allow multidisciplinary and inter-sectoral collaboration, encourage innovation in ideas and alternatives and can respond to the 'shock' of the changes required to the core culture of a system. It has been said that the 'lens that we use to investigate any phenomenon has a profound effect on what we see' (Anderson and McDaniel 2000, p. 83). The Resilience Alliance (2007, p. 3) notes that 'people base management actions on how they think the world works' and so identifying and understanding these 'lenses' or 'mental models' that policy makers and system planners use is vital if we are to understand how systems function, the level of their resilience and adaptability and how to transform them. In bringing different systems together, we are bringing together different cultures and understandings and often whole different vocabularies. Much of our understanding is based on conscious or unconscious assumptions and unless we can identify these assumptions we cannot develop a shared understanding.

It is important to remember that Australia does not exist in a vacuum and we are in the fortunate position of being able to draw on significant international experience, such as the 'Every Child Matters' program from the UK, incorporating 'Safeguarding Children' (United Kingdom Government Department for Children, Schools and Families 2009) and the USA's 'ABCD' and 'Sure Start' programs (Halfon et al. 2009). Halfon et al., in their 2009 comparison of early childhood services in the US, UK, Canada and Australia noted: 'approaches that align strategies across multiple levels of government (local, state and national) and that integrate services from different sectors (health, education, family support) are proving most successful.

Adoption of a common framework is an effective tool to get stakeholders on the same page and accountable to each other' (Halfon *et al.* 2009, p. x). There is now a large body of evidence demonstrating that integrated, family-centred policies and programs produce the most effective and efficient outcomes in early childhood development. Australia must ensure that their various systems can work together to achieve this.

## Conclusions

In Australia considerable reform activity is currently underway, in terms of resources, time and policy development, in early childhood development systems and services. These achievements, particularly in terms of policy, must be commended. As the policies and frameworks begin implementation, Australia can draw on lessons learned both internationally and nationally, not only in the area of early childhood development but also in the area of resilience theory. Australia has made key contributions to the theory and practice of the application of resilience theory in examining both ecological and socio-ecological systems (Resilience Alliance 2009). Resilience theory provides ideas about how to build new early childhood development systems that will not only achieve desirable outcomes but will also continue to deliver those outcomes in the face of future challenges. Resilience theory, however, also alerts us to the high levels of potentially undesirable resilience that appear to exist in the old systems and the need to overcome this resilience if desirable changes are to be achieved.

While significant reform processes have begun at State and Commonwealth level to bring the early childhood care and learning systems together with the education system, the policies and processes for linking these with the health and child protection systems is much less clear. A number of major policy initiatives have been developed by the Federal Government and the Council of Australian Governments (COAG) and it is now time to consider properly how they can be effectively implemented. Resilience theory tells us that Australia must begin a process of mapping and understanding its early childhood development systems to identify the specific elements that relate to early childhood and to try to identify facilitators and barriers to these elements interrelating effectively. Mapping these systems and, more importantly, their intersections and interactions, provides many challenges, but this is a key task if duplication is to be avoided and any form of integration achieved. It will then be possible to determine exactly how the various systems that will contribute to these shared understandings can come together to develop a sustainable way forward.

The challenge then that faces Australia in transforming its early childhood development systems is not insignificant. The push for reform, with the provision of supporting resources, is a key enabler of change; as is the now very large bank of evidence around the importance of the early years. There are also many examples of how services can be flexible and adaptive and provide care that meets the needs of children and families in their local communities. The importance of the willingness of the various key stakeholders to come together to drive reform should not be underestimated. Resilience theory provides a way to harness these very important positive drivers of change and use their strength to develop strategies and interventions that can assist in overcoming the existing barriers to integration between disparate systems.

*Teresa Burgess is a senior lecturer in the School of Population Health and Clinical Practice at the University of Adelaide, working in the area of primary care/primary health care research. She has extensive experience in the areas of evaluation, health services research (particularly models of primary health care service delivery and the integration of health and community services), evaluation of medical education and end-of-life care. She has recently worked on a range of programs including the national evaluation of the Asthma 3+ Visit Plan and the Evaluation of*

*GP Plus Health Networks in South Australia. Teresa has been a member of the Public Health Association of Australia (SA Branch) Executive Committee since 2002 and she was the Convener of the South Australian Refugee Health Network (SARHN) from 2005 to 2009. She is the Manager of Australia21's Project on Resilience in Early Childcare Systems.*

## References

Anderson R and McDaniel R (2000) Managing health care organizations: Where professionalism meets complexity science. *Health Care Management Review* **25**, 83–92.

Angus M (2007) 'Commonwealth–state relations and the funding of Australian schools. Making federalism work for schools: due process, transparency, informed consent'. NSW Public Education Alliance, Sydney, Australia.

Australian Government Department of Education, Employment and Workplace Relations (2009) Belonging, Being and Becoming. The Early years Learning Framework for Australia. Australian Government Department of Education, Employment and Workplace Relations, Canberra, <http://www.deewr.gov.au/EarlyChildhood/Policy_Agenda/Quality/Pages/EarlyYearsLearningFramework.aspx >.

Australian Government Department of Education, Employment and Workplace Relations (2008) Early Childhood Overview. Australian Government Department of Education, Employment and Workplace Relations, Canberra, <http://www.deewr.gov.au/earlychildhood/Pages/Overview.aspx>.

Australian Government Department of Families, Housing, Community Services and Indigenous Affairs (2008) Closing the Gap on Indigenous Disadvantage: the Challenge for Australia. Australian Government Department of Families, Housing, Community Services and Indigenous Affairs, Canberra, <http://www.fahcsia.gov.au/sa/indigenous/pubs/general/documents/closing_the_gap/foreward.htm>.

Australian Research Alliance for Children and Youth (2008) Inverting the Pyramid. Enhancing Systems for Protecting Children. Australian Research Alliance for Children and Youth, Canberra, <http://www.aracy.org.au/index.cfm?pageName=protecting_children>.

Bonanno GA, Wortman CB, Lehman DR, Tweed RG, Haring M, Sonnega J, Carr D and Nesse RM (2002) Resilience to loss and chronic grief: a prospective study from preloss to 18-months postloss. *Journal of Personality and Social Psychology* **83**, 1150–1164.

Challen A, Noden P, West A and Machin S (2009) UK Resilience Programme Evaluation. Interim Report. United Kingdom Government Department for Children, Schools and Families, London, <www.dcsf.gov.uk/research>.

Council of Australian Governments (2009) Investing in the Early Years – A National Early Childhood Development Strategy. Council of Australian Governments, Canberra, <http://www.coag.gov.au/coag_meeting_outcomes/2009-07-02/docs/national_ECD_strategy.pdf>.

Dowling A (2007) 'Australia's school funding system'. Australian Council for Educational Research, Camberwell, Australia.

Earvolino-Ramirez M (2007) Resilience: a concept analysis. *Nursing Forum* **42**, 73–82.

Garling P (2008) Final Report of the Special Commission of Inquiry Acute Care Services in NSW Public Hospitals. Overview. State of NSW through the Special Commission of Inquiry: Acute Care Services in New South Wales Public Hospitals, Sydney, <http://www.lawlink.nsw.gov.au/lawlink/Special_Projects/ll_splprojects.nsf/vwFiles/E_Overview.pdf/$file/E_Overview.pdf>.

Gillard J (2008) Media Release. Delivering Australia's First National Curriculum. 5 April. Australian Government Department of Education, Employment and Workplace

Relations, Canberra, <http://mediacentre.dewr.gov.au/mediacentre/gillard/releases/deliveringaustraliasfirstnationalcurriculum.htm>.

Halfon N, Russ S, Oberklaid F, Bertrand J and Eisenstadt N (2009) An International Comparison of Early Childhood Initiatives: From Services to Systems. The Commonwealth Fund, Canberra, <http://www.commonwealthfund.org/Content/Publications/Fund-Reports/2009/May/An-International-Comparison-of-Early childhood-Initiatives.aspx>.

Iles V and Sutherland K (2001) 'Organisational change. A review for health care managers, professionals and researchers'. London School of Hygiene and Tropical Medicine, London.

Mooney-Somers J and Maher L (2009) The Indigenous Resiliency Project: a worked example of community-based participatory research. *NSW Public Health Bulletin* **20**, 112–118.

National Health and Hospitals Reform Commission (2009) A Healthier Future for All Australians. Final Report. Recommendations. National Health and Hospitals Reform Commission, Canberra, <http://www.nhhrc.org.au/internet/nhhrc/publishing.nsf/Content/nhhrc-report>.

org/crc/index_30160.html>.

Resilience Alliance (2007) Assessing and Managing Resilience in Social–Ecological Systems: A Practitioners Workbook. The Resilience Alliance, Stockholm, <http://www.resalliance.org/3871.php>.

Resilience Alliance (2009) Key Concepts. The Resilience Alliance, Stockholm, <http://www.resalliance.org/564.php>.

Schweitzer R, Greenslade J and Kagee A (2007) Coping and resilience in refugees from the Sudan: a narrative account. *Australia and New Zealand Journal of Psychiatry* **41**, 282–288.

Sturmberg J and Martin C (2009) Complexity and health – yesterday's traditions, tomorrow's future. *Journal of Evaluation in Clinical Practice* **15**, 543–548.

UNICEF (2008) Summary on the United Nations Convention on the Rights of the Child. UNICEF, New York.

United Kingdom Government Department for Children, Schools and Families (2009) Every Child Matters. United Kingdom Government Department for Children, Schools and Families, London, <http://www.dcsf.gov.uk/everychildmatters/about/>.

Walker B, Carpenter S, Anderies J, Abel N, Cumming GS, Janssen M, Lebel L, Norberg J, Peterson GD and Pritchard R (2002) Resilience management in social–ecological systems: a working hypothesis for a participatory approach. *Conservation Ecology* **6**, 14 <http://www.consecol.org/vol6/iss1/art14/>.

Wood J (2008) Report of the Special Commission of Inquiry into Child Protection Services in NSW Executive Summary and Recommendations. NSW Government Department of the Premier and Cabinet, Sydney, <http://www.dpc.nsw.gov.au/publications/news/stories/?a=33794>.

# CHAPTER 13

# Population health – a forgotten dimension of social resilience

Richard Eckersley

## Abstract

The health of populations is an important, but neglected, aspect of the resilience of societies. Not only does population health affect the ability of societies to withstand adversity, it can shape how they respond to it – whether in ways that make things better or worse. The orthodox view of health is that it is continuing to improve in line with historic trends, but this is debatable. Common measures of health and well-being, notably life expectancy, self-reported health and happiness, do not give a full and accurate picture; among young people, in particular, it is arguable that health and well-being are in decline (even as life expectancy rises). This has important implications for future population health – and so resilience. To address this situation we must reconceptualise health and healthcare, re-orient education and set stricter standards for the corporate sector, especially in media and marketing. To enhance Australia's resilience, we need to make 'better health' (in the broadest sense), not 'greater wealth', the nation's defining goal.

## Introduction

The health of a population is a critical dimension of the resilience of a society. Population health is both a consequence and a cause of social changes, an important component of social systems that shapes their capacity to weather adversity and to maintain their essential structure and function under the pressure of hostile events and circumstances.

This is not generally recognised. A false dichotomy often characterises debate and discussion about national and international affairs. On the one hand, these matters are seen as shaped by large, external forces such as economic developments, technological change, environmental degradation and resource depletion and war and conflict. Population health may be affected by these forces, although this is often assumed rather than explicitly examined (except in the case of war and natural disasters), but health itself is not usually seen as a contributor to larger-scale social developments. The perspectives of economics, politics and, increasingly, environmental sciences dominate the discourse. On the other hand, considerations of health focus on internal, psychological and physiological processes and personal attributes, circumstances and experiences. The dominant frame of reference is a biomedical model of health (or more accurately, ill-health) as an attribute or property of individuals.

This separation is misleading. The reality is that change in both the social and personal worlds is shaped by a complex interplay between the world 'out there' and the world 'in here' (in our minds and bodies). We need to understand this interplay to comprehend what is happening in both worlds. In other words, human 'subjectivity' plays an important part in the functioning of social systems, including their resilience; this is what most distinguishes them from other, biophysical systems, such as ecologies and climate.

The dichotomy is also paradoxical in that with the possible exception of increasing wealth, improving health is the most widely used measure of human development. Wealth has only ever been a means to the end of a better life; health is a core component of that end. If population health is not improving, it is hard to sustain the belief that, as a society, we are making progress. And if heath is declining, this not only reflects social regression, it can reinforce it: if people are getting 'sicker and sadder', this weakens the confidence and resolve we need to face and overcome threats and adversities.

## Challenging the orthodoxy of improving health

Is health an issue for us in these times?

The orthodox view of population health in Australia and, indeed, most of the rest of the world, is of continuing improvement in line with historic trends (Eckersley 2008a). This view is based mainly on declining mortality and so rising life expectancy, as well as high levels of self-reported health and life satisfaction. Globally, life expectancy has more than doubled in the last 100 years and is still rising; it is one of humanity's greatest achievements.

While mortality might once have been a good summary measure of health, this is now questionable. The orthodox view underestimates the growing importance to overall health and well-being of non-fatal, chronic illness, especially mental disorders. Similarly, high levels of self-reported health and happiness cannot be taken at face value. Self-reported health is not an accurate measure of health status: many people with serious health problems will still say their health is excellent or very good. Likewise, happiness measures do not reflect all aspects of well-being.

The 'mismeasure' of health is especially relevant to young people. Their health is not only important in its own right, or for their sake; it is crucial to assessing the overall state and future of society. The young reflect best the tenor and tempo of the times by virtue of growing up in them. Because of their stages of biological and social development, they are most vulnerable to social risks and failings. Many of the attitudes and behaviours – even the illnesses – that largely determine adult health have their origins in childhood, adolescence and early adulthood. Thus, the health of young people shapes the future health of the whole population and, in a broader social sense, the health and resilience of society.

To take Australia as an example of the developed world, the historic fall in mortality rates means death now strikes very few young people: about 40 in every 100 000 aged 12–24 each year (Eckersley 2008a). Also, the major causes of death do not necessarily reflect underlying changes in physical and mental health (especially the biggest killer, road accidents). On the other hand, research in Australia and other developed nations suggests 20–30% of young people (20–30 000 per 100 000) are suffering significant psychological distress at any one time, with less severe stress-related symptoms such as frequent headaches, stomach-aches and insomnia affecting as many as 50%. Mental disorders account for almost half the total 'burden of disease' in young Australians, measured as both death and disability – far more than the second biggest contributor, injuries.

A few examples demonstrate the extent to which the high prevalence of diminished well-being amounts to a problem for social resilience. A recent survey (Bernard *et al.* 2007) of more than 10 000 Australian students from Prep school (aged 4–6) to Year 12 (aged 17–18) found that about 40% scored in the lower levels of social and emotional well-being. Between about a fifth and a half of students said they were lonely (18%); had recently felt hopeless and depressed for a week and had stopped regular activities (20%); were very stressed (31%); had difficulty controlling how depressed they got (32%); lost their temper a lot (35%); worried too much (42%); and had difficulty calming down when upset (a measure of resilience) (48%). (Yet, to illustrate the point above about the inadequacy of happiness measures, 89% of the students said they were happy.)

Several surveys by the Australian Childhood Foundation (Tucci *et al.* 2005, 2006, 2007) of children 10–14 or 10–17 produce a similar picture of high levels of stress, worry and anxiety. For substantial minorities, increasing to majorities for some questions, their sense of confidence in themselves, their community and their place in the world is under threat. Based on one survey (Tucci *et al.* 2007), the Foundation established three categories of children: those who felt well-connected and supported (52%); a 'worried' group (42%); and a 'disconnected and insular' group (the most vulnerable, 8%).

While such findings of high levels of emotional stress imply a worsening situation, long-term trends in mental health are very difficult to establish conclusively because of the lack of good, comparative data (Eckersley 2008a). The issue remains contentious. The weight of international evidence, however, indicates the prevalence of psychological problems among young people has risen in developed nations in recent decades, with the latest US research suggesting a five- to eight-fold increase in the proportion of college students scoring above cut-off points for psychopathology over the past 70 years. The trends are despite the increased treatment of mental disorders.

There are also other adverse patterns and trends in young people's health, including rising obesity and obesity-related diseases such as diabetes; high levels of physical inactivity; poor nutrition; increasing allergies; more young people in care and protection; and rising rates of violent crime (which mainly involves young people as both victims and perpetrators) (Eckersley 2008a).

These arguments also apply to overall population health, but with some important qualifications (Eckersley 2008a). Mental disorders are the third largest contributor to the total burden of disease, after cancer and cardiovascular disease and the largest contributor to the non-fatal component of the disease burden. The proportion of all Australians reporting 'mental and behavioural problems' as long-term conditions increased from 6% in 1995 to 11% in 2005. This picture, however, is offset by declining death rates for leading health problems, including the degenerative diseases of cancer, heart disease and strokes, which are also major causes of disability. (These diseases have relatively little impact on young people's health because of the time it takes for them to develop so, to some extent, current mortality rates reflect a way of life that has long past, for better or worse.)

Recent international research suggests the disease burden of mental illness has been underestimated, which would further challenge the orthodoxy of improving health. One study (Ormel *et al.* 2008) found people attributed higher disability to mental disorders than to the commonly occurring physical disorders, especially with respect to their 'social and personal role functioning'; with 'productive role functioning', the disability of mental and physical disorders was comparable. Another analysis (Prince *et al.* 2007) argues that the burden of mental disorders is likely to have been underestimated because of inadequate appreciation of the connection between mental illness and other health conditions. Mental disorders increase the risk of both communicable and non-communicable diseases and contribute to unintentional and intentional injury. Conversely, many health conditions increase the risk of mental illness.

## Public moods and attitudes

The discussion of health so far has focused mainly on clinically significant illness. If we go beyond this focus to consider people's morale and vitality, moods and attitudes, the evidence adds to the disturbing picture of poor personal and social resilience.

Many studies over the past decade, both qualitative and quantitative, reveal levels of anger and anxiety about changes in society that were not apparent 30 years ago (Eckersley 2005). The studies show many people are concerned about the materialism, greed and selfishness they believe drive society today, underlie social ills and threaten their children's future. They yearn for a better balance in their lives, believing that when it comes to things like individual freedom and material abundance, people don't seem 'to know where to stop' or now have 'too much of a good thing'.

A report on 'the mind and mood' of Australians (Ipsos Mackay 2005) says there is growing concern about the state of Australian society – rougher, tougher, more competitive, less compassionate – that is producing stress, edginess and a feeling of personal vulnerability. Australians feel they 'seem to lurching from one difficulty to another with the prospect of a serious crisis emerging'. One survey (Tucci et al. 2005) reported 'a growing sense among parents that childhood is at risk because the daily environment in which children live is perceived to be increasingly less safe, stable and predictable'. It found that 80% or more of parents believed children were growing up too fast, worried about their children's futures and felt children were targeted too much by marketers.

The concerns people express about life today and in the future are important to social cohesion and resilience because they weaken people's belief in a broader social ideal and a commitment to the common good, so reinforcing individual goals and priorities. They can also impact on personal well-being (Eckersley 2005, 2008a). Psychological research shows that viewing the world as comprehensible, manageable and meaningful is associated with well-being. Biomedical research shows that people become more stressed and more vulnerable to stress-related illness if they interpret the stress as evidence that circumstances are worsening, feel they have little control over its causes and don't know how long it will last.

## Population health's social impacts

Health, in both the narrower (clinical) and broader (well-being) sense, is an important consideration in determining whether societies flourish or languish, including how they cope with adverse events and conditions. The historian Kenneth Clark (1993) observed that civilisation, however complex and solid it seemed, was really quite fragile. After reviewing thousands of years of the rise and fall of civilisations, he warns that 'it's lack of confidence, more than anything else, that kills a civilisation. We can destroy ourselves by cynicism and disillusion just as effectively as by bombs'.

The interplay between psychology and history can be dramatic. The historian Norman Cohn (1957), in his study of the revolutionary chiliastic or millennialist movements that swept Europe in the Middle Ages, said the movements represented a 'collective paranoiac fanaticism'. He argued that societies became vulnerable to revolutionary chiliasm when the existing structure of a society was undermined or devalued and the normal, familiar pattern of life had undergone 'a disruption so severe as to seem irremediable'. It was then that particular calamities would appear particularly calamitous, producing 'an emotional disturbance so widespread and acute, such an overwhelming sense of being exposed, cast out and helpless, that the only way in which it can find effective relief is through an outburst of paranoia, a sudden, collective and fanatical pursuit of the Millennium'.

Cohn saw this paranoid response in the 20th century totalitarian movements of Communism and Nazism. All its ingredients also exist in the 21st century. The resulting social pathology is evident in today's fundamentalist cults and terrorist groups, such as the al-Qaeda terrorist network. There have also been signs of millennialist fervour in the United States in the wake of the September 11 terrorist attacks.

Diminished well-being, then, not only affects people's capacity to respond to adversity in a generic sense; it can dramatically influence the course their response takes. This is apparent in the 'psychosocial dynamics' of global threats such as climate change (Eckersley 2008b). People appear to be responding in at least three different ways to 'apocalyptic suspicions' about the 21st century: nihilism (the abandonment of belief in a social or moral order), fundamentalism (the retreat to certain belief) and activism (the transformation of belief). Each of these responses represents a way of coping, so producing benefits to people's individual well-being and resilience, but in quite different ways: nihilism through a disengagement and distraction from frightening possibilities and prospects; fundamentalism through the conviction of righteousness and the promise of salvation; and activism through a unity of purpose and a belief in a cause. Yet only activism (which arguably demands more collective resilience, energy and resolve) will allow us to deal constructively with global threats.

## Public policy implications

We need to think of health not just as an individual illness that requires treatment, but also as an issue having national, even global, causes and consequences. We need to think of health as a way of understanding ourselves better, how we should live and the societies we live in. Just as someone who is unwell, physically or mentally, will be less able to function effectively and withstand adversity, so too will an unhealthy population make a less resilient society. More than this, people's health and well-being can be an important factor in determining whether societies respond effectively to adversity and make the most of their opportunities – or react in ways that make the situation worse.

Global warming and the global financial crisis demand greater national and international intervention and regulation to avert potentially catastrophic outcomes. So, too, do the trends in population health. These include (Eckersley 2008a):

- thinking of health as more than a matter of healthcare services. This should include increasing the proportion of the health budget allocated to prevention and public health. The tradition bias in healthcare, especially medicine, against mental health also needs to be removed.
- reorienting education to give it a clearer focus on increasing young people's understanding of themselves and the world to promote human growth and development, not just materially, but socially, culturally and spiritually.
- setting stricter standards for the corporate sector, especially the media and marketing industries. Just as quality of life depends on the regulation by government of the natural environment and goods and services such as food to protect our physical safety and health and of the economy to ensure national economic benefits and financial propriety, we need to manage cultural influences better to guard against moral hazard and psychological harm.

At the most fundamental level, however, addressing the challenges of population health means changing the stories or narratives by which Australians define themselves, their lives and their goals. These changes should include making better health (in the broadest sense), not greater wealth, the nation's defining goal. This, in turn and in part, would shift the emphasis of economic activity away from private consumption for short-term, personal gratification towards social investment in building a more equitable, healthy and sustainable way of life.

*Richard Eckersley is a Director and Fellow of Australia21. His work explores progress and well-being, including measures of progress; the relationships between economic growth, quality of life and ecological sustainability; the social and cultural determinants of health and happiness; visions of the future; and young people and their world.*

## References

Bernard ME, Stephanou A and Urbach D (2007) 'The ASG student social and emotional health report'. Australian Scholarships Group, Oakleigh, Victoria.

Clark K (1993) *Civilisation.* Four-volume video series, BBC Enterprises Ltd., London.

Cohn N (1957) *The Pursuit of the Millennium.* Secker and Warburg, London.

Eckersley R (2005) *Well & Good: Morality, Meaning and Happiness.* 2nd ed. Text Publishing, Melbourne.

Eckersley R (2008a) 'Never better – or getting worse? The health and well-being of young Australians'. Australia21 Ltd, Canberra.

Eckersley R (2008b) Nihilism, fundamentalism, or activism: Three responses to fears of the Apocalypse. *Futurist* **42**, 35–39.

Ipsos Mackay (2005) 'Mind & mood'. The Ipsos Mackay Report no. 116. Ipsos Mackay Public Affairs, Sydney.

Ormel J, Petukhova M, Chatterji S *et al.* (2008) Disability and treatment of specific mental and physical disorders across the world. *British Journal of Psychiatry* **192**, 368–375.

Prince M, Patel V, Saxena S *et al.* (2007) No health without mental health. *Lancet* **370**, 859–877.

Tucci J, Mitchell J and Goddard C (2005) 'The changing face of parenting'. Australian Childhood Foundation, Melbourne.

Tucci J, Mitchell J and Goddard C (2006) 'Every child needs a hero'. Australian Childhood Foundation, Melbourne.

Tucci J, Mitchell J and Goddard C (2007) 'Children's fears, hopes and heroes'. Australian Childhood Foundation, Melbourne.

# CHAPTER 14

# Education – revolution or resilience

Robert Lewis, Jim White and Wayne Chandler

## Abstract

The purpose of education is, as it has always been, to initiate the young into those aspects of our culture on which their (and our) humanity depend. We are in an era of unprecedented challenge and change but, in spite of rhetoric about an education revolution, the national education system, on which the future resilience of Australian society depends, shows no signs yet of changing from the now outmoded 'factory educational model. There is not yet a shared bipartisan national vision for the new education system and the three-year electoral cycle means that key priorities for education one year can be off the agenda the next.

## Introduction

In Australian education there are three main areas where resilience is important. Firstly, there is the resilience of the educators, the people working in schools and other educational institutions. Secondly, there is the resilience of the students who are in the system and who eventually graduate from the system. Finally, there is the resilience of the entire education system and this is reflected in how well young Australians are prepared to face future challenges. This chapter will discuss the third area, the resilience of our current education system.

Bernard (2005) provides the following definition: 'resilience as a personal capability involves your use of rational thinking and a variety of coping skills that help you regulate the intensity of your emotional response to adverse events in your life'.

'The purpose of education in the 21st century is exactly the same as it was in the 19th and 20th centuries, that is to initiate the young into those aspects of our culture upon which their (and our) humanity depends' (Woodhead 2000). This definition has been widely accepted by Australian governments of all persuasions. This should not be confused with a definition of schooling, which is based on principles first espoused during the Industrial Revolution, that created a system based on training people for factory employment and aimed to 'school' the masses as efficiently as possible. This concept of schooling is no longer applicable to modern society. As a consequence a resilient Australian education system has been founded on a number of other key characteristics:

- a commitment has been made, by all governments, to the notion of education for all. This has developed in its scope and inclusivity and provided education in all locations from the one teacher bush school to the metropolitan areas. There was a recognition that some students needed additional support, including those with disabilities, students from non-English speaking countries and, more recently, Indigenous students. The resilient nature of this approach was readily seen as emerging challenges were addressed as they arose;

- wider access to tertiary education, provided initially by the Whitlam Government of the 1970s; and
- access to technology has been a major focus taken up by all sides of politics.

## Changing landscape

Former Prime Minister Paul Keating (Keating 2008), in an address to the Melbourne Writers Festival, said, 'we are living through one of those rare yet transforming events in history, a shift in power in the world from West to East. For 500 years Europe dominated the world; now, for all its wealth and population, it is drifting into relative decline'.

Wallis (2008) talks of three 'global awakenings' in history and believes that the world may be seeing the beginning of a fourth. Flannery (2005) presents a frightening picture of our future if as a global society we are unable to change the way we treat our planet. If we are to bring about the necessary change in human behaviour we need to mount a worldwide concerted effort based on educating our society in what needs to be done and how. The World Bank has accepted the proposition that the alleviation of poverty in developing countries is dependant upon education; not just literacy but the education of the whole person.

We are in an era of unprecedented change, both in its scope and in its speed. The resilience that Australia's education system currently has – founded on manageable, incremental change – may well prevent it from adapting to contemporary challenges.

In January 2007 the Australian Labor Party (ALP) launched its paper, 'The Australian Economy Needs An Education Revolution' (ALP 2007). The paper states that, 'we need to set ourselves a new national vision for Australia to become the most educated country, the most skilled economy and the best trained workplace in the world'. Unfortunately, the paper fails to outline any plans or strategies as to how this will be achieved.

Since the ALP's election to Federal Government, Kevin Rudd, Prime Minister and Julia Gillard, Deputy Prime Minister and Minister for Education, have made many speeches and announcements about the education revolution. These have culminated in the implementation in 2009 of the 'National Partnership Agreement (the Agreement)' and the 'Digital Education Revolution', where every Year 9 student in the country will receive a laptop computer.

This agreement supports a suite of school and broader reforms designed to transform the way schooling takes place in targeted schools in disadvantaged communities. The agreement aims to 'improve student engagement, educational attainment and well-being in participating schools, make inroads into entrenched disadvantage (including Indigenous communities), contribute to broaden social and economic objectives and improve understanding about effective intervention that can be implemented beyond the schools participating in this agreement' (Council of Australian Governments 2009a, b).

The economic downturn in 2008 also triggered a Federal Government stimulus package with billions of dollars available for buildings and maintenance in all schools in Australia. In some cases this helped overcome lengthy waiting times for buildings such as school halls.

Unfortunately the National Partnership funding of more than $3 billion does not address the inequity that still exists in the funding of different school systems. Public education remains the poor cousin of the elite schools, who continue to attract significant Federal funding.

## Change without change?

Dr Jim McMorrow (McMorrow 2008), author of a review commissioned by the Australian Education Union, a former senior ALP adviser and education consultant in Australian and NSW Governments, says in his report, 'The Rudd Government has inherited a set of arrangements for schools' funding that is lacking in rationality, integrity and transparency. Given the absence of any simple political remedies for dealing with these flaws the Government has opted to avoid disturbing the arrangements so early in its term of office. It has, therefore, accepted most of the Howard legacy and defaulted on policy reform in the medium term'.

Journalist Ross Gittins (Gittins 2008) comments, 'Kevin Rudd promised us an Education Revolution that would bring us better schools, universities and technical colleges and so more of the highly skilled, better paid jobs we need to prosper in a more competitive world. But, not to worry, that would not involve interfering with the Howard Government's scheme for making grants to the public and private schools'. Gittins continues: 'the state education bureaucracies and their unions have their own reasons for continuing to resist Federal pressure to publish performance indicators. But Rudd is giving them valid argument that his competition is biased against them. That's the kind of problem you strike when you pursue change without change'.

Is the 'Education Revolution' simply more political rhetoric, in the tradition of past Prime Ministers and Premiers who have seen education as a convenient pole from which to hang their flag? (Bob Hawke's was 'the Clever Country'; Bob Carr was dubbed 'the Education Premier'). At present 'smart politics' may be taking precedence over 'good policy'. The $16.2 billion 'Building the Education Revolution' is good policy, but the helter-skelter rush to have projects completed by early 2011 puts politics in front of policy. With a little more time for consultation and planning many schools could have found more innovative ways of addressing the educational needs of their communities.

The 20th century model of Australian education was a refined model of 19th century schooling. The fact that the model has survived, long past its use-by date, is indicative of its resilience. Despite its past achievements major issues remain, for example:

- national investment in education in Australia has not been keeping up with the rest of the world and has slipped by 7% since 1995;
- the 'public education' versus 'private education' debate is debilitating and detrimental to the education of *all* children in the nation;
- compulsory education is based upon a 'factory production model', in buildings that are increasingly costly to maintain, not conducive to modern learning and largely inaccessible to the majority of the community for the majority of the year;
- teaching is not seen as a preferred career and faces a crisis of self-confidence and low public self-esteem;
- three- or four-year political terms prevent long-term planning and increase unnecessary intervention as every new minister tries to make his or her mark;
- an ageing general population means that education is not seen as a 'number one priority' for the electorate;
- entitlement to education is a fundamental human right, but many of our less fortunate, less able, rural or remote students do not have equal access to this right;
- starting under the previous Federal Government and, unfortunately, continued by the appeasement policy of the current Government, the public education system, particularly in secondary schools, is becoming the residual system. NAPLAN results and trends in enrolments demonstrate that those who have access and ability and can afford it are electing to attend the private education system. Unless the current Government commences to implement the rhetoric of written policy, then the writing is on the wall:

the public education system will cater for the least able, being taught the least possible, by the least capable, with the least appropriate resources;

- former Chief Executive of the English Qualifications and Curriculum Authority and previously Director-General of Education in New South Wales, Dr Ken Boston (Boston 2009) said: *'Initiative, enterprise, self management and a thirst for learning are created by building, from the early primary years, respect for individual creativity and real achievement, through recognition and reward. Competitiveness and striving for individual success, is at the heart of teaching and learning in initiative, planning, personal organisation, problem solving and enterprise. None of these educational outcomes is achieved or enhanced by national testing or league tables'*;

- skill shortages are almost at crisis level in many professions and trades and our productivity growth has been steadily falling despite 'good' economic times; and

- recent changes to the Youth Allowance demonstrate the difficulty that the Government is having in implementing its Education Revolution. Julia Gillard has stated publicly that she is worried about the performance gap between rural and metropolitan students and that she intends to bridge this gap. But she has made alterations to the Youth Allowance that now make it far more difficult to qualify for financial assistance. Thus rural students, who often have to live away from home to attend university, are under a severe disadvantage when compared to metropolitan students who can access the same universities while living at home.

## The window is open

Change in the Australian education system is slow and depends on the capability of the educational leaders, particularly within each school, whether they are public or private. The motivation for change includes the adoption of new technologies, such as interactive whiteboards, connected classrooms with videoconference facility and the Year 9 laptops for learning. The installation of such technology does not guarantee that the teacher will use it effectively. In fact, the technology may simply replace other poor teaching technique. The true educational revolution will happen when quality teaching and learning is happening in the full diversity of learning environments.

Quality teaching is about engagement, building a relationship between the teacher and the learner and creating a stimulating learning environment that fosters the need to know and the techniques to know how. Children are information rich with an almost unlimited access to information via the internet. Unless this information can be turned into knowledge it is of little practical value without context.

A number of public schools across Australia provide high quality education for children with incredible social disadvantage. The resilience of these educators is to be applauded but unfortunately the continued disparate funding by the Australian Government of elite private schools only helps to widen the gap. It is time to drop the politics and genuinely fund less affluent community schools so that they can provide the quality of education necessary to help the next generation break the poverty cycle.

The opportunity for change is ripe with the planned implementation of the National Curriculum in 2011. The Australian Government is using funding to States as the incentive for accepting a national model. This may be the catalyst for some alignment of educational delivery between States but will not change the fundamental quality of teaching in the classroom. For Australia to continue to develop resilient students there needs to be an alignment of curriculum, public funding of education for the public good and a fundamental understanding of the measures necessary to overcome disadvantage. This will include attracting high quality leaders and teachers to low socio-economic and remote areas.

The existing resilience in Australian education is such that the situation can be addressed through a national approach to policy setting, increased funding to public and rural schools and a renewed emphasis on teaching as a profession. The challenge is for governments of all persuasions, teacher unions and the general public to commit to change to ensure that Australian education does not reach a situation where its resilience impedes necessary change.

## Winds of change

Education in the 21st century is vastly different to that for which our current education system was designed. 'Schools must ensure they remain relevant to their students' future life and there is rather too much evidence that they are failing in this regard' (Hawkes 2008).

A number of trends can be identified that will drive education in this century (Caldwell 2000; Dawkins 2002; Frey 2007; Wallis 2008; Australia 2020 Summit 2008):

- a transition from teaching to learning, with students learning anytime, anywhere and anything, with flexibility and at a pace comfortable to them, on topics that are relevant to them. Teachers will transition from topic experts to guides, facilitators and coaches where *'imagination is more important than knowledge'* (Albert Einstein);
- exponential growth of information, the technology to access, interpret, manipulate and communicate it and the application of this information and technology to care for, sustain and develop the planet;
- an increase in number and diversity of places where we come into contact with the rest of the world and where we learn, encompassing whole-of-life experience;
- a transition from a society of consumers to producers, where there is a real need to participate in creating, recording, interpreting and communicating history, current events, facts and news (e.g. YouTube and MySpace);
- the shift from West to East and Australia's place as a 20th century Western culture with a 21st century Eastern population and position;
- a transformation from a regional to a world citizen as the pace of change mandates that we produce faster, smarter, more capable, more flexible and more adaptable human beings (Frey 2007). Current systems prevent this from happening. *'We have to educate for what we can't imagine'* (Bill Gates);
- changes in demand for education, with education as a traded service for the whole of life and from throughout the world. A new definition of education will be shaped by such things as educational franchising; corporate training; distance learning; greater business and industry involvement in vocational education and training; privatisation and market economy forces. Education is a service that people will require all their life and therefore everyone will demand an entitlement and access to education;
- the role of government will be more sharply focussed on education for the public good and it will set priorities, establish funding structures and build frameworks that facilitate this in a full range of environments that will have the authority to deliver a world-class education with appropriate accountability;
- education will be a means to change, which is as unprecedented as it is unpredictable; and
- there will be no 'typical' student, but our current 'five-year-old' may mix in multicultural, multifaith settings; have a strong focus on the Asia–Pacific; be more imaginative and flexible learners; consider earth as a living organism to be nurtured not exploited; and structure work and career choices to fit lifestyle (see '*I am the future's child*', Beare 2001).

## Phoenix rising

Wallis (2008) wrote his book prior to the current economic crisis, but its publication during this crisis only strengthened the argument for a 'Fourth Global Awakening'. Hargreaves (2009) identifies a future for education that is defined by inspiration, innovation, social justice and sustainability rather than data-driven intervention, has less bureaucracy and more democracy and is collaborative rather than competitive. He envisages a model that will spread influence, not in buildings or programmes but in the principles it stands for and the people that it has touched.

'The Productivity Agenda – Education, Skills, Training, Science and Innovation' (Australia 2020 Summit 2008) provides a thoughtful foundation for debate to take place. Its ambitions, themes, challenges, ideas and well-constructed statements give rise to hope.

- We need to prepare our young people to be flexible workers as they will change occupations many times throughout their lives and increasingly operate as part of global production and knowledge systems. A true education revolution is needed if Australia is to stand in the world as a smart economy.
- Education must foster creativity since it is one of the greatest contributors to productivity in the 21st century.
- We need to seriously re-examine the governance system around education, at all levels, which are presently undermining effective education and creating enormous wastage.
- We must rethink funding structures to encourage flexibility.
- We must take innovative approaches to training and education.
- Long term planning must be encouraged.
- We need high aspirations and expectations for all our children.
- We need to move on from the old paradigm of 'public' versus 'private'. People have a right to choose where they study. We must accept that there are many ways we can educate people in Australia and they all should be valued and we must concentrate on developing every Australian to their full potential to enhance individual worth, social capital and the public good.

The continuing lack of a national vision for education may mean that the current education system, which has relied upon a slow rate of change and ad hoc management of that change, may flounder. Clearly the development of a shared vision for education in Australia is essential. Senge (2006) notes, 'you cannot have a learning organisation without a shared vision'. Leading educationalist Michael Fullan (Fullan 2001) supports this notion: 'structure does make a difference, but it is not the main point in achieving success. Transforming the culture – changing the way we do things around here, is the main thing'.

While successive Australian Governments have been able to demonstrate a commitment to education, they have lacked a strategic perspective, focusing instead on short-term political gain. This has resulted in unsustained priorities, a lack of coordination and fiscal waste. As political parties seek to provide a political alternative the change process is often confined to a three-year cycle. Key priorities one year can quickly be off the agenda when Government changes.

Desirable change may not be happening in the Australian education system due to the 'smart politics' rather than 'good policy' approach of all political parties. It may be time for the politicians to take a step back, listen to professionals, professional organisations, business leaders, unions and community groups. This opportunity has been created through the Australia 2020 Summit (2008), but, to-date, there is little practical evidence of the ambitions, themes, challenges and 'top ideas' contained in the paper 'The Productivity Agenda – Education, Skills, Training, Science and Innovation' guiding good policy.

The rapidity of change in today's world makes it an imperative that a unilateral approach is taken to position Australian education strategically to adapt to emerging challenges. If this is not done the resilience of 'schooling' may continue but the resilience of Australian education cannot be assured. The role of education in the resilience of future Australians has never been more important. We are faced with a technological revolution were students can access more information at a younger age than ever before. The challenge is to ensure that future educational delivery develops the techniques in our young people to turn information into knowledge. At the same time there needs to be a focus on what students need to develop to be resilient when coping with a world of continuing change.

*Robert Lewis (M Ed Admin.; B Phys. Ed; Dip. Teach; FACEL) is an Education Project Manager, who is currently working with government schools, non-government schools, the NSW Health Department, the University of New England and non-government organisations to improve planning, implementation and outcomes for success in the 21st century. He has previously been a senior educational leader NSW Department of Education and Training and provided educational consultancy services in Australia and the United Kingdom.*

*Jim White (M Ed; BA; Dip. Teach. Ag/Sc) is a senior educator in the NSW Department of Education and Training. During the past 34 years he has been involved in leadership in a variety of positions including standing as Principal of several successful schools. Jim currently works as a Regional Director in northern NSW.*

*Wayne Chandler (BA; Grad. Dip;. Ed. M Ed. Admin.; FACEL) is a highly experienced educator who has worked in the Senior Executive service in both NSW and the ACT since 1990. Positions he has occupied have included Cluster Director, Director of Education, District Superintendent and Schools Director (ACT). He has led a range of departmental portfolio areas including School Review and Development, International Education and Indigenous Education. Mr Chandler's previous positions included teacher, school executive, consultant and Principal in small rural schools, a Special Education school and large primary schools. Mr Chandler's contribution to education has been recognised through the award of a Fellowship by the Australian Council of Education Leaders.*

## References

ALP (Australian Labor Party) (2007) The Australian Economy Needs An Education Revolution. Australian Labor Party, Canberra, <http://www.alp.org.au/download/now/education_revolution.pdf>.

Australian Government Department of the Prime Minister and Cabinet (2008) The productivity agenda: Education, skills, training, science and innovation. In 'Australia 2020 Summit Final Report'. (Eds Department of the Prime Minister and Cabinet) pp. 5–32. Australian Government, Canberra, <http://www.australia2020.gov.au/docs/final_report/2020_summit_report_full.pdf>.

Beare H (2001) *Creating the Future School.* Routledge, Abingdon, Oxfordshire, UK.

Bernard ME (2005) *You Can Do It.* University of Melbourne, Melbourne.

Boston K (2009) Our early start on making children unfit for work. *Sunday Times*, UK, April 26, <http://www.timesonline.co.uk/tol/incomingFeeds/article6168874.ece>.

Caldwell B (2000) A 'public good' test to guide the transformation of public education. *Journal of Educational Change* **1**, 307–329.

Council of Australian Governments (2009a) National Partnerships Agreement on Low Socio–Economic Status School Communities. Council of Australian Governments, Canberra, <http://www.coag.gov.au/intergov_agreements/federal_financial_relations/docs/national_partnership/national_partnership_for_low_socio-economic_school_communities.pdf>.

Council of Australian Governments (2009b) National Partnerships Agreement on Literacy and Numeracy. Council of Australian Governments, Canberra, <www.coag.gov.au/... agreements/.../national_partnership/national_partnership _on_literacy_and_numeracy.rtf>.

Dawkins J (2002) Education at the leading edge – understanding the changes. The 2002 William Walker Oration, the Australian Council for Education Leaders/ LETA Conference, October 2, Adelaide.

Flannery T (2005) *The Weather Makers.* Text Publishing, Melbourne.

Frey T (2007) The Future of Education. Da Vinci Institute, Louisville, CO, USA, <http://www.davinciinstitute.com/papers/the-future-of-education-by-thomas-frey/>.

Fullan M (2001) *Leading in a Culture of Change.* Jossey-Bass, San Francisco.

Gittins R (2008) Rudd's big idea: change nothing. *Sydney Morning Herald*, 3 September.

Hargreaves A (2009) The Fourth Way of Educational Reform. ACEL Monograph Series 45, ACEL, Penrith, NSW, Australia.

Hawkes T (2008) The failure of schools to educate. *Sydney Morning Herald*, 8 September.

Keating P (2008) Template for peace in a more inclusive world structure. *Sydney Morning Herald*, 25 August.

McMorrow J (2008) Reviewing the Evidence: Issues in Commonwealth Funding of Government and Non-Government Schools in the Howard and Rudd years. Australian Education Union, Canberra, <http://www.aeufederal.org.au/Publications/2008/JMcMorrowpaper.pdf>.

Senge P (2006) *The Fifth Discipline – The Art and Practice of The Learning Organisation.* Doubleday, New York.

Wallis J (2008) *Seven Ways to Change the World: Reviving Faith and Politics.* Lion Hudson PLC, Oxford, UK.

Woodhead C (2000) 'Annual Report of Her Majesty's Chief Inspector of Schools: Standards and Quality in Education 1998/1999'. Office for Standards In Education, Manchester, UK.

# ENVIRONMENT AND SOCIETY

# CHAPTER 15

# Resilience of social–ecological systems

Steven Cork

## Abstract

Over the past four decades, research on ecological and human social systems has generated a body of theory about resilience and related concepts like adaptability and transformability. While the requirements for resilience to specific challenges vary with the nature of the challenge, general resilience is thought to depend primarily on the diversity of species, people and institutions that are in a given system, its modularity (which influences how the system deals with local failures), and the tightness of feedbacks (which influences how quickly changes in one part of the system are detected and responded to by other parts). Building and/or maintaining social and ecological resilience are high priorities in most major government and non-government strategies for managing Australia's natural resources. Organisations are seeking ways to move from traditional approaches to policy development and implementation that either do not encourage diversity, modularity and tightness of feedbacks or actively erode them, but progress is slow. Particular attention needs to be paid to developing governance systems that allocate authority and responsibility at scales appropriate for detecting and responding to ecological change, and understanding the dependency relationships between human and ecosystems and managing to meet these needs in an uncertain future.

## Introduction

Much has been written about the decline in extent and condition of ecosystems in Australia and globally (National Land and Water Resources Audit 2002; Cork *et al.* 2006; Rockström *et al.* 2009). Over the last decade and a half, in particular, there has been increasing focus on the relationships between humans and the 'natural environments' that they live in and depend on for life-support and fulfillment in its many forms (Daily 1997; Cork *et al.* 2001, 2007). The concepts of 'ecological footprint', 'industrial metabolism' and 'ecosystem services' are examples of metaphors and frameworks developed to explain human dependence and impacts on nature and to enable those dependencies and impacts to be considered in decision-making processes (Ayres and Simonis 1994; Daily 1997; Rapport 2000).

Research into the dynamics of ecological systems and the links between these and human social and economic systems has generated a body of theory about resilience that has posed challenging questions for not only managing ecosystems but also managing development of human settlements, industries and well-being (Walker *et al.* 2004; Walker and Salt 2006). This chapter outlines current thinking about resilience in relation to coupled social–ecological systems, comments on trends in the resilience of these systems in Australia and highlights some of the challenges in diagnosing and managing resilience using environmental and social policy.

## The concept of resilience in relation to social–ecological systems

Resilience is a term used in virtually all disciplines and fields of human endeavour (van Opstal 2007; Cork *et al.* 2008). It has long been a key concept in engineering (Holling 1996). It has become especially popular recently in business and economics and in mental and physical health, as academics and practitioners are being asked to address perceptions of growing risks and threats and an increase in the severity and frequency of 'surprise events' (Starr *et al.* 2003; van Opstal 2007). Across these disciplines and others, the word 'resilience' is used in widely different ways and is frequently not defined or explained, even within disciplines.

Over the past four decades, research on ecological and human social systems has drawn on empirical observations of how systems have responded to perturbations in the past and developed theories about resilience and related concepts like robustness, adaptability (the capacity of actors in a given system to influence resilience), and transformability (the capacity to create a fundamentally new system when ecological, economic, or social, including political, conditions make the existing system untenable) (see Resilience Alliance 2009 for various reviews of research in this area). The research was initially based on observations about cycles of resource capture and exploitation (Figure 15.1), which appear to apply to both ecological and human social systems (Resilience Alliance 2009).

Several conclusions that emerge from research on resilience of coupled social–ecological systems are discussed below (see Walker and Salt 2006 for further discussion of these).

### *It is not useful to think of resilience as 'staying the same'*

Efforts to find a definition of resilience that is consistent with what has been observed in ecological and social systems have revealed that complex adaptive systems like these never return to exactly the same condition after a perturbation as they were in previously. Individuals, organisations, societies and ecosystems all change in subtle ways after being perturbed. Walker

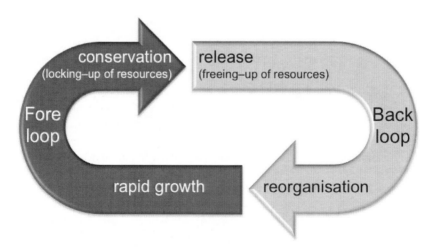

**Figure 15.1**   Simplified version of the adaptive cycle (adapted from Walker and Salt 2006)

*et al.* (2004) recognise this by defining resilience as 'the capacity of a system to absorb disturbance and reorganise while undergoing change so as to still retain essentially the same
function, structure, identity and feedbacks'.

Holling (1996) distinguished ecological from engineering resilience by suggesting that
engineers build resilience into structures to ensure that they return to essentially the same
condition after perturbation, while the ability to change within limits is vital if ecosystems are
to keep performing the same essential functions in the face of environmental variability and
shocks.

Thus it has been proposed that ecological resilience can be assessed in terms of four key
attributes: (1) latitude – the maximum amount the system can be changed before losing its
ability to recover; (2) resistance – the ease or difficulty of changing the system; (3) precarious-
ness – how close the system currently is to a limit or 'threshold' which, if breached, makes
recovery difficult or impossible; and (4) panarchy – how the above three attributes are influenced by the states and dynamics of the (sub)systems at scales above and below the scale of
interest (Walker *et al.* 2004;Walker and Salt 2006).

## General versus specified resilience

A system can be generally resilient (i.e. able to absorb a range of disturbances) or specifically
resilient (i.e. resilient to certain disturbances) (Walker and Salt 2006). Often, there is a trade-
off between these two types of resilience in both ecosystems and social systems. For example,
an ecosystem that is highly resilient to fires might not be resilient to impacts of land clearing
and/or use of agricultural chemicals. Similarly, human communities that are found to be
susceptible to specific challenges, such as bushfires, often display remarkable general resilience
in supporting one another and recovering socially from the disaster.

## Desirable versus undesirable resilience

Whether or not resilience in an ecological system is desirable or undesirable to humans
depends on whether we would like to see status quo functions and structure maintained (i.e.
the system is meeting our needs), or not (i.e. we would like to move the system to a different set
of functions). For example, changing land management practices can be difficult due to the
resilience of social–ecological systems that has served them well in the past but might no
longer be in their best interests or those of society.

## A systems-thinking approach is vital

These systems are complex and adaptive (i.e. they contain many more links than we can comprehend with simple cause and effect models and the rules by which the systems work change
as the system adapts to change). Ignoring these connections and interactions is a recipe for
unintended consequences and policy failure (Sterman 2000; Pannell 2008).

## Change often is not gradual or obvious

Some change happens quickly and obviously, while other change occurs slowly until the
conditions are right for a period of rapid 'threshold' change after which the system's functions
and structures are different and might not be able to return to their original conditions. One
example is the slow rise of salty water tables in many Australian landscapes due to removal of
the trees that once kept water tables much lower. Once the salty water rises to within about two
metres of the surface its rate of progress increases dramatically and landscapes appear to
become saline almost over night. Another example is loss of soil nutrient and carbon recycling
and the process by which young plants replace old and spread throughout landscapes. The

structure of vegetation and litter in most landscapes determines how well they retain water, seeds, nutrients and other resources. Once a critical loss of this structure is passed, landscapes rapidly lose functionality, start to 'leak' resources and fail to support the species that would otherwise have sustained the system (Tongway and Hindley 2004).

### Social–ecological systems go through cycles of complexity that affect their resilience

Both social and ecological systems go through cycles of building up and breaking down links. In what has been described as 'adaptive cycles', these systems tend to grow rapidly, accumulating resources, species, ideas and ways of doing things (Table 15.1). They grow in complexity until they reach a point at which that complexity starts to cause stagnation. Sometimes disturbances like fire, floods, drought, diseases, revolutions, loss of key leaders, economic crises, or wars move the system back into its less complex phase. Sometimes they cause it to break down and reorganise into a different system. Both outcomes can be desirable at different times and in different circumstances.

Contemplating these cycles has led researchers to conclude that resilience cannot be considered in isolation from 'adaptability' – the collective capacity of the human actors in the system to manage resilience – and 'transformability' – the capacity to create a fundamentally new system when ecological, economic, or social conditions make the existing system untenable (Table 15.1).

### Perturbations are important for maintaining resilience

The process of regular, but often unpredictable, challenges from disturbances that happens in nature tends to retain multiple species that can perform essential functions under different conditions (Walker *et al.* 1999). In this way, natural systems have changed in many respects over time but have continued to find ways to utilise the air, water and soil nutrients that are their fundamental resources. A major issue of concern in the modern world is that humans have dampened the processes of disturbances on both the natural and man-made environments, causing loss of diversity of form and function among non-human species and loss of diversity in thought, skills and outlook among humans. This means that when a challenge arises there are fewer potential solutions on offer.

## Key components of resilience

A wide range of processes and attributes have been suggested in the literature as being important for conferring resilience on social–ecological systems (Table 15.1). While the

**Table 15.1** Attributes of systems indicating resilience, adaptability or transformability (adapted from Walker and Salt 2006, and Resilience Alliance 2009b)

| General resilience | Adaptability | Transformability |
|---|---|---|
| Diversity (e.g. of skills, ideas, functions) | Social capital (leadership, trust) | Experimentation |
| Modularity (failure in one part of the system does not cause failure of the whole system) | Human capital (skills, education, health) | Support for change |
| Awareness of cross-scale processes | Adaptive governance | Trust |
| Tight feedbacks (early detection of emerging change, effective transfer of information and rapid and appropriate responses) | Financial resources | Human, built and natural capital |
| Overlapping institutions and reserves of human and other resources | Natural capital | Cross-scale awareness |
| | Social and ecological memory and ongoing learning | |

requirements for resilience to specific challenges vary with the nature of the challenge, general resilience is thought to depend primarily on three key factors:

- *diversity* – the number and variety of species, people and institutions that are in the system
- *modularity* – the connections between parts of the system and how they affect the ability of the system to keep functioning if some bits fail
- *tightness of feedbacks* – how quickly changes in one part of the system are detected and responded to by other parts

In the policy section later in this chapter the consequences of diversity, modularity and feedbacks are explored in relation to strategies for conserving biodiversity in Australia.

### Resilience of what, to what?

Resilience thinking poses many questions about the relationship between humans and nature, including:

- when and where is resilience desirable and when is it not?
- what functions and structures do we want from our social–ecological systems (and can we even answer this question)?
- how much resilience is enough?
- what sorts of shocks and surprises might we need our social–ecological systems to be resilient to?

These questions can be summed up in the question: 'resilience of what, to what?' (Carpenter *et al.* 2001). One attempt to answer this question has been to identify a set of so-called 'ecosystem services'. These are the benefits that humans get from ecological systems, including regulatory services, like regulation of water flows in rivers, regulation of water tables, regulation of pests and diseases and regulation of atmospheric composition; provisioning services, like provision of food, clean water, fibre, building material, pharmaceuticals; cultural services, like maintenance of spiritual, educational and recreational values; and supporting services, like maintenance of soil fertility, creation of soil and maintenance of genetic diversity (Daily 1997; Binning *et al.* 2001; Cork *et al.* 2001; Abel *et al.* 2003).

Defining the benefits that people expect from ecological systems helps us consider the first part of the question above; 'resilience of what?' Addressing the second part of the question ('to what?') requires us to think about the future. At the moment we are consumed with thoughts about how climate might change and how much oil is left in the world. Climate change in particular will have important direct impacts on ecosystems. But the decisions that humans make to deal with climate change, energy and other issues will have at least as great an impact as the physical changes themselves. Hence the suggestions later in this chapter for achieving greater resilience in Australia's social–ecological systems are largely about bringing better thinking to the consequences of decision-making.

## Trends in biodiversity and its interactions with human societies

The loss of biodiversity that Australia has experienced in the last two centuries is massive by international standards. Over 100 species of plants and animals have become extinct (Williams *et al.* 2001). Globally, two-thirds of the mammals that have become extinct since the 1600s are Australian (National Land and Water Resources Audit 2002). In a recent assessment, Rockström *et al.* (2009) produced a set of nine indicators of 'safe operating limits' for this planet and suggested that at least three of these – rate of biodiversity loss, climate change and the nitrogen cycle – have already been far exceeded.

Despite some recent positive outcomes in threat abatement, recent national assessments of the condition and trend of biodiversity in Australia (Williams *et al.* 2001; Cork *et al.* 2006; National Land and Water Resources Audit 2002) indicate that it is in more peril than ever with greater than 1000 entire regional ecosystems now recognised as threatened (National Land and Water Resources Audit 2002). Internationally, Australia is identified as one of the world's regions most likely to undergo large losses of biodiversity in the next few decades (Sala *et al.* 2000).

Opinions about the scale and urgency of action required vary more widely within Australia, ranging from the view that incremental progress is all that can be expected (e.g. with regard to emissions reform) to the assertion that only an emergency response of unprecedented scale and resourcing can hope to avoid major ecosystem decline and human suffering in the near future (Spratt and Sutton 2008). At a deeper level, some argue that modern Western societies are at, or near, a stage in their adaptive (organisational) cycles at which they are so overconnected and complex that they have to either drastically reform their institutional and governance structures or go through some form of uncontrolled institutional collapse and reorganisation in the face of approaching challenges (Marshal 2005, 2008; Homer-Dixon 2009; International Monetary Fund 2009).

What do assessments of ecosystem decline in Australia tell us about the resilience of these systems and their ability to keep producing ecosystem services? There are several indications that both could be reaching dangerously low levels, possibly approaching threshold changes:

- it was estimated in 2001 that 39% of Australia's 85 bioregions have more than 30% of their ecosystems described as threatened;
- clearing of vegetation has already turned large areas of Australia's agricultural land saline and much more is poised to turn saline in the near future;
- water flowing from many catchment areas for Australian cities requires extensive filtration to meet quality standards (although some catchments, like that for Melbourne, produce much higher quality water because of good vegetation cover);
- appropriation of water for human use in southern Australia has reached a point where shocks like drought force us to make serious trade-offs between ecosystem functions, economic growth and perhaps even basic human welfare; and
- habitat for birds, mammals, reptiles and other animals as well as plants, fungi and invertebrates in the sheep and wheat belt of Australia has been reduced substantially since the arrival of Europeans (Cork *et al.* 2006). As climate change threatens to change temperature, rainfall and other determinants of where plants and animals can live, many will be unable to move because the habitat they need does not exist in the new climatically suitable areas. The interaction of climate change with habitat fragmentation is likely to affect processes like pollination of native plants and crops by native insects, birds and mammals (thus reducing yields), natural control of pests and diseases by native insects and birds, erosion control by native vegetation, regulation of stream flows, water runoff into streams and storages and water infiltration to soil and water tables. It will also affect a range of cultural services provided by ecological systems, including provision of a sense of place for Australians.

Most of Australia's ecosystems have changed considerably since the arrival of European people. They also had changed substantially under the influence of Aboriginal people before that. From a resilience perspective one might ask 'are Australian ecosystems different functionally and structurally than they used to be?'. The answer to this question depends on what we think the essential functions and structures of these ecosystems are. For example, although many species have disappeared, we could argue that most Australian ecosystems still perform the same set of functions with many of the same sorts of interactions among species as they once did. On the other hand, some would argue that an agricultural or urban landscape is fundamentally different from a forest of a native grassland or wetland.

This is where it is important to consider what we expect from ecosystems and how we define 'function' and 'structure'. There are currently many views on these issues but little dialogue to help Australians understand one another's different viewpoints.

## Policy challenges

Resilience in social–ecological systems requires diversity, modularity and tightness of feedbacks (manifested as a variety of skills and ideas, connectedness, openness, reserves of resources, and institutions that overlap so that issues do not fall between the institutions and responsibility and authority that match the scale and location of challenges and opportunities and lead to capacity for early detection and quick responses; Table 15.1). Unfortunately, many traditional approaches to policy development and implementation either do not encourage these factors or actively erode them. Marshal (this volume), for example, explores the reluctance of Australian governments to devolve decision-making authority and responsibility despite mounting evidence of the undesirable consequences of overly centralised governance models.

### *Being transparent about the 'real policy problem'*

Wilson *et al.* (2009), among others, have highlighted poor problem definition as one of the biggest obstacles for achieving effective ecosystem and biodiversity conservation in Australia (and elsewhere for that matter). Poor problem definition usually occurs because of inadequate consideration of underlying influences that results in the problem being defined in terms of the symptoms rather than the causes. When this happens there is a high risk that strategies and tactics will not only fail to solve the problem but may make it worse (Sterman 2000; Pannell 2008).

Most major government and non-government strategies for conserving Australia's biodiversity and managing natural resources more generally identify the encouragement and maintenance of resilience as a high priority; that is, they frame the policy problem at least partly in terms of resilience (Western Australian Government Department of Environment and Conservation 2006; Sattler and Taylor 2008; Australian Government Department of the Environment, Water, Heritage and the Arts 2009; New South Wales Government Department of Environment, Climate Change and Water 2009; Northern Territory Government Department of Natural Resources, Environment, the Arts and Sport 2009; Queensland Government Department of Environment and Resource Management 2009; South Australian Government Department for Environment and Heritage 2009; Victorian Government Department of Sustainability and the Environment 2009). Most, if not all, government departments and non-government organisations, however, implement these strategies via compartmentalised programme areas and predetermined targets that hark back to centralised, command-and-control approaches to policy and management. This appears to occur because implementation strategies and resourcing are driven by other elements of the problem not overtly stated (e.g. political agendas, issues relating to the culture of agencies and the government of the day, traditional views on how to approach conservation problems and financial constraints).

One of the most elegant demonstrations of this is Connell's (2006, 2007) analysis of the development of policies and plans for managing water and other environmental assets in the Murray–Darling Basin (MDB). Connell argues that jurisdictional impediments to cooperation drove the Murray–Darling Basin Commission (MDBC) to adopt a philosophy of incremental progress that had little chance of achieving the objective of sustainability. On the other hand, there is a danger that initiatives like the National Water Initiative and the Commonwealth takeover of the MDBC, which have set high-level strategic objectives, will struggle because they do not address the underlying jurisdictional and other constraints on cooperative action.

## *Avoiding partial solutions*

One enemy of resilience is partial policy and management solutions that do not consider the important systems links at the right scale. Simplistic responses to habitat fragmentation, such as planting trees of any sort anywhere in the landscape (which was one response in the past), risk not only failing to provide new habitat but also risk compromising other ecosystem services like water runoff and pest control. Solutions to habitat decline need to consider the types of species that used to be in landscapes and the functions they performed. They also need to consider the ways in which those landscapes have changed, which might mean that the same species will no longer survive there. Most importantly, we need to understand and address the underlying processes that continue to drive decline, even after tree clearing has ceased. In many parts of Australia's agricultural landscapes, for example, the conditions for germination of new seedlings of native plants no longer exist and this must be addressed before progress can be made towards restoration of the functions of these landscapes.

## *Moving to adaptive governance*

Governance systems that involve people who live closest to environmental change as key decision makers are more likely to detect and respond to change quickly than centralised governance systems far from the sites of change. Australia has moved towards regional models of governance in recent years. There have been successes but many improvements have been suggested (including in other chapters in this volume).

## *Encouraging diversity, modularity, tight feedbacks and self-organisation*

Perhaps the biggest challenge for rebuilding resilience in Australia's ecosystems is that something needs to be done urgently before many landscapes pass through thresholds and become something other than what we would like. Urgent environmental action usually means some trade-offs with economic growth. An underlying driver of future habitat decline will be climate change and there is a raging debate about how to bring about urgent action to reduce emissions of greenhouse gases while managing impacts on economic growth. It will be important that Australian decision-makers think broadly about resource allocation, avoid the pitfalls of narrow approaches to efficiency (Table 15.2), and seek solutions that encourage diversity of function, structure and ideas in both the ecological and social parts of systems so that both parts are able to generate a range of potential solutions.

For example, reducing expenditure on research into the extent and nature of decline in Australian ecosystems (there is still very little support for ongoing data collection to support

**Table 15.2**  Postulated effects on resilience of applying traditional command and control management, based on simple notions of economic efficiency, to conservation policy and management (adapted from Walker *et al.* 2004, and Walker and Salt 2006)

| Key elements of resilience | Effects of 'narrow' efficiency |
|---|---|
| Diversity (of ideas, skills, resources, etc.) | Elimination of 'spare capacity; focus on what we need now leaving us unprepared for later |
| Modularity (failure in one part does not bring down the whole) | Centralised functions can leave a system vulnerable if the centre fails; humans tend to create unstable networks – nature tests its vulnerabilities constantly |
| Tight feedbacks (effective two-way information flows) | Centralised control can reduce intelligence from the 'coal face' and delay response |
| Self-organisation | The more we try to control a system the more we risk reducing resilience |

State of the Environment Reporting, for example) and limiting training and job opportunities for environmental scientists are trends that are likely to reduce resilience rather than build it. Local governments, which are at the coalface of environmental decision-making, struggle to be able to afford environmental officers and even if they have the resources to fund these posts, they struggle to find qualified people to fill positions. Universities and other research organisations are being forced by funding limitations to address only the issues that are apparent today. Similarly, the current tight control of policy development by politicians and their advisors discourages new thinking about possible alternative policies and fails to make use of the potentially huge amount of talent existing in public servants and others who could contribute to policy development.

A lesson learned in the past is perhaps worth remembering. The failure of the 1961 invasion of Cuba by the USA (the Bay of Pigs invasion) is an ideal example in which rapid consensus decision-making was encouraged and alternative solutions ignored (Janis 1972). In the subsequent Cuban Missile Crisis, President Kennedy invited outside experts to share their viewpoints and allowed group members to question them. He also absented himself from meetings to avoid implied pressure and encouraged diverse thinking in many other ways, even dividing the decision-making group up into sub-groups to break up too much group cohesion. The peaceful resolution of this crisis is attributed to these resilience-building measures. In my view, such measures are under-employed in development of environment policy at present, although the recent 2020 Summit convened by the Australian Government is a step in this direction.

*Steven Cork, BSc, PhD, is an Australia21 Fellow and Leader of Australia21's Resilience Project. He is also an ecologist and futurist who, over the past 26 years, has been a senior researcher with CSIRO and played a lead role in developing ecological scenarios for the world's future in the United Nations' Millennium Assessment. He now works as a private consultant (EcoInsights).*

# References

Abel N, Cork S, Gorddard R, Langridge J, Langston A, Plant R, Proctor W, Ryan P, Shelton D, Walker B and Yialeloglou M (2003) 'Natural Values: Exploring options for enhancing ecosystem services in the Goulburn Broken Catchment.' CSIRO, Canberra.

Australian Government Department of the Environment, Water, Heritage and the Arts (2009) Caring for our Country Business Plan 2009–10. Australian Government, Canberra, <http://www.nrm.gov.au/business–plan/index.html#priority>.

Ayres RU and Simonis UE (1994) *Industrial Metabolism: Restructuring for Sustainable Development.* United Nations University Press, Tokyo.

Binning C, Cork S, Parry R and Shelton D (2001) 'Natural assets: An inventory of ecosystem goods and services in the Goulburn Broken catchment'. CSIRO, Canberra.

Carpenter SR, Walker BH, Anderies JM and Abel N (2001) From metaphor to measurement: Resilience of what to what? *Ecosystems* **4**, 765–781.

Connell D (2006) The chariot wheels of the Commonwealth. PhD thesis, Centre for Resource and Environmental Studies, Australian National University, Canberra.

Connell D (2007) *Water and politics in the Murray–Darling Basin.* Federation Press, Sydney.

Cork S, Sattler P and Alexandra J (2006) 'Biodiversity theme commentary prepared for the 2006 Australian State of the Environment Committee'. Australian Government, Canberra, <http://www.deh.gov.au/soe/2006/commentaries/biodiversity/index.html>.

Cork S, Shelton D, Binning C, Parry R (2001) 'A framework for applying the concept of ecosystem services to natural resource management in Australia'. In Third Australian

Stream Management Conference. 27–29 August, Brisbane. (Eds I Rutherford, F Sheldon, G Brierley and C Kenyon) pp. 157–162. Cooperative Research Centre for Catchment Hydrology, Brisbane.

Cork S, Stoneham G, Lowe K, Gainer K and Thackway R (2007) 'Ecosystem services and Australian natural resource management (NRM) futures. Paper to the Natural Resource Policies and Programs Committee (NRPPC) and the Natural Resource Management Standing Committee (NRMSC)'. Australian Government, Canberra, <www. environment.gov.au/biodiversity/publications/ecosystem–services–nrm–futures/pubs/ ecosystem–services.pdf>.

Cork S, Walker B and Buckley R (2008) 'How Resilient is Australia?' Australia21, Canberra, <http://www.australia21.org.au/whats_new.htm>.

Daily GC (1997) *Nature's Services – Societal Dependence on Natural Ecosystems*. Island Press, Washington, DC.

Holling CS (1996) Engineering resilience versus ecological resilience. In *Engineering Within Ecological Constraints*. (Ed. PC Schulze) pp. 31–34. National Academy Press, Washington, DC.

Homer-Dixon T (2009) When wise words are not enough. *Nature* **458**, 284–285.

International Monetary Fund (2009) 'Financial stability report April 2009: Responding to the financial crisis and measuring systemic risks. Chapter 2. Assessing the systemic implications of financial linkage'. International Monetary Fund, Washington, DC, <http://www.imf.org/External/Pubs/FT/GFSR/2009/01/pdf/chap2.pdf>.

Janis, IL (1972) *Victims of Groupthink: A Psychological Study of Foreign-Policy Decisions and Fiascoes*. Houghton Mifflin, Boston.

Manyena SB (2006) The concept of resilience revisited. *Disasters* **30**, 433–450.

Marshall GR (2005) *Economics for Collaborative Environmental Management: Renegotiating the Commons*. Earthscan, London.

Marshall GR (2008) Nesting, subsidiarity and community-based environmental governance beyond the local level. *International Journal of the Commons* **2**, 75–97. <http://www. thecommonsjournal.org/index.php/ijc/article/viewFile/50/19>.

McGregor A, Coffey B, Deutsch C, Wescott G and Robinson J (2008) 'Ecological Processes in Victoria. Policy Priorities for Sustaining Biodiversity.' Victoria Naturally Alliance, Melbourne.

National Land and Water Resources Audit (2002) 'Australian Terrestrial Biodiversity Assessment'. Commonwealth of Australia, Canberra, <http://audit.ea.gov.au/ANRA/ vegetation/docs/biodiversity/bio_assess_contents.cfm>.

New South Wales Government Department of Environment, Climate Change and Water (2009) The NSW Biodiversity Strategy. New South Wales Government, Sydney, <http://www.environment.nsw.gov.au/biodiversity/nswbiostrategy.htm New South Wales Government>.

Northern Territory Government Department of Natural Resources, Environment, the Arts and Sport (2009) Biodiversity Conservation. Government of the Northern Territory, Darwin, <http://www.nt.gov.au/nreta/wildlife/index.html>.

Pannell DJ (2008) Environmental Policy for Environmental Outcomes. INFFER Working Paper 0804. University of Western Australia, Perth, <http://cyllene.uwa.edu. au/~dpannell/dp0804.htm>.

Queensland Government Department of Environment and Resource Management (2009) Conserving Biodiversity. Queensland Government, Brisbane, <http://www.derm.qld.gov. au/wildlife–ecosystems/biodiversity/conserving_biodiversity/index.html>.

Rapport DJ (2000) Ecological footprints and ecosystem health: Complementary approaches to a sustainable future. *Ecological Economics* **32**, 367–370.

Resilience Alliance (2009) Research on Resilience in Social–Ecological Systems – A Basis for Sustainability. Resilience Alliance, Stockholm, <http://www.resalliance.org>.

Rockström J, Steffen W, Noone K, Persson Å, III FSC, Lambin E, Lenton TM, Scheffer M, Folke C, Schellnhuber H, Nykvist B, Wit CAD, Hughes T, Leeuw Svd, Rodhe H, Sörlin S, Snyder PK, Costanza R, Svedin U, Falkenmark M, Karlberg L, Corell RW, Fabry VJ, Hansen J, Walker B, Liverman D, Richardson K, Crutzen P and Foley J (2009) Planetary boundaries: exploring the safe operating space for humanity. *Ecology and Society* **14**, 32 <http://www.ecologyandsociety.org/vol14/iss2/art32/>.

Sala OE, Chapin FS, Armesto JJ, Berlow E, Bloomfield J, Dirzo R, Huber-Sanwald E, Huenneke LF, Jackson RB, Kinzig A, Leemans R, Lodge DM, Mooney HA, Oesterheld M, Poff NL, Sykes MT, Walker BH, Walker M and Wall DH (2000) Biodiversity – global biodiversity scenarios for the year 2100. *Science* **287**, 1770–1774.

Sattler PS and Taylor MFJ (2008) 'Building Nature's Safety Net 2008. Progress on the Directions for the National Reserve System'. WWF–Australia, Sydney.

South Australian Government Department for Environment and Heritage (2009) Biodiversity. Government of South Australia, Adelaide, <http://www.environment.sa.gov.au/biodiversity/index.html>.

Spratt D and Sutton P (2008) *Climate Code Red: The Case for Emergency Action.* Scribe Publications, Melbourne.

Starr R, Newfrock J and Delurey M (2003) Enterprise resilience: Managing risk in the networked economy. *Strategy + Business* **30**, [online], <http://www.strategy–business.com/article/8375>.

Sterman JD (2000) *Business Dynamics. Systems Thinking and Modeling for a Complex World.* Irwin McGraw-Hill, Boston.

Tongway DJ and Hindley NL (2004) Landscape Function Analysis: Procedures for Monitoring and Assessing Landscapes. CSIRO Sustainable Ecosystems, Brisbane.

van Opstal D (2007) 'The resilient economy: Integrating competitiveness and security.' Council on Competitiveness, Washington, DC, <http://podcast.tisp.org/index.cfm?pk=download&id=11018&pid=10261>.

Victorian Government Department of Sustainability and the Environment (2009) Victoria's Biodiversity Strategy. Victorian Government, Melbourne, <http://www.dse.vic.gov.au/DSE/nrence.nsf/childdocs/–8946409900BAC6344A256B260015D4AF–F20C24316259FF3FCA256EE700077CB3?open>.

Walker B and Salt D (2006) *Resilience Thinking: Sustaining Ecosystems and People in a Changing World.* Island Press, Washington, DC.

Walker B, Holling CS, Carpenter SR and Kinzig A (2004) Resilience, adaptability and transformability in social–ecological systems. *Ecology and Society* **9**, 5 [online], <http://www.ecologyandsociety.org/vol9/iss2/art5/>.

Walker B, Kinzig A and Langridge J (1999) Plant attribute diversity, resilience and ecosystem function: The nature and significance of dominant and minor species. *Ecosystems* **2**, 95–113.

Western Australian Government Department of Environment and Conservation (2006) Draft – A 100-year Biodiversity Conservation Strategy for Western Australia: Blueprint to the Bicentenary in 2029. Government of Western Australia, Perth, <http://www.naturebase.net/haveyoursay>.

Williams J, Read C, Norton A, Dovers S, Burgman M, Proctor W and Anderson H (2001) Biodiversity, Australia State of the Environment Report 2001 (Theme Report). CSIRO Publishing on behalf of the Department of the Environment and Heritage, Canberra.

Wilson K, Carwardine J and Possingham H (2009) Setting conservation priorities. *Annals of the New York Academy of Sciences* **1162**, 237–264.

# CHAPTER 16

# Climate change – a resilience perspective

Paul Barratt, Graeme Pearman and Mike Waller

## Abstract

In fashioning its adaptive response to climate change, Australia needs to be resilient not only to changes in precipitation, temperature and weather patterns, but also to changes in our terms of trade, destruction of our tourist icons, changes in the social, economic and environmental circumstances of countries in our region and increasing demands upon the humanitarian capabilities of the Australian Defence Force and Australian non-government organisations. Our domestic policies and measures must be deeply integrated into global discussions and agreements. Uncertainty on this issue is not a reason for delaying decisions but flexibility can be maintained through application of a portfolio approach to energy options while national and international experience are developed.

## Introduction

The climate of the earth is changing, , and the evidence is strong that this is as a result of human activities (IPCC 2007; Richardson *et al.* 2009). Climate change as an issue includes the science that underpins our knowledge of how and why these changes are unfolding, the physical and biological consequences of these changes, how ecosystems may adapt and the societal consequences in response to the changes. The issue presents a striking case study of the need for resilience, first in the need for policies that deliver resilience in the face of risk and uncertainty, and second in the need for public policy which is itself resilient.

It also presents a classic illustration of the requirement to analyse resilience at geographical scales above and below the scale in question. Thus, to analyse the impact of climate change on Australia as a whole we need to consider the impact of climate change on the nation in the context of changes globally and regionally, and sub-nationally and locally.

## Characteristics of the climate change issue

Climate change as an issue is characterised by great complexity in the mathematical sense; it has a great number of interconnected variables. Everything is connected to everything else and small changes in one variable can have profound consequences for other aspects of life, in different and sometimes unexpected geographical locations. Geophysical changes have ecological and economic consequences. Economic conditions affect the technical options that are available to us and the rate at which they are developed, which in turn affect the growth trajectory of the whole family of greenhouse gas emissions.

This complexity means, in turn, that we are forced to make our decisions in circumstances of great uncertainty and under circumstances in which we cannot afford to wait until all or even most of the uncertainties are resolved. As Professor Ross Garnaut put it in the final report of his Review (Garnaut 2008 p. 300), important climate change decisions must be made now despite innumerable scientific, geopolitical and economic uncertainties about the:

- strength of the tendency for global emissions to continue increasing;
- relationship between the accumulation of greenhouse gases in the atmosphere and global warming and in particular the regional manifestations of climate change;
- nature, timing and extent of local biophysical effects on  Australia and elsewhere as a result of the extent of climate response;
- level of ambition and the likelihood of international cooperation to reduce greenhouse gas emissions;
- development and costs of new technologies that reduce our reliance on emissions-intensive processes; and
- adaptation choices that will be available domestically and internationally, and their cost.

The combination of great complexity and a large portfolio of uncertainties means, in turn, that there is great unpredictability. Small changes in any of the variables can produce large and unexpected changes: changes that may not necessarily be incremental, but potentially precipitous; changes that may be irreversible over timescales of centuries to millennia. The policy framework required for an adequate response to climate change needs to be able to cope with that unpredictability and those timescales.

The reason that decisions must be made with urgency against the background of all of this uncertainty is that we face potentially very serious consequences, many of them irreversible, and there is reason to believe that they are approaching us more rapidly than conservative scientific assessments have indicated. Since the Fourth Report of the Intergovernmental Panel on Climate Change was published in 2007, there has been significant change in both scientific understanding and the observed impacts of climate change. The onset of measurable phenomena appears to be running ahead of projections. These include sea-level rise and temperature change (Rahmstorf et al. 2007), the summer melting of Arctic sea ice (NSIDC 2009), and other observed changes to polar ice sheets (Velicogna 2009), the rate of carbon dioxide emissions and atmospheric accumulation (Canadell et al. 2007; Raupach et al. 2007), changes in plant and animal species related to climate change in the terrestrial (Rosenzweig et al. 2008) and marine biota (Polovina et al. 2008), to name just a few. The question, 'have scientists been conservative in their assessment of the risk associated with climate change,' is a complex and important one (Pittock 2006).

Assessment that climate change poses severe risks to the planet reflects not perfect knowledge of what may happen, but rather significant probabilities of the occurrence of change combined with the potential for those changes to have huge and perhaps quite sudden impacts (Lenton et al. 2008). To add to this, there is the potential that many of these changes will be irreversible, such as the loss of particular species, or effectively so over long periods of time, such as the potential to reach points where we see the breakdown of large ice sheets (Pritchard et al. 2009) and/or the release of gases from below the frozen Tundra or from the deep ocean.

From an economic perspective, there is very substantial controversy about whether and how catastrophic climate-change risk should be calculated and alternative responses evaluated. From one point of view, the existence of small-probability extreme events renders both the estimates of damage and the resulting trajectory of insurance-based carbon prices highly speculative. From another, the appropriate response to extreme risks (assuming these exist) is to allow for mid-course corrections in pricing and other climate change response strategies (Aldy *et al.* 2009).

Further, what one person or nation might see as an economically advantageous outcome of climate change might seem disadvantageous from another perspective. For example, the demise of the Arctic ice cap might be seen as a huge opportunity, perhaps worth billions of dollars each year, in terms of reduced shipping costs in trade between the countries of the region or increased access to the resources on the seabed of the Arctic Ocean. On the other hand, currently there is no clear agreement concerning ownership of such resources, so that this change brings a potential risk of international conflict over these resources, or at least calls for the development of rules governing this economically and strategically vital region (Borgerson 2008). Alternatively, it might be concluded that these potential economic gains weigh poorly against the massive changes to the environment or to the regional energy budget with consequences for natural ecosystems of the region and potentially the further destabilisation of the Greenland ice sheet.

Finally, fashioning an appropriate response to climate change raises very important equity issues, both between nation states at different stages of industrialisation and within Australia. Dealing with these equity issues will constrain the available portfolio of responses.

The equity issue between nation states is largely a function of the length of time that key greenhouse gases, notably carbon dioxide, are resident in the atmosphere once they are emitted. This means that most of the total volume of anthropogenic carbon dioxide that is currently in the atmosphere and approaching dangerous levels is an accumulation of the emissions released by the key industrialised nations over the last century or more. Even rapidly developing countries like China and India have made a relatively modest contribution to the historic accumulation of greenhouse gases. The poorest countries in the world have barely begun to contribute. They cannot raise their living standards without raising their energy production, and they cannot be expected to remain poor because they have come late to the game and there is now a call to limit their emissions.

This international equity issue will continue to be a fundamental driver of any internationally negotiated climate change settlement.

Within Australian society, equity issues arise because energy costs and the cost of embedded energy in basic goods and services like food and transport form a much higher proportion of the budgets of low-income households than they do for the better-off in our society. Accordingly, responses to climate change that use market-related mechanisms, like energy price, or regulated responses requiring electricity distributors to use a mandated proportion of higher cost electricity from renewable sources, will have a disproportionate impact on people on low incomes. Policy will need to compensate for this, and the extent and nature of the compensation will feed its own consequences into the climate system and all that issues from it. Further, across the subregions of Australia, the largely different levels and nature of expected climate change and the different socio-economic activities mean that each region has contributed, and will contribute, differently to the climate change issue. Each region also is likely to be differently affected by climate change and will have different capacity to respond to it.

Surprisingly, therefore, unlike the member states of the European Union, where several years ago recognition of the economic and development inequities led to agreed differentiation of emissions reduction targets, such discussion in Australia has only just surfaced in the late stages of planning for a national emissions trading scheme. Indeed, often such issues have been raised largely as a reason for inaction that adds to the overall tendency to blame others and avoid personal or regional responsibilities.

The key point to be borne in mind is that small adjustments in any of the variables can produce large and unexpected changes in other parameters, leading to a requirement for the policy framework itself to be resilient.

Of course, climate change as an issue does not exist in a vacuum, but rather in the real world of concomitant yet diverse needs relating to health, water and the economic development of different nations. Likewise, those sectors of the Australian economy likely to be affected by climate change such as water, agriculture, coastal settlements, biodiversity, energy and their interactions, call out for policy in which benefits can be achieved simultaneously in multiple sectors. Such multi-sectoral planning is largely inconsistent with existing systems of sectorally divided:

- knowledge-generation within research organisations, that often fails to underpin decisions that need to be inclusive of wealth generation, social realities and broader human aspirations and environmental imperatives that span the realms of economics, physical and social sciences;
- activities in the corporate world, in which the nature of an individual enterprise can work against the incorporation of other views/ideas about directions and the future; and
- modes of operation of government departments.

Accordingly, we will now explore the attributes of a policy framework that would itself be resilient in addition to delivering resilience.

## Key attributes of polices that are resilient in the face of climate change

We propose the following as key attributes of any public policy framework that would be resilient in the face of substantial and unexpected change.

### *It will still be applicable if matters do not turn out quite as we expect*

Resilient policy will not seek to alight on a single projected point in the future, or a narrow range of points, because we can never know the future with sufficient precision. This is particularly the case with complex non-linear systems, like the climate and some systems such as ecosystems that depend on it, because small departures from the projected trajectory can produce very large changes in the system as a whole, potentially tipping it into a different state altogether. Also, the potential changes are so large that not only are the direct effects of climate change important but so are the second-order effects – how ecosystems re-balance their composition and how agriculture or energy systems adjust.

Accordingly, resilient policy will aim to cover as wide a range of credible outcomes as possible. Second-order effects in relation to climate change include changes in our terms of trade and destruction of our tourist icons. These lead to changes in the patterns of tourism, the sourcing and delivery of energy and consequential changes in the patterns of investment and employment. Other second-order effects include changes in the social, economic and environmental circumstances of countries in our region and increasing demands upon the humanitarian capabilities of the Australian Defence Force and Australian NGOs.

The requirement for policy to remain applicable if things do not turn out as we expect is particularly important in the field of climate change because the levels of certainty required for scientific 'proof' are quite different from the probabilistic approaches that inform risk management (Pearman and Härtel 2010). The requirement for a resilient policy framework is also very clear because, to the extent that mitigation fails to be sufficient to keep global warming within 'safe' limits (and we are not really sure what those 'safe' limits are), the policy framework needs to be able to bring into play measures that:

- are directed to extracting carbon from the atmosphere, rather than just abating emissions, and
- enable Australia to adapt to the changed circumstances including, *in extremis*, to respond to any irreversible tipping points that the world climate system might pass.

Current political arguments appear to be focused on the European Union position that the global mean temperature rise needs to be contained at or below 2°C (approximately equivalent to the stabilisation of greenhouse-gas concentrations at 450 ppmv $CO_2e^1$) to avoid dangerous consequences:

> *'the Council ... ACKNOWLEDGES that to meet the ultimate objective of the UNFCCC to prevent dangerous anthropogenic interference with the climate system, overall global temperature increase should not exceed 2°C above pre-industrial levels '* (European Council 2004, p. 29).

Yet recent analyses (Parry *et al.* 2009) show that even a peaking of global greenhouse gas emissions as early as 2015 would lead to ~50% chance of temperatures exceeding this level, and that it may not avoid more substantial changes to glaciation in both hemispheres and to the biosphere. Thus within the science community there are concerns that this agreed target itself may be too high (e.g. Hanson *et al.* 2007) and many scientists are now proposing that a global target of 350 ppmv $CO_2e$ will be required to avoid reaching this 2°C level and avoid concomitant consequences. If nothing else, this simply suggests that there is a risk that they are correct and that current policy development should be cognisant of this and appropriately structured to allow for changes to these targets. If they are correct it also implies that the task is not just about lowering greenhouse-gas emissions, but it is also about removing these gases from the atmosphere and this raises, in some cases, significantly different challenges.

## It is supported by the available evidence

This is a weaker test than requiring unassailable proof that the policy is 'the best' or that 'it works'. We may not have the necessary evidence to meet those sterner tests and we may have to exercise a considerable degree of judgement, but we ought to be able to expect that policy will not fly in the face of current human knowledge and understanding. Policy must be consistent with all of the knowledge and evidence that we have, even if there are gaps in our knowledge that we have to fill as best we can with informed judgements; even if this evidence flies in the face of conservative or ideologically held views of the way things are and the way they therefore should remain. Waiting for 'perfect' knowledge will probably ensure phenomena that threaten a resilient future.

## It commands wide public understanding and support

There are two levels of understanding and support that contribute to resilience. The first level is when the public understands that there is a problem and agrees that action must be taken.

The deeper level is reached when the public understands the arguments for the particular measures that are adopted to address the problem and agrees that those are the best available measures on the basis of current knowledge. Policy that is not understood by the public cannot be considered resilient. The public's understanding must extend to an understanding of the scale of a relevant policy response. There is not much point in mobilising public support for climate change action if the public is left with the impression that the singular actions like signing the Kyoto Protocol or putting solar collectors on the rooftops of schools, as useful as they might be, will suffice.

### It commands support across a broad range of the political spectrum

This is a weaker test than 'bipartisanship', which is often a chimera. It is not necessary that our two main political parties agree on the policy solution in precise detail. All that is required is that there is a sufficient measure of agreement that a change of government is not likely to produce radical change in the policy. This was a key idea, emerging from the Prime Minister's 2020 Summit in 2007, of the establishment of a statutory body to deal with the issue of climate change, designed to be the keeper of emerging and ongoing knowledge and the non-political resource for underpinning the strategic directions of overall policy. The purpose was clear: climate change is too important an issue and the political responses likely to be so significant that short-term and politically motivated diversions from long-term imperatives should not dominate; rather there should be more of a multi-partisan approach.

### It is practical and can be implemented

Allowing for lags in effecting results, the policy will mitigate or resolve the problem(s) it sets out to address. As Professor Garnaut notes in his Final Report (Garnaut 2008, p. xxviii):

> 'The climate change policy discussion has been bogged in delusion, in Australia and elsewhere. Mitigation targets are defined and sometimes agreed internationally without the difficult work being done, to make sure that the separate numbers add up to desired solutions and to make sure that there are realistic paths to where we commit ourselves to go'.

### It is equitable

Policy will be neither resilient nor sustainable if significant sectors of society are left feeling that they are carrying a disproportionate share of the burden or receiving an inadequate share of the benefits. This imposes strong obligations upon government to engage in a sustained public education campaign to ensure that the public understands the policy framework and to compensate the less well off in society for the disproportionate impact that the vagaries of regional change and the emissions abatement measures will have upon low-income households.

## Significant barriers to resilient policies to deliver resilience

There are several characteristics of any society that stand as major impediments to the resilience of policy frameworks that are designed to confer resilience in the face of rapid and surprising change. It is important that they be understood and taken into account when constructing the resilient policy framework, because they indicate that there is more to policy success than explaining what needs to be done, important as that is, and also that the failure of organisations and individuals to behave as the policy-maker might wish is not necessarily a function of ignorance, ill-will, irresponsibility or failure to 'get it'. Some of the most important social and institutional barriers are outlined below.

### Human behaviour

One of the biggest and least understood impediments to implementation appears to be psychological responses to highly threatening situations. The behaviour of individuals is strongly preconditioned by culture, circumstances, education, perceptions of what constitutes personal success, consumerism, markets and advertising and, in some cases, genetics (Hulme 2000; APS 2008; Adger *et al.* 2009; APA 2009; Pearman and Härtel 2010).

By and large, this behaviour is consistent with past or current paradigms but may not be applicable in a future world. For example, the way individuals are emotionally affected by threatening situations and indeed how they cope with these emotions varies widely. Each approach is important to the individual and no one response is necessarily right or wrong. The reality is that as humans we have a diversity of coping responses that include, for example:

- active denial (*'climate change is not happening'*; *'it is a millennarian cult'*);
- passive denial (*'I don't want to think about it, it is all too complicated'*);
- blame (*'Australia is an insignificant proportion of total emissions, nothing we do can make any difference'*; *'It's all the Prime Minister's fault'*; *'It's all China's fault'*);
- vested interests (insistence that we should not do anything until everyone else agrees to tackle the problem; defence of existing values; *'something must be done but not at the expense of jobs, trade competitiveness, personal welfare or lifestyle, etc.'*); and
- narrow perspective (enthusiastic support for poorly evaluated and thus not very helpful options; *'it can all be done with renewable energy'*).

A specific aspect of the role of human behaviour as a barrier to resilient policy resides in the fact that human experience is no guide to the magnitude and urgency of the climate change issue. For example, human experience is well versed in the influence of day-to-day or month-to-month variations of temperature that in magnitude far exceed those experienced or antici-pated as global average changes. There is no cognisance of or experience within individuals concerning the importance of such 'small' changes in global average temperature. This is something that the geological record teaches the scientific community about the sensitivity of systems, but not something that individuals understand.

### Societal norms

Accumulated sets of individual behaviours make up socially acceptable patterns of behaviour and accepted notions of important issues like what constitutes success, the engagement in work, the pursuit of wealth and the concept of happiness and well-being. Many of these norms have evolved and are held, largely unconsciously, by individuals, reflecting cultural, educa-tional, family and geographical preconditions. Significantly, the combined influences of these, over time, have underpinned the evolution of the kinds of social infrastructure we have today; our governance structures, social institutions and community-held norms of behaviour. All of these have influenced why we have the created the climate change issue – and perhaps other issues that suggest a non-sustainable future (Pearman and Härtel 2010) – and why, without better understanding of these human conditions, they threaten the timely response required to manage the issue.

### Institutional rigidities

The organisations and rules that are central to the way modern society operates have strong biases in favour of preserving existing norms and power structures. This is a source of strength in periods of stability, allowing people to plan and commit the time and money needed to provide the infrastructure and services that underpin modern economies. It can, however, become a major problem when external circumstances demand significant structural change. In defending their turf, entrenched special interest groups can become a major impediment to change as the possible costs to their own sectional interests dominate consideration of the wider societal benefits of the structural changes required to respond to a changed external environment. Australia confronted exactly these tensions in the early 1980s in relation to the arguments over tariff reform and floating the currency.

### Knowledge capture

This refers to the means by which new or newly relevant knowledge is assimilated by those who need to use it or whose behaviour needs to be modified in the light of it. The processes are largely *ad hoc*. There are multiple pathways, some of which are open to abuse, and there are few rules of engagement. What is more, knowledge concerning complex issues such as climate change is generated within an operating environment of broad disciplinary areas: physical and biological sciences, social sciences, economics and engineering. Interpretation of this knowledge in appropriate descriptions of the world and establishing real-world options is a challenge with current knowledge-generation frameworks.

## Accepting the challenges

The mitigation of the climate-change issue presents Australian policy makers and the community at large with a diabolical problem.[2] The effects of climate change will manifest themselves over a long period of time but we must make decisions about them now. We must make those decisions in the face of considerable uncertainty about the full extent and nature of the effects of climate change, or the times at which any of the diverse effects will become important enough to make a difference to our lives. We are not able to say with certainty how much climate change is 'dangerous', although there is good reason to believe that we are close to that point now and there is some reason to say that we have already passed the level of aggregate emissions that will give rise to 'dangerous' climate change. Nor are we able to say with any certainty what balance we should strike between mitigation of climate change and adaptation to it.

We must make important decisions in the face of uncertainty about the performance and cost of the various technological options that are still in the development stage and at this stage we are not sure what everyone else is going to do. And, as noted above, small changes can have major and unexpected effects because of the non-linear nature of the mathematics of complex systems.

As Professor Garnaut noted in his Final Report, it is an error to think that uncertainty provides good reason for delaying decisions to start effective mitigation. Delay is itself a decision. Uncertainty surrounding climate change is a reason for disciplined analysis and decision, not for delaying decisions (Garnaut 2008, p. xxviii).

As part of this process, it is important to make two important distinctions: the distinction between uncertainty and risk, and the distinction between the standards of certainty that would satisfy a scientist and the levels of risk that a risk manager would take seriously.

### Uncertainty and risk

Risk relates to an event that can be placed on a known probability distribution. We know when we toss a coin that, over enough trials, it will come down heads 50% of the time. There are many situations that are similar enough to other situations experienced in the past for us to have a good 'feel' for where an outcome would sit on the probability distribution.

There is uncertainty when an event is of a kind that has no close precedents, or we have insufficient knowledge about it, for the probability distribution of outcomes to be defined with precision or where an event is too far from understood events for related experience to be helpful in foreseeing possible outcomes (Garnaut 2008, p. 8).

Although there is a clear conceptual distinction between risk and uncertainty – one that is very important for industries like the insurance industry – they are in fact the ends of a single spectrum. In climate change, much of the time we are at the 'uncertainty' end of the spectrum rather than the 'risk' end; we have a poor understanding of the probabilities of the potentially catastrophic outcomes we are attempting to address but we know they are potentially important.

### 'Proof' versus risk management

Scientific argumentation looks for 'proof' that meets very strong tests of probability; usually a hypothesis under test is accepted if there is 99% certainty it is proven. The International Panel on Climate Change (IPCC 2005) uses phrases like 'virtually certain' when the probability is >99%, 'very likely' when the probability >90%, and so on. Science also looks for causal pathways that explain why the observed phenomena occur, not simply correlations of statistical data.

Risk managers, on the other hand, apply a quite different discipline. They have to match the probability of an outcome with its potential consequence. An event in the scientist's 'very unlikely' category (10% > probability >1%) would, if it has seriously adverse consequences, be something that a risk manager would take very seriously and act to protect against.

The stringent tests of proof characteristic of the scientific community mean that the projected extent and consequences of global warming will always be on the conservative side, as comparison of each of the four reports of the International Panel on Climate Change with subsequent scientific measurements suggest. In every case the observed trajectory has been significantly faster than the projections based upon conservative readings of the science.

### Spreading the risk: a portfolio approach

It is not possible at this stage to be prescriptive about the optimum technical/policy mix that will deliver the deep cuts we will be required to achieve by the middle of the century, because of the uncertain technical and commercial trajectories of the alternative technologies that will be on offer. This reflects the intrinsic technical risk associated with the engineering and process design, uncertainty about how domestic and international greenhouse policies will evolve, unforeseen costs of the changing levels of demand and timescales for delivery and resource availability.

A number of major technical and commercial uncertainties about new emissions reduction technologies are likely to be resolved in the period 2015–2025. In the face of these uncertainties, a resilient policy would be one that minimised large-scale but irreversible commitments of capital and other scarce resources to technology options with successful payoffs that only deliver in a narrow range of circumstances. Instead, it will be important for Australia to put itself in a position to be a smart utiliser of appropriate new technologies as they are proven to be both technically and economically viable. In the meantime, risk should be minimised through the portfolio approach described below.

In the present climate of uncertainty, the need is to establish and sustain a portfolio of options that, in its entirety, is robust under a wide range of technical and commercial and/or policy settings. This involves promoting options on potential component technologies and emission-reduction measures that exhibit the following characteristics:

- **feasibility** – deliver the target emissions reductions over the policy period (this is, to some, what can be delivered without changes from current paradigms of behaviour and development);

- **adaptability** – prepare the economy to be adaptable enough to take up opportunities quickly and effectively as they emerge;
- **backup capacity** – retain spare capacity to be called on in the event of difficulties (e.g. from international resource pressures) or the need for further action (e.g. in the light of new climate knowledge);
- **no-regrets/low risk** – take no-regrets/low risk measures and satisfy short term needs while delaying large irreversible commitments to uncertain technologies where possible;
- **learning through experience** – learn about the relevant developments, including exploratory demonstration/pilot programs, for the most promising options; and
- **building technological skill** – build technological skill and diversity so as to be in a position to take advantage of new technologies as uncertainties are resolved.

### Start early

Starting now will reduce the risk of disruptive change in the future. Time is a critical advantage in addressing the challenges of the stiff targets we will face and the uncertainties of the optimal adjustment path. Making steady progress now, within the framework of the portfolio approach described above, will both promote learning and avoid the need for major and disruptive change later on and avoid the social and economic cost of a crash program later in the century.

### Market-based solutions

The most economically efficient way to achieve the optimum technology and policy mix over time will be to place maximum reliance on solutions created within a framework that maximises the effective application of market forces to the climate change problem. Over time the climate change and environmental costs of greenhouse-gas emissions should be internalised through measures that attach a price to carbon, such as carbon trading. This will enable both investors and consumers to make rational choices between the available low emission technologies on the basis of price, performance and reliability.

For maximum effectiveness, however, this requires governments to establish a set of pre-conditions: the rule of law and sanctity of contracts; recognition and regulation of non-market 'externalities'; an incentive-compatible and equitable tax regime; perfect competition; and symmetry in international trade in which all nations possess open capital accounts and floating exchange rates.

Many of these pre-conditions are honoured as much in the breach as in the observance, giving rise to significant challenges for policy design and implementation and reduced resilience of climate change policies:

- while pricing carbon is unarguably a move in the right direction by assisting to internalise the external environmental costs of carbon emissions, there is a large degree of uncertainty and disagreement about the scale of the externality and hence the appropriate price;
- the markets for important elements of carbon-producing activities are far from perfect, either involving major barriers to entry (e.g. in the form of regulations and pre-existing, often state-financed, energy infrastructure) – there are also significant areas of energy demand where information/split incentives provide major barriers to pricing mechanisms and hence call for alternative/complementary approaches; and
- even where internalising costs is practically possible and desirable from a broad societal perspective, narrow sectional interests can either blunt or largely avoid the implementation of effective price signals, for example:

- the granting of excessive amounts of free permits to large emitters, thereby shifting the costs to the broader community; and
- resistance to, or rejection of, road-pricing that offers multiple and broad-scale social and economic benefits in terms of avoided economic costs of congestion, lower emissions and more efficient use of scarce infrastructure.

## Non-partisanship

It will be clear from the above that the establishment of an appropriately resilient response to the challenge of climate change is a complex and difficult task and one that will require frank and forthright communication with the public; for without public support it will fail.

It is vital, therefore, that the legitimate debate that is to be had about many aspects of our national response be based upon the science as we know it and the facts of the situation being addressed. To the extent that political point-scoring results in the spread of disinformation, the difficulty of the task and the cost to our society will be greatly increased.

## Conclusions

Australia faces a diabolical problem in confronting the issue of climate change. The effects of climate change will manifest themselves over a long period of time but we must make decisions about them now. We must make those decisions in the face of considerable uncertainty about the full extent and nature of the effects of climate change, or the time at which the effects will make a significant difference to our lives.

In order to meet this challenge we must adopt a policy framework that confers resilience in the face of risk and uncertainty and which itself is resilient; able to continue to function in a relevant manner if the future trajectory of climate impacts diverges markedly from what we currently expect.

This means, *inter alia*, that we must develop policy frameworks that are consistent with all of the available evidence, that command wide public understanding and support, including support across a broad range of the political spectrum, that are practicable, can be implemented and on a scale that delivers changes of the magnitude that we require, that are equitable and that take account of the human factors that are barriers to effective change.

We must start taking effective action now in order to avoid having to undertake a costly crash program later. We should take a 'portfolio' approach, so that we are not over-reliant on a narrow range of measures that may not live up to their promise and recognise that the most economically efficient way to achieve the optimum technology and policy mix over time will be to place maximum reliance on market-based solutions.

What all of the above adds up to is that our policy response must be flexible and adaptable and be able to respond to new climate knowledge and new technologies as they become available.

*Paul Barratt AO is a Director of Australia21 and a former Secretary of the Departments of Primary Industries and Energy, and Defence. He has an honours degree in physics and an arts degree in Asian Civilisations and economics.*

*Dr Graeme Pearman AM is an Australia21 Fellow and Leader of the Australia21 Energy Project. He has been Chief of the Division of the CSIRO Climate Program. In 2003 he was awarded a Federation Medal for services to science.*

*Mike Waller is a director of Heuris Partners, a consulting company specialising in strategy development. Prior to establishing Heuris, he spent nearly six years with BHP Ltd, as Chief Economist and head of environment and community-relations policy. Before that, Mike held senior positions in the UK Treasury and Australian public service. He holds an honours degree in economics and has undertaken executive training at the London Business School. Mike is a Director of Australia21.*

## Endnotes

1    Each greenhouse gas has a different molecular structure, absorption capacity and residence time in the atmosphere. While carbon dioxide is the key greenhouse gas, the effect of the others, particularly methane, nitrous oxide and some chlorofluorocarbons, is added as if it were replaced by an amount of carbon dioxide having an equivalent effect over 100 years ($CO_2e$).

2    The term 'diabolical' was used to describe the climate change issue by Garnaut (2008). Other terms appropriate in considering such multi-dimensional problems might be 'complex adaptive systems', 'chaotic systems' or 'non-linear systems'.

## References

Adger NW, Dessai S, Goulden M, Hulme M, Lorenzoni I, Nelson DR, Naess LO, Wolf J and Wreford A (2009) Are there social limits to adaptation to climate change? *Climatic Change* **93**, 335–354.

Aldy JE, Krupnick AJ, Newel RG, Parry IWH and Pizer WA (2009) Designing Climate Mitigation Policy. Resources for the Future, Washington, DC, <http://www.rff.org/RFF/Documents/RFF-DP-08-16.pdf>.

APA (American Psychological Association) (2009) *Psychology and Global Climate Change: Addressing a Multi-faceted Phenomenon and Set of Challenges.* The American Psychological Association, Washington, DC, < http://www.apa.org/science/climate-change/>.

APS (Australian Psychological Society) (2008) *Climate Change: What You Can Do.* Australian Psychological Society, Melbourne, <http://www.psychology.org.au/publications/tip_sheets/climate/>.

Borgerson SG (2008) The economic and security implications of global warming. *Foreign Affairs* **87**, 63–77.

Canadell JG, Le Quéré C, Raupach MR, Field CB, Buitehuis ET, Ciais P, Conway TJ, Gillett NP, Houghton RA and Marland G (2007) Contributions to accelerating atmospheric $CO_2$ growth from economic activity, carbon intensity and efficiency of natural sinks. *Proceedings of the National Academy of Science* **104**, 18866–18870.

European Council (2004) Spring European Council, 25–26 March 2004 – Key Messages from Sectoral Councils. Document 7631/04 (Annex), Council of the European Union, Brussels, <http://www.consilium.europa.eu/uedocs/cms_data/docs/pressdata/en/misc/79589.pdf>.

Garnaut R (2008) *The Garnaut Climate Change Report – Final Report.* Cambridge University Press, Cambridge.

Hansen J, Sato M, Ruedy R, Kharecha P, Lacis A, Miller R, Nazarenko L, Lo K, Schmidt GA, Russell G, Aleinov I, Bauer S, Baum E, Cairns B, Canuto V, Chandler M, Cheng Y, Cohen A, Del Genio A, Faluvegi G, Fleming E, Friend A, Hall T, Jackman C, Jonas J, Kelley M, Kiang NY, Koch D, Labow G, Lerner J, Menon S, Novakov T, Oinas V, Perlwitz Ja,

Perlwitz Ju, Rind D, Romanou A, Schmunk R, Shindell D, Stone P, Sun S, Streets D, Tausnev N, Thresher D, Unger N, Yoa M and Zhang S (2007) Dangerous human-made interference with climate: a GISS modelE study. *Atmospheric Chemistry and Physics* **7**, 2287–2312.

Hulme M (2000) *Why We Disagree about Climate Change: Understanding Controversy, Inaction and Opportunity.* Cambridge University Press, Cambridge.

IPCC (Intergovernmental Panel on Climate Change) (2005). Guidance Notes for Lead Authors of the IPCC Fourth Assessment Report on Addressing Uncertainties. Intergovernmental Panel on Climate Change, Geneva, <http://www.ipcc.ch/pdf/assessment-report/ar4/wg1/ar4-uncertaintyguidancenote.pdf>.

IPCC (Intergovernmental Panel on Climate Change) (2007) 'Climate Change 2007. The Physical Science Basis'. Working Group I of the IPCC Fourth Assessment Report. (Eds S Solomon *et al.*, Cambridge University Press, Cambridge, <http://www.ipcc.ch/ipccreports/ar4-wg1.htm>.

NSIDC (National Snow and Ice Data Centre) (2009) State of the Cryosphere. Is the Cryosphere Sending Signals About Climate Change? National Snow and Ice Data Centre, Colorado, <http://nsidc.org/sotc/sea_ice.html>.

Lenton TM, Held H, Kriegler EW, Hall JW, Lucht W, Rahmstorf S and Schellnhuber HJ (2008) Tipping elements in the Earth's climate systems. *Proceedings of the National Academy of Science* **105**, 1786–1793.

Pearman GI and Härtel CEJ (2010) Climate change: Are we up to the challenge? In *Greenhouse 09: Living with Climate Change.* (Eds I Jubb, P Holper and W Cai) pp. xx–xx. CSIRO Publishing, Melbourne.

Pittock AB (2006) Are scientists underestimating climate change? *Eos Transactions of the American Geophysical Union* **87**(34), 340.

Polovina JJ, Howell EA and Abecassis M (2008) Ocean's least productive waters are expanding. *Geophysical Research Letters* **35**, L03618, doi:10.1029/2007GL031745.

Pritchard HD, Arthern RJ, Vaughan DG and Edwards LA (2009) Extensive dynamic thinning on the margins of the Greenland and Antarctic ice sheets. *Nature* **461**, 971–975.

Rahmstorf S, Cazenave A, Church JA, Hansen JE, Keeling RF, Parker DE and Somerville RCJ (2007) Recent climate observations compared to projections. *Science* **316**, 709, doi: 10.1126/science.1136843.

Raupach MR, Marland G, Ciais P, Le Quéré C, Canadell JG, Klepper G and Field CB (2007) Global and regional drivers of accelerating $CO_2$ emissions. *Proceedings of the National Academy of Science* **104**, 10 288–10 293.

Richardson K, Steffen W, Schellnhuber HJ, Alcamo J, Barker T, Kammen DM, Leemans R, Liverman D, Munasinghe M, Osman-Elasha B, Stern N and Wæver, O (2009) 'Climate Change: Global Risks, Challenges and Decisions. Synthesis Report of the Climate Congress, Copenhagen, March 10–12, 2009'. International Alliance of Research Universities, University of Copenhagen, Copenhagen.

Rosenzweig C, Karoly D, Vicarelli M, Neofotis P, Wu Q, Casassa G, Menzel A, Root TL, Estrella N, Seguin B, Tryjanowski P, Liu C, Rawlins S and Imeson A (2008) Attributing physical and biological impacts to anthropogenic climate change. *Nature* **453**, 353–358.

Velicogna I (2009) Increasing rates of ice mass loss from the Greenland and Antarctic ice sheets revealed by GRACE. *Geophysical Research Letters* **36**, L19503, doi: 10.1029/2009GL040222, 2009.

# CHAPTER 17

# Resilience to global change

Nicky Grigg

## Abstract

Is it possible to thrive in 'the anthropocene', a world characterised by human-induced global change? To do so would be to be resilient to the impacts of global change. What such resilience would look like and how it can be achieved are highly uncertain. Nevertheless, viewing the problem through a systems-resilience lens offers insights to inform a wise mixture of mitigation and adaptation strategies. A common and significant barrier to action is the various ways in which actions are separated from impacts. Time and space separate impacts from actions, but there are also more subtle drivers of separation: the classification of knowledge into different disciplines; decision-making confined to narrow terms of reference; the interplay between individual and collective interests; and, ironically, a focus on local efficiency. These forms of separation lead to a significant barrier to action: the distribution of people wanting change is very different in time and space to the distribution of people with the means to make the changes. Shared global ethical principles are needed to negotiate this barrier and mediate a more resilient relationship between humans and Earth.

## A safe operating space for humanity

Earth scientists argue that the planet has been so changed by human activity that our era warrants being viewed as a new geological epoch, one characterised by the impact of humans: 'the anthropocene' (Steffen *et al.* 2007). 'Global change' is the term used to refer to this suite of human-induced changes. Global change encompasses climate change, but includes a myriad of other changes that are having global-scale impacts.

To tackle climate change requires a focus on the global carbon cycle, whereas to tackle global change requires an expanded view. An analysis in Nature written by members of the Stockholm Resilience Centre (Rockström *et al.* 2009) suggests a scope that encompasses nine aspects of global change:

1. climate change;
2. ocean acidification;
3. stratospheric ozone depletion;
4. changes to global nitrogen and phosphorus cycles;
5. global freshwater use;
6. land-use change;

7. loss of biodiversity;
8. build up of particulate material in the atmosphere; and
9. chemical pollution.

These biophysical changes warrant urgent attention in the assessment of leading earth scientists and in the paper published in *Nature*, the authors offer a set of measurable limits defining boundaries within which there is a 'safe operating space for humanity'. Cross these boundaries and humans risk pushing the planet into an entirely different way of functioning. Such change – irreversible on the time scale of a human lifetime – would jeopardise the natural systems we depend upon. The authors suggest that three such boundaries have been crossed already: those for climate change, biodiversity loss and the global nitrogen cycle.

Within the community of international earth-system scientists there is very little argument that human activities are having a rapid, detrimental impact in many crucial parts of the earth system. It is also evident that exceedingly little is known about how far these systems can be changed without causing irreversible damage – the authors readily admit that some of their proposed boundaries are highly uncertain and speculative.

## Missing institutions

Driving the biophysical changes are powerful social forces and in an analysis published in *Science* (Walker *et al.* 2009), again by authors from the Stockholm Resilience Centre, a strong argument was made for the need for social institutions capable of addressing not just the biophysical dimensions of global change but also the human dimensions (including population increase, increasing urbanisation, increased per capita resource use, terrorism, increased antibiotic resistance and increased global connectivity in transport and information networks). The focus of the paper is on the current failure of international institutions (such as international agreements) to tackle these global problems successfully. The authors explain that cooperation in international agreements is difficult to achieve in situations where nations stand to gain from collective cooperation, but stand to gain even more by not cooperating and 'free-riding' on the cooperation of other nations. Furthermore, they point out that all too often international agreements focus on single issues, ignoring the fact that these global problems are overlapping and intertwining.

The authors spell out elements of change that would enable international institutions to be designed so that individual countries are better off participating than not participating, and so that complex interactions between interconnected issues are handled in an intelligent manner. They propose a variety of instruments for facilitating different kinds of interactions. These include international norms that facilitate local understanding of global-scale problems (interactions relating local to global), agreements that account for links between different dimensions of global change (interactions across problem domains), and incentive structures that make cooperation more rewarding than 'free-riding' (interactions between individual and collective interests).

## Resilience to global change

What changes will contribute to resilience to global change, given the nature of the biophysical and human forces involved? The two papers from the Stockholm Resilience Centre point to ways forward, identifying both the aspects of global change needing attention and the nature of global institutions required to deal with such global interconnected problems. Both papers stressed the need to consider connections – connections that link issues across time and space, across topic area and across individual and collective interests. It is customary to conceptualise problems and other systems using diagrams with boxes and arrows, but typically time and funding are allocated to the boxes and not the arrows (Campbell 2006). A characteristic that distinguishes organisations interested in resilience, complex systems or global change is that the arrows, the links between the boxes, are in fact a central focus of their activities.

What are some of the challenges in working on interconnections? It is instructive to consider a climate change example. At a most basic level, responses to climate change fall into two categories: mitigation and adaptation. To mitigate is to recognise the processes responsible for climate change and take actions to slow, stop or reverse those processes. To adapt is to respond to events when they occur or to anticipate likely impacts of climate change and take action to reduce our vulnerability to those impacts. Surprisingly, adaptation and mitigation are usually considered in isolation. An obvious insight from resilience and systems thinking is to consider mitigation and adaptation in tandem and build reinforcing loops between the two so that each support the other (i.e. focus on the connections).Principles for designing such integration between mitigation and adaption strategies, however, are remarkably difficult to develop (Swart and Raes 2007). The difficulties stem from the difference in scale of impact of the two approaches; as a gross generalisation, the benefits of mitigation are felt globally, whereas the benefits of adaptation are experienced locally. The mismatch in scale leads to unwanted trade-offs. For example, using more fossil-fuel based energy to cool buildings and desalinate water may contribute to local adaptation but undermines global carbon emission mitigation efforts. The connections do matter: more attention can be paid to avoiding trade-offs and seeking synergies between adaptation and mitigation, but the separate scales of impact are a key barrier to achieving this.

## Factors working against resilience

It is possible to work conceptually with the system links called for by resilience and systems thinkers, but in practice many system properties act to reinforce separation. Put most simply: actions are separated from impacts and this separation prevents integrated systems approaches in tackling global change. Forms of separation include:

- separation in space. The term 'teleconnection' was originally used by atmospheric scientists to describe a relationship between atmospheric phenomena across large distances. More recently the term has been used to mean any cause–effect relationship that is separated by large distance in the earth system (Adger *et al.* 2009);
- separation in time. Impacts of decisions taken by one generation will be felt by future generations. A stark reminder of this effect is analyses demonstrating that at least 1.4°C of 'committed' global warming is the result of past and current generations' greenhouse gas emissions (Ramanathan and Feng 2008);
- separation due to knowledge classification into different disciplines (e.g. physics, biology, hydrology, ecology, economics, psychology) or due to decision-making being limited to specific foci without a broad enough scope to consider connections (e.g. biodiversity loss or climate change);
- separation due to counter-intuitive chains of cause and effect, typical of highly connected systems with feedback loops;
- separation due to the measurable insignificance of individual actions (e.g. in a world of over six billion people, whether an individual chooses to eat meat or not tomorrow will be measurably insignificant, yet the cumulative impact of more and more people choosing to eat meat is a significant factor for change in humanity's impact on global

biodiversity, water use, carbon emissions and biogeochemical cycles (McMichael *et al.* 2007);

- separation due to interplay between individual and collective interests: '*individually reasonable behaviour leads to a situation in which everyone is worse off than they might have been otherwise*' (Kollock P 1998) (tragedy of the commons and similar social dilemmas); and

- separation due to a focus on efficiency. Concentrating on resource-use efficiency without taking a broader systems view leads to Jevons' Paradox or the 'rebound effect' where improvements in efficiency inadvertently lead to greater overall rates of resource consumption (Polimeni and Polimeni 2006; Turner 2008).

As well as making genuine integration difficult, these many forms of separation lead to a perverse distribution of motivation for change. Local and immediate concerns are more tangible and influential drivers for change than global and future concerns, yet local and immediate concerns have 'non-local' and historical antecedents. When local and immediate concerns are separated in time and space from their cause then there is a systemic problem: the distribution of people wanting change is very different in time and space to the distribution of people with the means to make the changes. This is yet another form of separation – separation in motivation. To express it more poetically, 'Song of the Children' written by Judith Clingan AM (Clingan 1989) had one generation sing to another to foster a shared motivation across generations:

'*Why, O our fathers,*
*Why, O our mothers,*
*Do you not stop the destruction?*'

## Questions of equity

These considerations bring us to questions of equity. As the global discourse slowly moves away from the question of whether to reduce greenhouse gas emissions to how to achieve reductions, the debate shifts from science to ethics: how are emission reductions to be allocated across people and across time? Professor Ross Garnaut couched his recommendations for emission reductions according to basic principles of fairness, outlining what Australia's 'proportionate part' in meeting a global concentration target would be (Garnaut 2008). In a more recent analysis, Dr Michael Raupach and colleagues have analysed mitigation pathways and allocation of emission reductions using the framework that 'cumulative $CO_2$ emissions since industrialisation are a non-renewable resource to be shared among nations' (Raupach *et al.* submitted). It is a well-argued case: peak global warming above pre-industrial temperatures can be predicted from total cumulative $CO_2$ emissions (i.e. the sum of all $CO_2$ since 1751) and these predictions are almost independent of the details of emissions trajectories over time. These features allow the analysis to focus on (a) the cap on cumulative emissions required to prevent dangerous climate change; and (b) the ways in which such a cap can be allocated among people on Earth. The authors explore emission allocation possibilities according to two criteria: equity of access to remaining $CO_2$ emissions and the attribution of past emissions. When constrained by a cap consistent with preventing dangerous climate change, clear insights into feasible and fair mitigation pathways emerged.

It is a powerful analysis, simultaneously highlighting the urgency of the problem (by demonstrating the dramatic impact of delay on the possible mitigation trajectories) and using principles of fairness and pragmatism to outline the range of possibilities for allocating emissions reductions among nations. The authors did not seek to combine the analysis with economic considerations and it would be interesting to do so. A contentious aspect of economic analyses is how to value future expenditure and costs relative to those in the present. Usually encapsulated in the 'discount rate', these assumptions have a significant impact on outcomes of economic analyses of mitigation pathways. Broadly speaking, the higher the discount rate the more delayed mitigation is favoured. The analysis by Raupach and his colleagues provides compelling, robust reasoning for the need for early and rapid mitigation. Their analysis provides a firm biophysical base that integrates ethical principles of fair allocation of a scarce resource and it would be fruitful to perform an economic analysis of mitigation that is grounded on this robust foundation.

Professor Elinor Ostrom won the Nobel Memorial Prize in Economic Sciences 'for her analysis of economic governance, particularly the commons'. Her work has emphasised the importance of institutional diversity, dialogue and conflict resolution, information, rules, infrastructure and readiness to learn and change (Ostrom *et al.* 1999; Dietz *et al.* 2003). According to her work, science has an important role to play, but many other roles and forms of human wisdom and expertise are required to integrate the science into the fabric of our society. Dr Donella Meadows reached very similar conclusions after a lifetime of studying and mathematically modelling human-ecosystem dynamics – the science is important but so too are other human qualities. It is interesting to note the hesitancy with which she and her colleagues voiced these qualities: 'We would like to conclude … by mentioning five other tools we have found helpful, not as the ways to work toward sustainability, but as some ways that have been useful to us. We are a bit hesitant to discuss them because we are not experts in their use and because they require the use of words that do not come easily from the mouths or word processors of scientists. They are considered to be too 'soft' to be taken serious in the cynical public arena. They are: visioning, networking, truth-telling, learning and loving.' (Meadows *et al.* 1993).

Dr Brian Walker and his colleagues anticipate the emergence of peremptory (or 'jus–cogens') norms (Christenson 1988) (such as those now in existence prohibiting slavery, torture and genocide) with a focus on environmental protection (Walker *et al.* 2009). Such a development would be significant as it would provide founding common principles to inform strategies dealing with the forms of separation discussed above and also for bringing out more of the human qualities that have been shown to be effective in tackling problems of global change.

## Conclusion

The Chief Scientist for Australia, Professor Penny Sackett, has stated that ours is a time where we need 'all hands on deck'. Earth-systems scientists have provided clear guidance on those aspects of global change that are of most concern and have indicated global rates and thresholds that we'd be wise to limit ourselves within. Resilience thinkers have indicated why our current institutions are failing us and described the kinds of institutions that would be more effective. A common theme is the need to pay attention to system interconnections and weaken those barriers that prevent integrated approaches. Shared, global ethical principles have a uniquely binding role in this regard, with the potential to allow humanity to build bridges where currently there are barriers.

*Nicky Grigg, BE (Hons), BSc, PhD, is a Research Scientist (aquatic systems modelling) at CSIRO Land and Water in Canberra. She started her studies in environmental fluid dynamics, moving to study sediment diagenesis processes. Her research in recent years has focused on aquatic system responses to human actions. Dr Grigg is a participant in the CSIRO Complex Systems Science initiative working on the implications of nonlinear dynamics on mathematical modelling of socio-ecological systems.*

# References

Adger WN, Eakin H and Winkels A (2009) Nested and teleconnected vulnerabilities to environmental change. *Frontiers in Ecology* **7**, 150–157.

Campbell A (2006) 'The Australian natural resource management knowledge system'. Land & Water Australia, Canberra, Product Number PR061081, <http://lwa.gov.au/products/pr061081>.

Christenson GA (1988) Jus cogens – Guarding interests fundamental to international society. *Virginia Journal of International Law* **28**, 585–648.

Clingan J (1989) Terra Beata – Terra Infirma [music]. National Library of Australia, Canberra, <http://catalogue.nla.gov.au/Record/2860531/Details>.

Dietz T, Ostrom E, Stern PC (2003) The struggle to govern the commons. *Science* **302**, 1907–1912.

Garnaut R (2008) 'The Garnaut climate change review: Final report'. Cambridge University Press, Melbourne, <http://www.garnautreview.org.au>.

Kollock P (1998) Social dilemmas: The anatomy of cooperation. *Annual Review of Sociology* **24**, 183–214.

McMichael AJ, Powles JW, Butler CD and Uauy R (2007) Food, livestock production, energy, climate change and health. *Lancet* **370**, 1253–1263.

Meadows DH, Meadows DL and Randers J (1993) *Beyond the Limits: Confronting Global Collapse, Envisioning a Sustainable Future.* Chelsea Green Publishing Company, White River Junction, Vermont, USA.

Ostrom E, Burger J, Field CB, Norgaard RB and Policansky D (1999) Sustainability – Revisiting the commons: Local lessons, global challenges. *Science* **284**, 278–282.

Polimeni JM and Polimeni RI (2006) Jevons' Paradox and the myth of technological liberation. *Ecological Complexity* **3**, 344–353.

Ramanathan V and Feng Y (2008) On avoiding dangerous anthropogenic interference with the climate system: Formidable challenges ahead. *Proceedings of the National Academy of Sciences of the United States of America* **105**, 14245–14250.

Raupach MR, Canadell JG, Briggs PR, Ciaisc P, Enting IG, Friedlingstein P, Le Quéré C and Peters GP (submitted) Beyond peak $CO_2$: sharing and timing of globally capped emissions. *Proceedings of the National Academy of Sciences.*

Rockström J, Steffen W, Noone K, Persson A, Chapin FS, Lambin EF, Lenton TM, Scheffer M, Folke C, Schellnhuber HJ, Nykvist B, de Wit CA, Hughes T, van der Leeuw S, Rodhe H, Sörlin S, Snyder PK, Costanza R, Svedin U, Falkenmark M, Karlberg L, Corell RW, Fabry VJ, Hansen J, Walker B, Liverman D, Richardson K, Crutzen P and Foley JA (2009) A safe operating space for humanity. *Nature* **461**, 472–475.

Steffen W, Crutzen PJ and McNeill JR (2007) The Anthropocene: Are humans now overwhelming the great forces of nature? *Ambio* **36**, 614–621.

Swart R and Raes F (2007) Making integration of adaptation and mitigation work: mainstreaming into sustainable development policies? *Climate Policy* **7**, 288–303.

Turner GM (2008) A comparison of The Limits to Growth with 30 years of reality. *Global Environmental Change* **18**, 397–411.

Walker B, Barrett S, Polasky S, Galaz V, Folke C, Engstrom G, Ackerman F, Arrow K, Carpenter S, Chopra K, Daily G, Ehrlich P, Hughes T, Kautsky N, Levin S, Maler K-G, Shogren J, Vincent J, Xepapadeas T and de Zeeuw A (2009) Looming global-scale failures and missing institutions. *Science* **325**, 1345–1346.

# DISASTER PREPAREDNESS
# AND RECOVERY

# CHAPTER 18

# Biosecurity – preparing for the unexpected

Stephen Prowse

## Abstract

Biosecurity is a community responsibility with wide-ranging implications for health, trade and tourism. Human, animal and plant health are inextricably interlinked. Considerable progress has been made in recent years in building essential links and networks to handle the unexpected emergence of new pathogenic agents and the dissemination of old ones. State and Commonwealth agencies are central players in this endeavour and the recently created Australian Biosecurity Intelligence Network and the Australian Biosecurity System for Primary Production and the Environment are building resilience into the way we will respond to future threats. But trained personnel and the way information is shared will be central elements that will determine our national capacity to respond adaptively to threats in the future.

## Biosecurity – what is it?

Biosecurity means different things to different people. In essence, it is the processes, programs and structures we have in place to protect people and animals from the adverse economic impacts of emerging-disease entry and spread.

In the broadest sense, biosecurity has pre-border, border and post-border dimensions and includes public health, livestock health, plant health and wildlife disease. Biosecurity also has research, operational and policy dimensions. The sector is complex with a broad spectrum of stakeholders.

In the biosecurity context, resilience should be seen as our ability to respond to unexpected outbreaks of disease or disease incursions. This requires the building of generic response capacity and capability underpinned by the appropriate networks in the biosecurity community and strong research to support evidence-based policy and practice.

## Biosecurity – who is involved?

Biosecurity is a community responsibility with many individuals and agencies playing a role. State and Commonwealth Governments working with key stakeholders in agricultural industries and the public health sector establish the broad framework. Operational responsibility lies with Commonwealth and State Government agencies working closely with CSIRO and industry/government agencies such as Animal Health Australia and Plant Health Australia. Other stakeholders such as environmental groups also play an important part. The activities are supported and underpinned by research providers such as universities, research institutes, CSIRO and Biosecurity Cooperative Research Centres. A number of private companies also have a role to play as service providers.

## Biosecurity challenges

Scientists work in an increasingly complex and technologically sophisticated environment. They need to consider a wider range of factors than ever before if their work is to be effective. Increasingly, trade and other policy considerations need to be taken into account.

Despite improved mobility and communications, researchers in the biosecurity community often do not know where to turn for collaboration and information. Researchers are expected to be generalists, crossing a range of disciplines and sectors. Thus rapid access to information and expertise becomes critical. Platforms for collaboration exist within specific research disciplines but numerous gaps inhibit them from operating effectively 'across discipline'.

Further, the connections and links between organisations involved in biosecurity research leave much to be desired with minimal sharing of data beyond personal contacts.

In the biosecurity sector, a wider range of skills is being developed and technologies adopted. These include biotechnology, epidemiology, disease modeling, GIS and mapping, social sciences, risk analysis, forecasting and predictive modeling. These tools and technologies are critical parts of contemporary research and often generate and use large amounts of information.

The information can exist in many forms and come from many sources. In the animal health sector the information includes laboratory results, property data, livestock identification and movement data, spatial data, climate information, vegetation data and feral animal data.

This information frequently lies in different hands and in various forms. At present, the individual researcher needs to discover potential sources of information and plot a course that will enable that information to be shared and utilised most effectively.

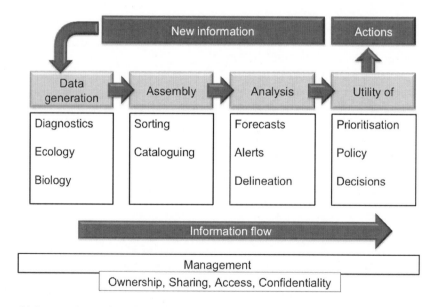

**Figure 18.1**  A new paradigm in connectivity and information collection, management and analysis.

This is particularly the case across disciplines where the personal relationships are less well established.

As an example, it may be that human health authorities notice an upsurge of a particular zoonotic infection as a result of medical surveillance systems. The animal health community becomes aware of that concern and must ask whether this is a result of a change in the behaviour of the disease agent. Perhaps there is a wildlife reservoir of this disease or perhaps wildlife has a changed vulnerability.

At present any initiative to harness all of this information, to analyse the results and to research novel approaches must tread a very precarious path. There is likely to be a disjuncture between those with a vested interest in the disease and those who need information to make decisions.

The cross-boundary nature of diseases and the observation that most disease outbreaks have both an animal and a human element means that a cross-jurisdictional and cross-sectoral approach is required. In particular this requires a close working relationship between emerging infectious disease practitioners in the human health, livestock disease and wildlife disease sectors.

New biotechnologies and information technologies have led to the need for a new paradigm in connectivity and information collection, management and analysis.

This is outlined in Figure 18.1.

## Biosecurity trends

### Increased EID risks

There is good evidence that there are increasing outbreaks of infectious disease and a majority of these are associated with animals (Jones *et al.* 2008). Disease emergence is the result of a complex interplay of many factors, including economic, social and scientific matters. Risk factors can be considered from the perspective of wildlife, livestock and human disease (PMSEIC 2009).

The destruction and manipulation of ecosystems has enhanced the risks associated with wildlife disease. Habitat loss and movement of wildlife has altered the spread of disease from wildlife to livestock and humans as the patterns of contact change. Increased demand for food and other agricultural products has altered irrigation practices, horticultural practices and animal production systems.

The impact of climate change remains to be elucidated though it may be expected to have a variety of effects on disease agents, hosts and the environment. As an example, the recent movement of bluetongue virus into northern Europe has been attributed to changing vector distribution that has in turn been attributed to climate change (Purse *et al.* 2005). Changing temperatures, patterns of rainfall and storms all have the potential to both increase and decrease the likelihood of disease emergence.

The risk of the entry and spread of infectious disease in human populations has been exacerbated by increased global travel. The global movement of animals and animal products may also contribute to increased risk of disease events and the magnitude of the impact of an event. The rapid cross-boundary movement of severe acute respiratory syndrome (SARS), H5N1 avian influenza and influenza A H1N1 2009 demonstrated how disease can move rapidly throughout the world. SARS was clearly spread by the movement of infected people (Heymann and Rodier 2004). The contribution of legal and illegal movement of poultry, wild bird migration and inappropriate vaccine usage to the spread of avian influenza remains to be determined.

Economic, cultural and social factors make a significant contribution to the risk of disease emergence and spread. Increasing wealth has also meant an increase in demands for animal protein. This has resulted in changing production systems with increased intensive animal production. This is often accompanied by poor development of appropriate infrastructure and quality control to support such production systems, again increasing the risk of adverse events including emerging infectious diseases. Poverty can also result in poor infrastructure and health care systems. Increasing populations of both people and animals associated with lifestyle choices may also contribute to disease risk.

The biology of disease-causing organisms is also a critical contributing factor. Changing environments allow increased opportunities for evolutionary change and the emergence of variant organisms. For example, the high levels of variation in influenza virus and the subsequent adaptation to different environments make this a difficult disease to control (Webster and Govorkova 2006).

### Bioterrorism

Following the incidents of September 11 2001, more attention has been focussed on the risks of bioterrorism. While there have been no major bioterrorism incidents since the 2001 terrorist attacks, the risk remains. The enhanced ability to respond to outbreaks of unknown diseases will also enhance our preparedness to respond to any bioterrorism incident.

### Reduced resources and a shift in responsibilities

Over the last two decades we have seen increased pressure on resources in the biosecurity sector and, in some areas, a shift in responsibility from government to an industry sector. In the agricultural sector this has resulted in the formation of Animal Health Australia (AHA) and Plant Health Australia (PHA). These organisations are government/industry partnerships that manage disease control programs. The companies foster a collective approach to disease management and response. An important element of the outbreak response process has been the development of agreements that define the way in which outbreak costs are shared between government and industry. This provides a level of confidence in responding to a disease outbreak.

### One-health approaches

'One-health' seeks to improve the health and well-being of all species by enhancing cooperation and collaboration across the public health, environment and livestock sectors to combat emerging infectious disease threats (American Veterinary Medical Association 2008). The concept of 'one-health' has been developed as a result of an increased understanding of the factors leading to the emergence of zoonosis and recognises that human and animal health are inextricably linked. The complexities of such a broad cross-sectoral approach, however, may make the implementation difficult.

## Building resilience

### Consolidation of biosecurity activity

State Governments in Queensland, Western Australia and Victoria are bringing together biosecurity activities across plants, insects, animals and aquaculture sectors. However, the difficulties in developing effective and functional linkages between animal/wildlife/environment and human health remain.

Perhaps the most advanced development is in Queensland where the State Government is developing a Health and Food Sciences Precinct in Brisbane, which will bring together animal health and production scientists, public health scientists and food scientists to create a vibrant knowledge centre for health and food. This Precinct, comprising about 700 scientists and support staff, will be a centre of excellence focusing on improving quality of life through advances in healthcare, medicine, food security, biosecurity and nutrition. The key design driver is the integration of existing human health sciences with animal and food sciences to develop a one-health approach to health and disease research.

Housing complementary animal, food and human science facilities near to each other will exploit opportunities for collaborative and whole-of-lifecycle (environment, food, animal, plant and human health) research, capitalise on sharing resources, scientific equipment, new and emerging generic and specific technologies and maximise diagnostic capacities in human–animal disease surge situations.

Scientists from across the sectors have been involved proactively in the design of the facilities as well as the development of collaborative projects.

## Collaborative research ventures

The Australian Biosecurity Cooperative Research Centre for Emerging Infectious Disease and the National Plant Biosecurity Cooperative Research Centre were established to improve Australia's capability and capacity to respond to emerging infectious disease outbreaks. The primary focus has been on zoonotic and exotic pests and diseases. These ventures act as a focus for collaborative research activities that bring together researchers across different agencies, jurisdictions and sectors. A number of other biosecurity and emerging infectious disease centres have also been established. Few if any, however, have the resources to achieve genuine collaborative partnerships.

## Enhanced planning

Following outbreaks of foot and mouth disease and mad cow disease in the United Kingdom and other countries and bird flu and SARS in Asia, the Federal Government and State Governments and industry have undertaken numerous planning and simulation exercises. These exercises have been important events in helping identify biosecurity response needs and set priorities. One key and common element in all the exercises and simulations is the need to improve information management (Australian Government Department of Agriculture, Fisheries and Forestry 2005a, b; Australian Government Department of Health and Ageing 2007).

## Broader responsibility in the community

The trend to broaden biosecurity responsibility will continue with increasing industry involvement in disease surveillance and in the management of outbreak responses. These significant behavioural and cultural shifts will improve our ability to respond to and manage disease outbreaks. Industry and community involvement will increase as technology to collect and analyse diverse sources of information improves. In addition, the biosecurity community will need to accept that alternative sources of information are of value and complement traditional disease information.

## Improving biosecurity information infrastructure

A significant challenge faced by all sectors is to convey the right information to the relevant people in a timely manner to allow them to make the best evidence-based decisions. In order to address this issue in part, the Australian Biosecurity Intelligence Network (ABIN) has recently been established with Federal Government funding.

The purpose of ABIN is to strengthen Australia's biosecurity research, surveillance and response capability, by enabling researchers, industry and government to connect with each other, utilise expertise, share data, information and generate disease intelligence using leading edge tools and technologies made available through online workspaces.

ABIN will make it possible for the biosecurity community of researchers, industry and governments to work together to address common problems or emerging biosecurity issues through access to data, information and know-how and the use of leading edge tools and technologies to generate biosecurity intelligence. In essence, ABIN will make it easier to connect, share, use and create biosecurity intelligence for biosecurity research, surveillance and response.

The use of ABIN will increase the quality and quantity of biosecurity intelligence that can be used for more informed and robust decision-making, policy development and operational response.

### A policy approach – AusBIOSEC

A policy initiative aimed at achieving a common approach to improved biosecurity has been developed by the Federal Government together with the State Governments. AusBIOSEC (AusBIOSEC Taskforce 2009) is a framework of common principles and guidelines to enable biosecurity arrangements to be applied consistently across Australia. The aim is to connect all biosecurity activities being undertaken by the Federal, State and Territory Governments, industry, landholders and other key stakeholders in primary production and the environment. The key outcome is the improved management of pests and diseases that have a negative impact on the environment, livestock or public health.

The scope of this work encompasses the entire biosecurity continuum and includes managing pests and diseases of terrestrial, freshwater and marine environments that could be harmful to primary industries, the natural and built environments and public health. It also covers the full biosecurity spectrum, including prevention and preparedness, emergency response and ongoing management of established species.

### Improving capability and capacity

A critical element of our national response capacity is an appropriately sized workforce with adequate skills and capabilities. Training programs to enhance the base and the level of skills are undertaken at multiple levels. These include professional and para-professional training, training in universities and training producers in disease response procedures. Such programs are developed and managed by AHA, PHA and the Biosecurity Cooperative Research Centres. A critical element of this is to develop a 'surge' capacity to mobilise the trained people in the face of an outbreak.

### National Animal Health Laboratory Strategy (NAHLS)

A National Animal Health Laboratory Strategy (Animal Health Australia 2009) is aimed at the development and delivery of a national animal health laboratory service capability for the effective control of animal diseases of major importance to Australia. This is in response to a recognition of the need to improve national collaborative arrangements between all animal health laboratories.

The Strategy will be based on a cohesive laboratory partnership involving commonwealth, state and territory governments, CSIRO, veterinary schools, private laboratories and industry, with a mutual understanding that threats to animal health in Australia are now threats that are of national significance rather than of significance solely to individual jurisdictions. The Strategy will be driven by the primary goal of ensuring Australia's animal health laboratories have the capability to rapidly and accurately diagnose exotic, new and emerging diseases that threaten market access, public health, food safety, biosecurity, animal productivity, wildlife health and biodiversity. Equally, it will ensure that Australia's laboratory system is able to meet requirements for ongoing disease surveillance, in-depth case investigations and surges in testing demand during emergency situations. Ensuring the availability of appropriately trained animal health diagnosticians across Australia's animal health laboratories will also be a key element of the Strategy.

A key priority for the Strategy will be to strengthen research activities within the animal health laboratory services. This research will underpin diagnostic and knowledge capability, allow the refinement and validation of existing tests, develop new techniques and technologies, investigate existing, new and emerging diseases and assess and develop new preventative and control measures.

### Forecasting and risk assessment

Emerging infectious diseases pose a growing threat to agricultural production, human health and the environment. Many of the world's epidemic diseases (particularly those transmitted by intermediate hosts) are known to be highly sensitive to changes in the broader environment. The application of environmental data to the study of disease offers the capability to demonstrate host–vector–environment relationships and potentially forecast the risk of disease outbreaks or epidemics. Disease forecasting systems have been developed to help primary producers to make economic decisions about disease management.

Accurate disease forecasting models would markedly improve epidemic prevention and control capabilities and minimise economic impact by determining the risk that a disease will occur, or that the intensity of the disease will increase. Existing systems for epidemic preparedness focus on disease surveillance using expert knowledge and statistical modelling of disease activity. Predictive health information systems would use monitored environmental variables, linked to a disease system, to provide early warning of possible outbreaks.

There has been an increase emphasis on forecasting with initiatives in the Australian Government Department of Agriculture, Fisheries and Forestry, the Australian Centre of Excellence in Risk Analysis and the Australian Biosecurity Cooperative Research Centre as well as in some State jurisdictions.

### Technology

Over the past 30 years there have been enormous advances in both scientific and information technology that have had a major impact on biosecurity. Technology will continue to advance rapidly and will have a huge impact on biosecurity policies and practices. In the context of the biosecurity sector, careful evaluation of new technologies is required to ensure scarce resources are wisely spent. It is easy to be seduced by technological solutions when often a 'low tech' solution is available, achievable and cost effective.

### Conclusions

In the biosecurity sector we must expect the unexpected. No one could have predicted the outbreak of SARS in 2002, which spread to 27 countries, infected 8273 people and caused 775 deaths. Hence, resilience lies in a better ability and agility to deal with the unexpected and unknown by adopting a cross-sectoral and cross-jurisdictional 'one-health' approach. This requires a commitment to develop the human disease, livestock disease and wildlife disease networks at research and operational levels. This can be achieved through genuine interdepartmental and inter-agency collaborative research and operational programs.

Training programs to increase capacity and capability and to improve the use of technology are also of great importance. Improved career paths for professionals in the sector are required. Perhaps the most significant trend that requires continued support is the participatory and collaborative approach to disease control and management. While the unexpected will always be a challenge, an increased attention to forecasting will also be important. Improved information management will contribute to improved forecasting and risk assessment that assists in setting priorities and in resource allocation. These processes will improve our ability to address risks associated with known diseases.

Australia has made substantial progress over the last decade in building disease response capability and capacity. This has been achieved in the face of pressure on resources. The maintenance of these resources will require ongoing attention to ensure that Australia is well equipped to address the disease challenges of the future.

*Dr Stephen Prowse is the Chief Executive Officer of the Australian Biosecurity Cooperative Research Centre for Emerging Infectious Disease.*

## References

American Veterinary Medical Association (2008) 'One health: a new professional imperative. One health Initiative Task Force: Final report'. American Veterinary Medical Association, Schaumburg, Illinois, USA, <http://www.avma.org/onehealth/default.asp>.

Animal Health Australia (2008) 'National Animal Health Laboratory Strategy'. Animal Health Australia, Canberra, <http://www.animalhealthaustralia.com.au/programs/ahsp/lab_network.cfm>.

AusBIOSEC Taskforce (2009) AusBIOSEC. Australian Government Department of Agriculture, Fisheries and Forestry, Canberra, <http://www.daff.gov.au/animal-plant-health/pests-diseases-weeds/biosecurity/ausbiosec>.

Australian Government Department of Agriculture, Fisheries and Forestry (2005a) 'National Emergency Zoonosis Exercise. Exercise Elausis '05. Evaluation Report – Key Findings.' Australian Government Department of Agriculture, Fisheries and Forestry, Canberra, <http://www.daff.gov.au/__data/assets/pdf_file/0004/146848/eleusis_key_findings_may06.pdf>.

Australian Government Department of Agriculture, Fisheries and Forestry (2005b) 'National Foot–&–Mouth Disease Simulation. Operation Minotaur. Evaluation Report'. Australian Government Department of Agriculture, Fisheries and Forestry, Canberra, <http://www.daff.gov.au/__data/assets/pdf_file/0005/146831/minotaurreport.pdf>.

Australian Government Department of Health and Ageing (2007) 'National Pandemic Influenza Exercise: Exercise Cumpston 06 Report'. Office of Health Protection Australian Government Department of Health and Ageing, Canberra, <http://www.flupandemic.gov.au/internet/panflu/publishing.nsf/Content/cumpston–report–1>.

Heymann D and Rodier G (2004) Global surveillance, national surveillance and SARS. Emerging Infectious Diseases 10, 173–175.

Jones KE, Patel NG, Levy MA, Storeygard A, Balk D, Gittleman JL and Daszak P (2008) Global trends in emerging infectious diseases. Nature 451, 990–994.

PMSEIC (Prime Minister's Science Engineering and Innovation Council) (2009) 'Epidemics in a changing world. Report of the expert working group'. Australian Government,

Canberra, <http://www.innovation.gov.au/ScienceAndResearch/prime_ministers_
science_engineering_innovation_council/Pages/twentiethmeeting.aspx>.

Purse BV, Mellor PS, Rogers DJ, Samuel AR, Mertens PPC and Baylis M (2005) Climate
change and the recent emergence of bluetongue in Europe. Nature Reviews Microbiology
3, 171–181.

Webster RG and Govorkova EA (2006) H5N1 influenza – continuing evolution and spread.
New England Journal of Medicine 355, 2174–2177

# CHAPTER 19

# Pandemic preparedness and resilience

Bob Douglas

## Abstract

Pandemics of disease can result from a range of previously known, or newly evolving pathogenic agents. They can decimate large populations, destroy businesses, immobilise armies and spread fear across society. If combined with other economic, resource or armed threat, they can impair the very survival of society. Australia has been preparing for a serious influenza pandemic for some years and a whole-of-government approach has been evident in our response to swine influenza, which has now achieved pandemic status. To enhance the resilience of Australia's pandemic preparedness, we need to review our constitutional arrangements, bring the community into the planning process and expand our thinking and planning beyond government. We need to prepare the community for a broad range of possible pandemic agents and the likelihood that pandemic assault could occur at the same time as other future systemic shocks.

## Introduction

Pandemic is the word used to describe an epidemic of disease that occurs over a wide geographic area and affects a substantial proportion of its population.

Resilience is the ability of a human community or other complex system to absorb disturbances so that it retains its essential characteristics, its function and its identity (Walker and Salt 2006; Cork *et al.* 2008). A society or community that is resilient to pandemics is one that will respond to the disturbance produced by such an event while retaining its central functions over time, emerging functioning and intact from the onslaught of a disease that infects, mains, kills or threatens the well-being of very large numbers of its inhabitants.

The term pandemic can refer to infectious or non-infectious diseases; the timeframe during which the pandemic affects the population can range from days to years and the impacts on the human population can range from high death rates, to massive absenteeism, to disability, overcrowding of hospitals and swamping the capacity of health professionals and/or supplies of life-saving drugs. Under certain circumstances pandemics can impair profitability and decimate businesses, destroy the effectiveness of armies, incapacitate schools, kill community leaders, contaminate water supplies, impede public transport, confine people indoors and spread fear and panic across society.

When such an event occurs, even in a previously stable and well-adjusted society, the impact can be very disruptive, threatening the breakdown of societal norms and institutions.

Where a pandemic arrives in company with other destabilising forces such as armed conflict, economic depression, poverty, food or resource shortage and environmental stress, it could threaten the very identity and survival of that society.

Globalisation, the quadrupling of the human population in the past hundred years, the transport and communications revolutions and the confluence of climate change and peak oil make the probability of a compounded scenario in coming decades disturbingly high.

## The avian flu scare prepared us for swine flu

The threat of a global pandemic amongst humans caused by a strain of avian influenza that has decimated many bird flocks around the world in recent years had the effect of galvanising governments across the world into developing plans to deal with an avian flu pandemic if and when the virus mutated sufficiently to be easily transmitted from human to human.

A large international effort was therefore put in place, linking national and international influenza pandemic preparedness plans when the alarm was sounded in response to a Mexican outbreak of influenza coming from a different animal source, swine flu. During 2009, swine flu spread widely in Australia, calling into play the nation's pandemic preparedness plan. So far, so good; the pandemic has been milder than was first feared. But we are still only in the first year of the pandemic and there remain concerns that the influenza virus will develop increasingly lethal capacity as it continues to spread across the world. Vaccines and specific antiviral drugs have been stockpiled; intelligence systems have been developed and the community is generally alert to the uncertainties ahead. Lines of command and decision points have been clarified and the community is regularly informed about progress of the pandemic.

But there are many other candidates besides influenza for a global pandemic that we already know about and others that could, like HIV, come upon us unprepared. The pandemic threat calls for a broad examination of the factors that will enable Australians to respond creatively to disease disturbances that we cannot at present predict or anticipate.

## Black Death, swine flu, HIV/AIDS, the African viruses and smallpox

Writing of the epidemic of plague that swept the world in the mid-14th century, which is generally assumed to have killed between one-third and one-half of the populace, Robert of Avesbury (Ibejii 2001) wrote:

> 'Those marked for death were scarce permitted to live longer than three or four days.
> It showed favor to no-one, except a very few of the wealthy. On the same day, 20, 40 or
> 60 bodies, and on many occasions many more, might be committed for burial together
> in the same pit'.

The influenza pandemic of 1918–1919 was another global disaster. It killed between 20 and 40 million people, more than had died in World War 1. More people died of influenza in a single year than in four years of the Black Death from 1347 to 1351.

In 1976, the spectre of 1918 loomed large when the re-emergence of the flu virus in an army population was seen as a threat to the entire United States population. Public health officials initiated a mass vaccination campaign but the anticipated pandemic did not occur. What did result, however, was an increase in incidence of a paralytic illness, Guillain Barre syndrome, attributed to a reaction to the vaccine, which highlights the fact that mass vaccination campaigns can bring with them unintended consequences (Pollak 2009).

In addition to swine flu, the world is currently in the throes of a slow burning pandemic of HIV/AIDS. In large areas of the developing world, the pandemic is producing massive dislocation of families, large numbers of orphans and infected adults, who will progressively die a slow lingering death unless they receive specific anti-retroviral treatment. In other countries, the HIV threat was faced squarely in the 1980s and a range of counter-measures has confined but not eradicated the threat.

Many viral agents, including a group of viruses that are at present confined to Africa, such as the Ebola virus, Marburg fever virus and Lassa fever virus, are believed to have the capacity to generate pandemic threats to humans. A number of these agents are transmitted from animal reservoirs and could cross to humans in a variety of ways.

There is also a plausible possibility that terrorists could obtain access to laboratory supplies and spread agents such as smallpox virus, which was eradicated from human populations in 1979 and to which the human population would now be very vulnerable.

## Australia's pandemic influenza preparedness

The National Action Plan for Human Influenza Pandemic (NAP) reaches into all aspects of Australian Government and was triggered by intelligence from sentinel surveillance activity across the world and coordinated by the World Health Organization (Council of Australian Governments Working Group on Australian Influenza Pandemic Prevention and Preparedness 2009). Seen originally as a problem to be managed by the health care system, the plan recognises that pandemic preparedness must be coordinated at the very highest levels of national and international administrations. A 'whole-of-government approach' has been instituted. The Australian Government Department of Families, Housing, Community Services and Indigenous Affairs (2009), for example, has an excellent web page on building resilience through business continuity and pandemic planning.

The NAP appears to deal competently with those logistics that are predictable. It concentrates almost exclusively on pandemic influenza occurring in a setting that, in other respects, is assumed to be operating on a 'business as usual' footing.

The NAP does not, and probably cannot because it is a government sponsored activity, easily call into question the controlling and dominant impact of economic efficiency and risk aversion that are inherent in all Australian bureaucracies and which are often in conflict with resilient systems. All of these, in addition to media blame-calling and fear-mongering, inevitably come into play when a pandemic strikes.

## Enhancing resilience to future pandemics

Resilient complex systems are diverse, connected, open, able to respond quickly, have reserves on which to draw and can benefit from overlapping structures and functions in systems above and below them. A resilient system at the State level derives its resilience from connections and flexibility at the scales above and below the State.

This raises the nature of the relationship between states, territories and local government in Australia and the national capacity for a coherent national response to the unexpected. Most observers agree that Australia is currently over-governed with these three levels of government that contain within them multiple impermeable silos of responsibility. In the long term, we must pay serious attention to major constitutional reform if we are to build a society that is capable of adapting at short notice to the potentially overwhelming pressures of an unanticipated fast-moving pandemic coming on top of the social upheaval associated with a profound economic downturn or an extreme weather event.

In considering this issue of constitutional reform (as we must in coming years) the case for abolition of the States and modification of both national and regional governance structures should be squarely on the national agenda.

Also, in the interest of obtaining rapid and flexible responses to the complex dilemmas that a fast moving pandemic will pose, we should be building into all of our bureaucratic structures the principle of 'subsidiarity.' This is the idea that a central authority should have a subsidiary function, performing only those tasks that cannot be performed effectively at a more immediate or local level.

## Measures that could enhance resilience in the short term

But, short of these desirable longer term constitutional and governance reforms, there are some ways in which we could quickly enhance resilience to a pandemic in the short term and prepare Australians for the kinds of hazards that almost certainly lie ahead. They include:

- calling a national pandemic planning summit that brings civil society from across Australia into a planning exercise that expands ownership of pandemic planning from government to the community at large and from influenza to a broad suite of pandemic scenarios;
- developing a series of 'hypotheticals' in communities across the nation, in which community leaders are encouraged to experiment with the ideas for managing catastrophe in their community (e.g. 'how would we cope with an 80% attack rate and a 50% death rate from the release of smallpox virus in our town or city?');
- involving the community (perhaps starting with high school students) in an open discussion about who should be the first recipients of limited supplies of life-saving drugs and prophylactic vaccines in their school and community;
- developing some realistic media productions about what makes some societies able to adapt and transform in response to catastrophic events while others spiral into chaos, as occurred in New Orleans following Hurricane Katrina;
- promoting discussion in schools, hospitals, churches and small businesses about 'first-aid community plans' for what to do if 40% of the population suddenly becomes seriously ill with a highly contagious infectious disease; and
- developing plans for substantial 'surge capacity' in the availability of emergency beds to care for victims of a fast-moving pandemic (this may require a capacity to build army tent hospitals on public recreational sites and a mobilisation of a reserve list of retired nurses and doctors to staff them).

Some will find these suggestions at first glance unduly alarmist. Yet we are now fully adjusted to the notion of preparing the whole community to be able to undertake cardiopulmonary resuscitation (CPR) and to deal with minor personal emergencies. The likelihood that we will need to deal with the catastrophic effects of a pandemic in our own lifetimes is now probably greater than the likelihood that most of us will need to carry out CPR. Understanding the nature of threat and being mentally ready to deal with it when it arises is one way to dispel fear and build resilience.

*Emeritus Professor Bob Douglas, AO, MD, FRACP, FRACGP, FAFPHM, is a Visiting Fellow at the National Centre for Epidemiology and Population Health at The Australian National University, where he was the founding director. He is the current Chair of the Board of Australia21.*

# References

Australian Government Department of Families, Housing, Community Services and Indigenous Affairs (2009) Building Resilience Through Business Continuity and Pandemic Planning. Australian Government, Canberra, <http://www.fahcsia.gov.au/sa/communities/progserv/Documents/pandemic_influenza/default.htm>.

Cork S, Walker B and Buckley R (2008) *How resilient is Australia?* Australia21, Canberra, <www.australia21.org.au>.

Council of Australian Governments Working Group on Australian Influenza Pandemic Prevention and Preparedness (2009). 'National Action Plan for Human Influenza Pandemic'. Australian Government, Canberra, <http://www.dpmc.gov.au/publications/pandemic/docs/NAP.pdf>.

Ibeji M (2001) 'Black Death' British History and Middle Ages. BBC, London, <http://www.bbc.co.uk/history/british/middle_ages/black_05.shtml>.

Pollak A (2009) Fear of a Swine Flu epidemic in 1976 offers some lessons and concerns, today. New York Times May 8, <www.nytimes.com/2009/05/09/health/09vaccine.html>.

Walker B and Salt D (2006) *Resilience Thinking: Sustaining Ecosystems and People in a Changing World.* Island Press, Washington, DC.

# CHAPTER 20

# The role of communication in supporting resilient communities

Susan Nicholls

## Abstract

Resilience is intimately associated with good communication. Without resilience, communities are not likely to recover after disaster. My contention in this chapter is that communication means more than simply delivering information. This is the case in all stages of the emergency process – prevention, preparedness, response and recovery. Recognition that communities may achieve resilience if they are enabled to do so with the help of two-way communication is an important concept to carry into the future.

## Introduction

This chapter is based on the premise that all successful social enterprises are built on good communication. Good communication is not the same thing as information. Good communication is two-way, a dialogue, a matter of hearing as well as speaking and of being willing to act on the mutual exchange of information, opinion and expressed wants and needs. While it is obvious that such precepts are vital for good interpersonal communication, it is less obvious that they are also essential where communities and government or other agencies are the parties communicating in a risk environment, or dealing with disaster. It is the practice of communication within the framework of disaster – that is, risk, response and recovery communication – and its relationship to resilience, that provide the focus for this chapter.

### Communication: dialogic or informational?

Dialogic communication arises out of philosophical notions of equality. Kent and Taylor (2002) state, 'The concept of dialogue has its roots in a variety of disciplines: philosophy, rhetoric, psychology and relational communication. Philosophers and rhetoricians have long considered dialogue as one of the most ethical forms of communication and as one of the central means of separating truth from falsehood'. According to Botan (1997), 'dialogue elevates [audiences] to the status of communication equal with the organization'. I argue that resilience can only be improved by a form of communication that takes as its starting point the efficacy and legitimate agency of audiences as co-authors of communication. While the greater part of communication emanating from government falls under the 'everyday information' category, where communities are faced with crisis, and when there is a strong need for information, there is also a strong need to enable communities by interacting with them in a process that allows a two-way interaction.

The academic field of public relations has devoted considerable research into examining how crisis is dealt with in organisations. Organisations that ignored the possibility of crisis had the least chance of surviving one, yet numbers of major US corporations do not have a crisis management plan, or at least one that is frequently updated or rehearsed (Penrose 2000). Public relations scholars have written copiously (e.g. Fink 1986; Coombs 1999; Fearn-Banks 2002; Seeger 2002) on how crisis communication should be managed, but the key notion is that crisis is to be expected at some stage. Without the conviction that this is the case, no planning will take place. Paton (2003), working in psychology, found that communities are quite resistant to the idea that something bad will happen, even those communities that have already experienced a disaster (presumably on the theory that 'lightning does not strike twice'). Paton's research indicates that much depends on the perceived trustworthiness of the communicator and in the reliability of messages. This has implications for the communicator in terms of establishing trust beforehand through dialogic communication.

Without information, communities and individuals under stress are unable to make good decisions. A sense of helplessness and despair follows. Without intelligent hearing on the part of the information givers, it is more difficult for individuals to express their situation; to understand or convey their informational needs. Through their own understanding they enable themselves to take the necessary steps to return to equilibrium. Communities that (re) build their own resilience after disaster and, for that matter, before – at the stages of mitigation and preparedness – are likely to experience a more robust and satisfactory outcome.

Emergency Management Australia (EMA), Australia's federal disaster management agency, reminds us that whether we wish to acknowledge it or not, we are very vulnerable to risk and disaster:

> 'Australia is a nation prone to a range of natural, technological and human-caused
> emergencies. Since 2000, on average each year 24 people have lost their lives as a direct
> result of natural disasters. Almost 600 have been injured and up to 390,000 affected in
> some way. The economic cost to communities of natural disasters has been in excess of
> $3.6 billion annually. Many more people are also affected by human caused emergencies
> and disasters, with a further significant cost to the nation' (Australian Government
> Attorney-General's Department 2009a).

### Community, resilience, disaster and recovery

As this chapter will refer frequently to community in the context of resilience to disaster contributing to recovery, I will define these terms as follows:

- a 'community' in this context is 'a social grouping that interacts, albeit inconsistently, on a number of levels – often but not necessarily bounded by a geographic commonality but bounded by the effects of the disaster – and is characterised by a self-recognised and self-defined commonality of experience which changes over time' (Nicholls 2006).
- 'resilience' is a term in danger of obsolescence. Preceded in the policy lexicon by the term 'sustainability', resilience now looks likely to be taken over by 'adaptability' despite distinctions understood in various scientific fields. For this chapter, however, I use and define resilience as 'the capacity of communities to respond to extreme adversity while maintaining social coherence and identity' (after Cork 2009).

- 'disaster' has a plethora of definitions depending on which discipline is using the term (Saylor 1993; Perry 2007). For this chapter I define 'disaster' as involving these factors (Eyre 2006):
    - an event in time that has an identifiable beginning and end;
    - the destruction of property, injury and/or loss of life;
    - affecting a large group of people adversely;
    - out of the realm of ordinary experience;
    - public and shared by members of more than one family;
    - the subject of intense media interest;
    - disrupting the normative or cultural system of a society; and
    - traumatic enough to induce stress in almost anyone.

I will define and examine 'recovery' later in this chapter.

## The role of communication

The role of communication in fostering community resilience in a disaster context is three-fold: to assist in preparation and mitigation through carefully designed communication campaigns; to facilitate response during a crisis; and to contribute to and, where possible, expedite recovery, also through a combination of information and dialogue.

### Preparation and mitigation

Preparation and mitigation are closely linked. Preparation for any kind of impact involves imagining what could happen and taking steps to be ready for that event. For example, a householder living in the bush could clear the ground of bush litter around their house, have independent water storage and a protected pumping system, ensure that hoses and sprinklers are in place and that the family has a clear emergency escape plan. Using the same example, mitigation means that the householder has built defence systems into their property in the expectation that, should a bushfire arrive, damage will be minimised by protective actions taken in advance.

In Australia, local and State Government agencies typically take responsibility for providing information about such preparation. Australian Government Attorney-General's Department (2009b) notes: 'The concept of the prepared community concerns the application of the comprehensive, all hazards and all agencies approaches at the local level (typically at local government level)'. The focus here is on what agencies do. The other part of the equation, the community that is supposed to be prepared, seems to be regarded as a monolithic receptor of the information and instructions that are thought by agencies to be helpful in facing risk.

Given that many individuals are resistant to warnings, and minimise risk preparation in the belief that 'it won't happen here/to me', persuasive and trustworthy communication plays a vital part in warning about risk realistically and credibly as a first step. Dialogue is a logical method to establish trust and to persuade an uncommitted audience. A second step, part of this dialogue, is to suggest a clear and practical set of actions that will mitigate the danger, taking feedback into account. A third is to present the means by which these actions can be accomplished to prepare effectively for impact. This advice should be formulated in such a way as to convince audiences that: a) if they make the effort, they have a reasonable expectation that they can accomplish this; b) it is a worthwhile thing to do; and c) there are advantageous and desired rewards for their effort (Vroom 1964, cited in Wood et al. 2004).

### Response communication

In this chapter I do not address operational communication engaged in by emergency responders.

'Response' refers to the immediate reaction to an emergency, involving the emergency services, associated government agencies and the affected community. Unfortunately, research about crisis communication focuses heavily on media management. While this is clearly a vital part of disaster response, and while media play a significant role in informing audiences about what measures are being taken in response to disaster, this focus ignores the capacity of affected communities to respond effectively in their own ways if given the opportunity – opportunity that dialogic communication can help provide. In fact, rendering communities powerless by disregarding their own agency in self-protection and resilience can be harmful to longer-term recovery. Moreover, the view that communities are helpless and prone to panic tends toward two unhelpful outcomes: it encourages an attitude within communities of over-reliance on government services that are often already at or beyond breaking point during disasters; and media is likely to exacerbate an audience's anxiety with alarmist and sensational coverage. It is also worthwhile pointing out in this regard, given the difficulties of giving accurate and timely information to affected communities during the response phase of a disaster, that the phenomenal growth of social media has already affected how information is shared among communities. Social media has tremendous potential to assist people facing disaster by providing trustworthy, timely contact and mutual support. Interestingly, it is characterised by the reciprocated responsiveness of sender and receiver.

### Recovery

Few studies have looked closely at how communication can assist recovering communities (Camilleri *et al.* 2007), but good dialogic communication is key to enabling communities to acquire agency in their own recovery. When a community is faced with disaster, individuals are in the curious dilemma of needing a great deal of information, often not knowing precisely what information they need, and not being able to effectively assimilate or act on information when it is received. These factors come into play to a greater or lesser extent before, during and after disasters (underscoring the connectedness of all stages of disaster in contributing to recovery). There is a particular difficulty when it is government, often mistrusted or held responsible by communities for their plight, that is attempting to communicate. This provides a challenge to communicators.

Following a major emergency such as bushfire or cyclone, communities immediately begin their own recovery by bonding together, often demonstrating notable altruism (Wraith and Gordon 1988). Emergent groups appear, combining individuals who may have little in common but their shared disaster experience and their desire to re-establish normality (Gordon 2004). These groups often apply to government agencies for help. If agencies are not in the habit of engaging in dialogic communication, groups can feel rebuffed and become politicised (Stallings and Quarantelli 1985). This, in turn, can result in conditions of conflict detrimental to resilience.

One of the difficulties of post-disaster or recovery communication is in understanding what actually constitutes recovery. This can be seen in a duality of attitudes toward recovery that I have called the 'soft-hat/ hard-hat' approaches:

> 'When the sewerage system is working again, the roads and bridges are useable, the electricity, gas and telephone connections are restored and the supply of food and goods is back to normal – is that recovery? Is the community recovered?' (Nicholls and Glenny 2005).

The restoration of essential infrastructure is one part of recovery and a very easily measurable one: for example, four out of five destroyed bridges rebuilt; 3000 metres of fencing repaired; six of eight settlements have telephone and electricity restored, and so on. We can see how well we are doing just by looking at the numbers. This is the domain of the hard-hats; people who put physical things back together again.

But some things are harder to measure.

How do we measure sleepless nights, sudden flashbacks, children wetting their beds or paralysing fear at the smell of smoke or the roar of high wind? It is not easy to measure tears nor to understand how to staunch them. This is the shadow side of recovery, the unglamorous, slow, painful journey with few milestones or signposts. This is the terrain of the soft-hats, the helpers, counsellors, psychologists, social workers and case managers who continue to work with disaster-affected communities for months and years after an event such as the Victorian firestorm. For a community to be resilient, the diverse approaches of soft-hat and hard-hat are needed, working together.

Following this notion, I define recovery as *an ongoing state of being, experienced differently by individuals in a community that has suffered disaster, in which there are varying states of restoration, recuperation, renewal and revival of physical, emotional, economic, and infrastructural conditions that had been damaged or destroyed by the disaster.*

The historical record tells us that biological systems that maximise diversity do best in the survival stakes, because diversity allows for and encourages adaptability. In human communities, communication has the capacity to encourage and defend diversity and to call forth diverse contributions to serve community needs preparatory to, during and after crisis. Diversity of reaction and capacity to cope are characteristic of individuals who have experienced disaster. This diversity is frequently misunderstood, even by people who have also gone through the disaster experience as well as by those wishing to help. There are no 'one-size-fits-all' solutions for individuals who are recovering from a disaster. Their needs are multiple. They include, differently for different people, material, emotional, aesthetic, social, environmental and spiritual assistance. Dialogic communication plays an essential role in elucidating and responding to diverse needs, thus encouraging and supporting resilience.

The Canberra experience of the aftermath of 18 January 2003 can teach us many lessons about recovery, especially about how extremely varied it can be from person to person. Research undertaken three years after the Canberra bushfire gave many contradictory indications about what helped and what hindered people's recovery. For example, some people found that media coverage repeatedly showing familiar places – even their own houses – engulfed in flame was deeply upsetting: others thought it was a good thing because it showed the rest of Australia, and the world, what they had gone through (Camilleri *et al.* 2007). A major finding was that people thought *Community Update*, the weekly recovery newsletter, a very great help and emphasised that they regarded it as 'their' newsletter. The structure of the recovery organisation itself was highly conducive to dialogic communication. A Community and Expert Reference Group was established, with representatives widely drawn from the community and relevant organisations, and the Recovery Centre was also a source of mutual exchange of information, views and needs. All of these fostered two-way communication (Nicholls and Glenny 2005).

Communication was seen to fail dramatically during Hurricane Katrina in the USA. When devastation of large areas of infrastructure in New Orleans and neighbouring cities combined with a society divided by poverty, an already weak system of governance struggling to respond was overwhelmed. Recovery communication brought to bear some time after Hurricane Katrina, like that following the 11 September attacks in 2001, was a highly sophisticated TV and print campaign designed to help a diverse group of people who were distressed (Nicholls and Healy 2008). An important aspect of both of these campaigns was their recognition that 'hard-hat' recovery is not all there is and that two-way communication was essential: every TV commercial and all printed material had a free call number so that personal support could be reached. This, in turn, provided authorities with a clearer idea of where people were in their recovery and what their concerns were (within the bounds of privacy). In addition, hard-to-reach communities – such as particular 'closed' ethnic groups and first responder teams – were recognised as having distinct communication needs and methods of access to help (April J. Naturale, Project Liberty, New York City pers.comm.).

## Conclusion: recovery and resilience

My contention in this chapter has been that communication means more than simply delivering information. This is the case in all stages of the emergency process – prevention, preparedness, response and recovery. Resilience is intimately associated with good communication as argued above. Without resilience, communities are not likely to recover after disaster. Recognition that communities may achieve resilience if they are enabled to do so with the help of dialogic communication is an important concept to carry into the future.

*Dr Susan Nicholls is an adjunct Associate Professor at the Australian Institute for Sustainable Communities. Over the past seven years she has taught Professional Communication at the University of Canberra (since 2003) and Environmental Communication at the Australian National University. Widely experienced as a metropolitan newspaper journalist and public affairs officer with the Commonwealth Government prior to becoming an academic, her current area of research interest is government communication, particularly in relation to risk and disaster recovery. She has undertaken research looking at the role of communication in risk management and disaster recovery, and has given seminars and workshops for Emergency Management Australia and the Australian Red Cross on these topics. She has also published a number of papers in the* Australian Journal of Emergency Management *and the* Asia-Pacific Public Relations Journal, *and has contributed chapters to books on risk and crisis management in public relations. She has also taught at the University of Wollongong and the University of New South Wales (ADFA).*

## References

Australian Government Attorney General's Department (2009a) Community Engagement. Australian Government, Canberra, <http://www.ema.gov.au/www/emaweb/emaweb. nsf/Page/EmergencyManagement_Communities_CommunityEngagement>.

Australian Government Attorney General's Department (2009b) Community Engagement. Australian Government, Canberra, <http://www.ema.gov.au/www/emaweb/emaweb. nsf/Page/EmergencyManagement_EmergencyManagementApproaches#PC>.

Botan C (1997) Ethics in strategic communication campaigns: The case for a new approach to public relations. *Journal of Business Communication* **34**, 188–202.

Camilleri P, Healy C, Macdonald E, Nicholls S, Sykes J, Winkworth G and Woodward M (2007) 'Recovering from the 2003 Canberra bushfire: A work in progress'. Emergency Management Australia, Canberra, <http://www.ema.gov.au/www/emaweb/emaweb.nsf/ Page/EMA_Library>.

Coombs, WT (1999) *Ongoing Crisis Communication: Planning, managing, and responding.* Sage, Thousand Oaks.

Cork S (Ed) (2009) *Brighter Prospects: Enhancing the Resilience of Australia.* Australia 21, Weston, Australian Capital Territory.

Eyre A (2006) 'Literature and Best Practice Review and Assessment: Identifying People's Needs in Major Emergencies and Best Practice in Humanitarian Response'. UK Government, London.

Fearn-Banks K (2002) *Crisis Communications: A Casebook Approach.* Lawrence Erlbaum Associates, Mahwah, New Jersey.

Fink S (1986) *Crisis Management: Planning for the Inevitable.* AMACOM, New York.

Gordon R (2004) The social system as site of disaster impact and resource for recovery. *Australian Journal of Emergency Management* **19**, 16–22.

Kent M and Taylor M (2002) Toward a dialogic theory of public relations. *Public Relations Review* **28**, 21–37.

Nicholls S (2006) Disaster memorials as government communication. *Australian Journal of Emergency Management* **21**, 38.

Nicholls S and Glenny L (2005) Communicating for recovery: A case study in communication between the Australian capital territory government and the ACT community after the ACT bushfires, January 2003. In *Public Relations Issues and Crisis Management.* (Eds C Galloway and K Kwansah-Aidoo) pp. 41–58. Thomson Social Science Press, South Melbourne.

Nicholls S and Healy C (2008) Communication with disaster survivors: towards best practice. *Australian Journal of Emergency Management* **23**, 14–20.

Paton D (2003) Disaster preparedness: a social-cognitive perspective. *Disaster Prevention and Management* **12**, 210–216.

Penrose R (2000) The role of perception in crisis planning. *Public Relations Review* **26**, 155–171.

Perry RW (2007) What is a disaster? In Handbook of Disaster Research. (Eds H Rodriguez, EL Quarantelli and RR Dynes) pp. 1–15. Springer, New York.

Saylor CF (Ed) (1993) *Children and disasters.* Plenum Press, New York.

Seeger MW (2002) Chaos and crisis: Propositions for a general theory of crisis communication. *Public Relations Review* **28**, 329–337.

Stallings R and Quarantelli EL (1985) Emergent citizen groups and emergency management. *Public Administration Review* **45**, 93–100.

Wood J, Chapman J, Fromholtz M, Morrison F, Wallace J, Zeffane RM, Schermerhorn JR and Osborn RN (2004) *Organisational Behaviour: A Global Perspective.* John Wiley & Sons Australia Ltd., Milton, Queensland.

Wraith R and Gordon R (1988) 'Human responses to natural disasters (series) Part 8: Community responses to natural disaster'. *Macedon Digest* **3**(2).

# CHAPTER 21

# Beyond resilience in the face of disaster – transforming adversity by transforming ourselves and our systems

Theresia Citraningtyas

## Abstract

Psychological resilience has often been referred to as the ability to 'bounce back' from difficult experiences. While such definition serves to acknowledge human beings' capacity to face incredible adversity, it may also create a potentially misleading aim of 'returning to normalcy'. In reality, dealing with adversities such as disasters is far beyond bouncing back to business as usual, not becoming adversely affected, or even achieving positive outcomes. Adversities such as disasters are often life changing, in a multidimensional way. While adversities can make people more vulnerable, they can also lead to growth and strength as people become aware of the need to change. On the other end, what is an advantage in ordinary times can sometimes become a vulnerability in disasters if and when it increases expectations and reduces a sense of personal capacity. To avoid this, systems need to work in ways that allow individuals to retain power in and over systems while feeling supported by them, particularly in face of the unexpected. Similar to what is found among individuals, the human element that appears to make a system most vulnerable could also be its greatest strength. Formal systems thus need to go beyond professional roles, clear job descriptions, mandates and hierarchies and focus on people, relationships, families and communities as a whole, in all aspects of life.

## Introduction

The concept of resilience has come to guide our thinking, particularly in the context of disasters in Australia. This chapter will look at different ways resilience from a psychological perspective has been conceptualised and it will discuss their benefits and limitations. It will then go beyond the concept of resilience to look more closely at how people respond to and potentially transform themselves in disasters and other adversities. This then highlights how vulnerability and advantage, which are generally considered to be distinct, can sometimes be two sides of one coin. This goes for individuals as well as systems. We will then discuss how we might be able to enhance our capacity to face disasters by focusing on the most vulnerable, which is also the strongest part of systems: the whole person, relationships and families.

## Conceptualisations of psychological resilience and their limitations

Psychological resilience has often been referred to as the ability to 'bounce back' from difficult experiences (American Psychological Association 2008). While such a definition serves to acknowledge human beings' capacity to face incredible adversity, it may also create a potentially misleading aim of 'returning to normalcy'.

Psychological resilience is also often presented as a lack of adverse consequences such as post traumatic stress disorder (PTSD) in spite of potentially traumatic exposure (e.g. Levine *et al.* 2009). This perspective has helped establish a general consensus that in the face of most adversities, resilience is the norm rather than the exception (e.g. Masten 2001). Attesting to this, despite an estimated 50% trauma exposure rates based on the National Comorbidity Survey, lifetime PTSD was estimated at 7.8% (Kessler *et al.* 1995). As Almedom and Glandon (2007) argue, however, just as health cannot be defined merely by an absence of disease, resilience is not merely an absence of PTSD. More importantly, the limited prevalence of conditions such as PTSD does not mean that people necessarily go through adversity unchanged.

## Looking more closely at how people respond to adversity

In reality, dealing with adversities such as disasters is far beyond bouncing back to business as usual, not becoming adversely affected, or even achieving positive outcomes (Masten 2001). These different paths can be presented as different trajectories (Bonanno 2004; Masten and Obradovic 2007), but this does not capture how adversity can incite tremendous change in a multidimensional way. The notion of positive adaptation gestures towards this (American Psychological Association 2008; Masten 2001, 2005; Masten and Obradovic 2006). The scale of change, however, is such that some affected individuals say that disaster is 'life changing'. Thus, it may be helpful to look beyond bouncing back or adapting, to transforming adversity by transforming in the face of adversity.

Changes that occur due to adversities can be simultaneously negative and positive (e.g. Aldwin 1994; Kessler *et al.* 2006). While adversity by default is undesired, human beings have incredible capacity to transform adversity into opportunity, what in popular terms have often been referred to 'turning lemons into lemonade' (American Psychological Association 2003). People affected by disaster, for example, have been able to achieve feats some of them never thought possible, such as winning awards or generating new organisations. More commonly, adversity often serves as impetus for post traumatic growth (PTG), a process whereby people report positive changes in relating to others, seeing possibilities, sense of personal strength, spiritual outlook and appreciation for life (Tedeschi and Calhoun 2004; Tedeschi *et al.* 1998). Adversities can act as reminders of what is truly important, helping one reorient life goals accordingly.

> 'You can actually make some changes and when you make the changes you actually feel better within yourself' (person who escaped burning home in 2004 Canberra bushfire, describing how he feels he became a better person because of the decisions he made following the bushfire).

## When vulnerability leads to strength: becoming aware of the need to change

While growth is generally seen as a positive outcome of traumatic events, unfortunately post-traumatic growth has also been correlated with post traumatic stress disorder (Calhoun and

Tedeschi 2004; Hobfoll *et al.* 2007; Linley and Joseph 2006). This may be because unlike the notion of resilience as resisting change, growth often occurs in face of conditions severe enough to demand changes to occur (Levine *et al.* 2009). Such conditions can remove the illusion of invulnerability, as people come to realise that their lives, selves and loved ones are subject to greater forces.

This greater awareness of vulnerability paradoxically allows greater awareness of responsibility, which can lead to greater strength. It has been suggested that, as long as people retain or develop a sense of coherence (Antonovsky 1987) or will to meaning (Frankl 1992), people can work through this realisation of vulnerability in order to achieve a more realistic sense of mastery and limitation. While this process can be arduous, the capacity built from overcoming previous hardship can potentially help people face subsequent adversities (Jackson 2007). As one person testified,

> 'Well, you're just coasting along and everything's going along nicely and that and then all of a sudden your father dies – or my father died. You have to sit up and start taking responsibility. And not only responsibility for your own life… our whole life changed' (interviewee, describing how their father's death in childhood was turning point in life that gave confidence to face subsequent life difficulties, including the 2004 Canberra bushfires).

## When advantage becomes vulnerability: when formal systems become the centre point

On the other end, what is an advantage in ordinary times can sometimes increase vulnerability if and when it creates exceeding expectations and reduces a sense of personal capacity. In other words, strength and vulnerability can sometimes be two sides of one coin, which disaster has the capacity to flip without warning. For example, people may feel vulnerable as they come to realise their own limitations or the limitations of the formal systems they have come to rely on.

> 'I rang triple-0 for some help and the poor girl at the end of the phone there just broke down and cried and said, 'I can't do anything for you'' (man, recalling burning home in Canberra 2004).

There is no question of the benefits of resource equity and well-developed systems. People with less access to resources are generally further disadvantaged in times of greater need. A common element of disaster, however, is that the situation is too severe for normal systems to cope.

When formal systems are unable to meet expectations, as often the case in disasters, people's sense of helplessness, disappointment, resentment and anger can be very severe (Kumagaia *et al.* 2006). The 2009 bushfire survival plan thus warns people not to expect fire trucks, not to wait for warnings, and not to rely on services such as telephone, electricity or public water.

Beyond being able to manage without the system, however, people need to retain or regain the capacity to manage the system. Individuals, relationships and communities often rely on formal systems without retaining a sense of authority over them. Formal systems are generally characterised by formal decision-making processes and high degrees of specialisation. Formal systems also tend to be made up of not individuals *per se*, but of professional roles with clear job descriptions, mandates and hierarchies. While meant to protect people from human weaknesses, this can have its drawbacks. And, as with working with any other highly complicated piece of machinery, individuals can feel subjected to or limited by the system rather than having power in and over it.

> *'[Before the bushfires] I was very much a sheep… [After that] I wouldn't sit idly by and ever again and do what people in authority just tell me to do because they're in authority and can tell you to do it'* (woman who lost home in 2004 Canberra bushfire).

The need to maintain power over the system is particularly crucial in the face of the unexpected. For example, disasters often call members of the system to take courage and accountability to quickly make crucial decisions and take important actions otherwise beyond their authority. It can also be difficult for people to suddenly have to make independent decisions after being used to following procedures or higher authorities, without feeling left to one's own devices.

> *'I was listening to the Walkman and even the announcer sounded panicky… so I'm thinking, wait a minute, they're out of control, they don't even know, I know more about the fire than the emergency services because the fire's actually [here]'* (a person who following radio instructions had taken flammables out of the house into closer reach of the bushfire, Canberra 2004).

## The most vulnerable is the strongest: the need to restore personal power in systems

This shows how disaster calls for formal systems to support the capacity of individuals and communities to deal with unexpected challenges and not to get in the way, such as through excessive bureaucracy. This is especially true during extreme duress, but should not be limited to disaster situations. At the same time, formal systems should not avoid accountability by leaving individuals to fend for themselves. Thus, the same principle of transformation needs to go beyond the level of individuals, to encompass systems as well. It is not sufficient for systems to aim to 'return to normal' functioning or continue on an expected trajectory. Just like individuals, systems may be called to be open to exploring new possibilities, enhancing ability to relate and even finding greater purpose.

It is important for systems to be able to negotiate authority, so that people retain the permission and develop the capacity to make decisions and take actions that have been otherwise institutionalised. Communities that retain and develop power and capacity to make autonomous decisions over local governance, public services, resource and environmental management have a greater likelihood of achieving better outcomes, as found among by the Harvard Project among First Nations (Cornell *et al.* 2002). Similarly in some regional parts of Australia:

> *'Because they're a bit to some extent isolated or removed from help and assistance and that sort of thing, they tend to build up a bit of confidence and initiative, I suppose. Because they've had to deal with not so much these days as they used to, but if you get an accident, you can't – ambulance is not going to be there straight away or you get – something else like police is not going to be there straight away. Over the years back before these times when we're more isolated if something happened like a drowning or an accident or something people like myself would be one of the first ones there'* (rural person, describing how the person's community succeeded in avoiding the 2004 bushfires by taking independent action).

Similar to what is found among individuals, what appears to make a system most vulnerable could also be its greatest strength – in this case the human element. Revalidating the human aspect of the system, for example, acknowledges the system's limitations while allowing for greater mastery and better prioritisation. Beyond that, the human aspect of systems is not only its most vulnerable part and its greatest asset, but it is its essence. Humans make up systems and systems are there for the people.

## The need to focus on families

Currently, the division between personal and professional lives is arguably the part of the system that requires a lot of attention. During ordinary times, many Australians already struggle with work–life balance. Family members tend to be tied to separate work or education places, which are rarely connected or coordinated and often create pressures in different directions. Even normal childhood illnesses can create incredible tensions in many working families, let alone disasters. Some people have had to choose between their relationships and their work demands or expectations.

In disaster situations, people who maintain formal systems can be just as affected as anyone else. Formal systems thus need to place people not just within the context of professional roles, clear job descriptions, mandates and hierarchies, but take into consideration the personal aspects of their lives. Otherwise, different expectations between a person's formal and personal roles and needs could create dilemmas (McFarlane and Norris 2006).

> 'One of the basic things of my profession is to help people. And I – even though I didn't work Saturdays, I felt after that, I should've reported to work … It's what you're supposed to be doing, that's the job. So it was sort of a thing of being torn between what my job is and my family, I guess. Obligations, yeah' (parent of young child, also an emergency serviceperson, who had been trapped in a burning building during the 2004 Canberra bushfire).

To illustrate how paramount this is, we could reflect on a series of questions, in the advent of an emergency, where would we want to be? Where would the staff of our formal systems want to be? Who will take care of our families? Can we afford to sacrifice our families? Should we have to? Such reflections can lead to the question of how systems can support individuals, relationships and families, instead of the other way around.

Families are not just the most vulnerable part of the system; they are also its greatest asset. Just like resilient individuals, resilient systems are flexible, adaptive and self-organising (Walker *et al.* 2002). At their best, relationships and family can epitomise such systems, because they focus on the changing needs, strengths and aspirations of their members instead of predetermined roles, functions and goals. In the advent of disaster, most people engage in affiliative behaviour to connect with and support each other (Mawson 2005). While formal support services are useful and necessary, they cannot take the place of personal relationships and networks. In times of need, most people take refuge in the homes of families and friends, not in offices or shelters. Unlike a counselor restricted by professional boundaries, a loved one's shoulder can be a place to cry on as well as muscles to help carry out debris.

The International Resilience Project (2006) researched 589 families of children from 30 countries who have been able to achieve positive outcomes despite adverse life circumstances. The resources that resilient children and families have can be simplified in terms of 'I have, I am, I can': I have (e.g. people around me I trust and who love me); I am (e.g. a person people can like and love); I can (e.g. talk about my problems) (Grotberg 1997). A consistent theme is that these resources underline the primacy of relationships, particularly those that touch them at a personal level. Other people make the biggest difference in how people go through the process of transformation. People affected by disaster often speak of how greatly they are touched by some people's kindness and how greatly they are disappointed by the apathy or callousness of others, as was found following the Canberra bushfires (Camilleri *et al.*

2007). Relationships not only can potentially provide support, they can provide meaning (Frankl 1992).

We are therefore called to take these personally experienced strengths further and bring them into the collective level, where systems can say 'We have, we are and we can'. Is it possible to create a formal system that can be trusted and loved, or perhaps even, that works like a good family?

## Conclusions: enhancing our capacity to deal with disasters

Enhancing our capacity to deal with disasters, thus requires not just enhancing the capacity of systems to deal with the unexpected, but also enhancing the capacity of the people and creating integration between people and formal systems. Places where people work and study must cater for the needs of families, just as families have adapted to the requirements of work and study. Greater communication between components of the system and across systems may pave the way to better negotiation of expectations and greater collaboration. Flexible partnerships that take into account persons as a whole and a part of community units may potentially reduce personal vs. professional conflicts.

In other words, there is a greater need for what is hereby referred to as People–Systems. These are systems with whole individuals, relationships and communities as their focus and basis, rather than depersonalised positions and functions. For example, one may want to learn from semi-formal, flexible community organisations, such as Community Fire Authority or Neighbourhood Watch, which can generally focus on, cater for and develop persons, relationships and communities, above roles, tasks, job descriptions or hierarchies. More than that, it may take collective ingenuity and effort to explore possibilities beyond what is already available.

Adversities such as disaster remind us that, as human beings, we are subject to, as well as part of, natural and social forces. Difficulties can serve as a reminder to what is truly important and awaken potentials that we never knew existed in us as individuals and as a part of greater systems. Disasters can serve as turning points to transform ourselves as persons, relationships, communities and systems and to take responsibility for the environment and for the local and global society. Instead of worrying that disasters may bring an end to civilisation as we know it, maybe we need to transform our civilisation and ourselves. Let's not wait for disaster.

*Dr Theresia Citraningtyas, MBBS (Indonesia), MWH (Melbourne), known as Citra, is a general practitioner from the One-Stop Crisis Centre, Cipto Mangunkusumo General Hospital, Jakarta, currently undertaking her PhD in Psychological Medicine at the Australian National University under the supervision of Prof Beverley Raphael. Her research looks at people's strength and resilience in disaster, in the context of the 2003 Canberra bushfire and 2004 tsunami in Aceh. Citra has a wealth of experience in capacity-building, medical education, women's health and mental health. She has worked as National Consultant for the World Bank Health Task Force and Services Project and with institutions such as the Department of Health of Indonesia. She has lectured at Universitas Indonesia (UI) and currently gives lectures at the Australian National University.*

## References

Aldwin CM (1994) *Stress, Coping and Development*. The Guilford Press. New York.

Almedom AM and Glandon D (2007) Resilience is not the absence of PTSD anymore than health is the absence of disease. *Journal of Loss and Trauma* **12**, 127–143.

American Psychological Association (2003) Turning lemons into lemonade: Hardiness helps people turn stressful circumstances into opportunities. American Psychological Association Online: Psychology Matters 23 December 2003, <http://www.psychologymatters.org/hardiness.html>.

American Psychological Association (2008) *The Road to Resilience*. American Psychological Association, Washington DC, <http://apahelpcenter.org/dl/the_road_to_resilience.pdf>.

Antonovsky A (1987) *Unraveling The Mystery of Health – How People Manage Stress and Stay Well*. Jossey-Bass Publishers, San Francisco, California, USA.

Bonanno GA (2004) Loss Trauma and Human Resilience American. *Psychologist* **59**, 20–28.

Calhoun LG and Tedeschi RG (2004) The Foundations of Posttraumatic Growth: New Considerations. *Psychological Inquiry* **15**, 93–102.

Camilleri P, Healy C, Macdonald E, Nicholls S, Sykes J, Winkworth G and Woodward M (2007) 'Recovering from the 2003 Canberra bushfire: A work in progress'. Australian Catholic University, Canberra.

Cornell S, Jorgensen M and Kalt JP (2002) 'The First Nations Governance Act: Implications of research findings from the United States and Canada – A Report to the Office of the British Columbia Regional Vice-Chief Assembly of First Nations'. Native Nations Institute for Leadership, Management and Policy, University of Arizona, Tucson, Arizona, USA.

Frankl VE (1992) *Man's Search For Meaning*. Beacon Press, Boston, Massachusetts, USA.

Grotberg EH (1997) The International Resilience Project: Findings from the Research and the Effectiveness of Interventions paper. In *Psychology and Education in the 21st Century: Proceedings of the 54th Annual Convention of the International Council of Psychologists*. 24–28 July 1996, Banff, Canada. (Ed. B Bain, HL Janzen, JG Paterson, LL Stewin and A Yu) pp. 118—128. IC Press, Edmonton, Canada.

Hobfoll SE, Hall BJ, Canetti-Nisim D, Galea S, Johnson RJ and Palmieri PA (2007) Refining our understanding of traumatic growth in the face of terrorism: Moving from meaning cognitions to doing what is meaningful. *Applied Psychology: An International Review* **56**, 345–366.

Jackson CA (2007) Posttraumatic growth: Is there evidence for changing our practice? The Australasian Journal of Disaster and Trauma Studies 1, <http://www.massey.ac.nz/~trauma/issues/2007-1/jackson.htm>.

Kessler RC, Galea S, Jones RT and Parker HA (2006) Mental illness and suicidality after Hurricane Katrina. Bulletin of the World Health Organization 84, 930–939.

Kessler RC, Sonnega A, Bromet E, Hughes M and Nelson CB (1995) Post-traumatic Stress Disorder in the National Comorbidity Survey. *Archives of General Psychiatry* **52**, 1048–60.

Kumagaia Y, Edwards J and Carroll MS (2006) Why are natural disasters not 'natural' for victims? *Environmental Impact Assessment Review* **26**, 106–119.

Levine SZ, Laufer A, Stein E, Hamama-Raz Y and Solomon Z (2009) Examining the relationship between resilience and posttraumatic growth. *Journal of Traumatic Stress* **22**, 282–286.

Linley PA and Joseph S (2006) The Positive and negative effects of disaster work: A preliminary investigation. *Journal of Loss and Trauma* **11**, 229–245.

Masten AS (2001) Ordinary magic. *American Psychologist* **56**, 227–238.

Masten AS (2005) Resilience in development. In *Handbook of Positive Psychology*. (Eds CR Snyder and SJ Lopez) pp. 74–88. Oxford University Press, New York, USA.

Masten AS and Obradovic J (2006) Competence and resilience in development. *Annals of the New York Academy of Sciences* **1094**, 13–27.

Masten AS and Obradovic J (2007) Disaster preparation and recovery: Lessons from research on resilience in human development. *Ecology and Society* **13**, 9, <http://www. ecologyandsociety.org/vol13/iss1/art9/>.

Mawson AR (2005) Understanding mass panic and other collective responses to threat and disaster. *Psychiatry* **68**, 95–113.

McFarlane AC and Norris FH (2006) Definitions and concepts in disaster research. In *Methods for Disaster Mental Health Research*. (Eds FH Norris, S Galea, MJ Friedman and PJ Watson) pp. 3–19. The Guilford Press, New York, USA.

Tedeschi RG and Calhoun LG (2004) Posttraumatic growth: Conceptual foundations and empirical evidence. *Psychological Inquiry* **15**, 1–18.

Tedeschi RG, Park CL and Calhoun LG (1998) Posttraumatic growth: Conceptual issues. In *Posttraumatic Growth: Positive Changes in the Aftermath of Crisis*. (Eds RG Tedeschi, CL Park and LG Calhoun) pp. 1–23. Lawrence Erlbaum Associates Inc., New Jersey, USA.

The International Resilience Project (2006) 'The International Resilience Project Report'. Dalhousie University, School of Social Work, Halifax, Canada,

Walker B, Carpenter S, Anderies J, Abel N, Cumming GS, Janssen M, Lebel L, Norberg J, Peterson GD and Pritchard R (2002) Resilience management in social–ecological systems: a working hypothesis for a participatory approach. *Conservation Ecology* **6**, 14 <http://wwwconsecolorg/vol6/iss1/art14/>.

# *Index*